For Humanism

# Marxism and Culture

Series Editors:
Professor Esther Leslie, Birkbeck, University of London
Professor Michael Wayne, Brunel University

# For Humanism

## Explorations in Theory and Politics

Edited by
David Alderson and Robert Spencer

PlutoPress
www.plutobooks.com

First published 2017 by Pluto Press
345 Archway Road, London N6 5AA

www.plutobooks.com

Copyright © David Alderson and Robert Spencer 2017

The right of the individual contributors to be identified as the authors of
this work has been asserted by them in accordance with the Copyright,
Designs and Patents Act 1988.

British Library Cataloguing in Publication Data
A catalogue record for this book is available from the British Library

ISBN    978 0 7453 3619 0    Hardback
ISBN    978 0 7453 3614 5    Paperback
ISBN    978 1 7868 0023 7    PDF eBook
ISBN    978 1 7868 0024 4    Kindle eBook
ISBN    978 1 7868 0022 0    EPUB eBook

This book is printed on paper suitable for recycling and made from fully
managed and sustained forest sources. Logging, pulping and manufacturing
processes are expected to conform to the environmental standards of the
country of origin.

Typeset by Stanford DTP Services, Northampton, England

Simultaneously printed in the United Kingdom and United States of America

# Contents

# Series Preface

This book is *for humanism* in a number of senses, not least as a kind of gift or service performed for an intellectual tradition that has been comprehensively displaced, its reputation traduced, its history crassly simplified and its multiple meanings homogenised, by wave upon wave of antihumanist thinking that has swept the academy since the 1960s. The common sense of several generations of intellectuals has been shaped by the moral-intellectual hegemony of antihumanism in its various philosophical manifestations. Structuralism, post-structuralism, postmodernism, postcolonialism and now today, in its most explicit form, post-humanism, all testify to academia's giddy intoxification with the rhetoric of epochal change and unlimited possibilities. What need have we in such circumstances for the outworn 'pre-post' ideologies of humanism, or indeed socialism, which was in part the real target of the assault on humanism? The latter we have been taught to 'know' was a bourgeois, Eurocentric ideology of capitalism, complacent, abstract, individualistic. To be sure, *liberal* humanism could be all those things and Marxism, surrounded by the material and intellectual authority of liberalism is bound to be influenced by aspects of this liberal humanism which it must in fact struggle to overcome. The struggle to preserve what is positive and discard what is negative within liberal humanism, the struggle to forge a socialist humanism, is bound to be difficult, bound to be a history with many dead ends and impasses. But this is true too of antihumanism, which is another version of liberalism, attuned to some of the most dynamic trends within advanced capitalism, that needed to offer a different model of the subject, of reality, of language, culture and taste. It seemed radical because it exploded one bourgeois model, but only to try and install another.

Humanism may have been less exciting to those driven by the commodification of knowledge, with its incessant need for 'innovation' and branding, but perhaps this book will help us discover by recovering its history and philosophical positions, that humanism was and is also rather more steadfast in its political-philosophical commitments, rather more nuanced, rather more patient, sober and perhaps serious about change, than its opponents. In an act of philosophical unpacking, *For Humanism* tells us that humanism was also more than the offspring of Western capitalist enlightenment thinking. Spatially and temporally it is wider and deeper than that. Politically it is very far from being antithetical to an authentic Marxism, something which the reflex action of contemporary theory, with its infatuations for structures on the one hand or explosive decentrings and fragmentations of the subject and reality on the other, is likely to forget.

Despite Althusser's influential book *For Marx*, which lent political respectability to attacks on humanism from the Left, Marx's thought is of course a humanism. Althusser's book was not for Marx, but against. Marx's critique is fired by a moral-normative standard that enables him to dismantle a system based on things, and offer an alternative: people before profit, as the contemporary slogan puts it, is a morally informed critique of capitalist political economy impossible to voice without a humanist conception. A Marxism shorn of humanism is a Marxism no longer interested in human emancipation. Is to talk of 'humans' a humanist error? People, humans, of course are organised into classes, of course they are differentiated and of course they are internally contradictory; a Marxist humanism seeks to overcome the first, organise a society that genuinely recognises the second and in doing so, not abolish contradiction as such, but give individuals and societies the means for addressing them productively rather than getting locked into self-destructive spirals of intensification. Humanisation of both nature and social nature, that is the shaping of our environment to meet the needs of humanity, provides an essential moral yardstick by which the judgement delivered against the dehumanisation prevalent within the capitalist mode of production, must be severe.

The undifferentiated assault on humanism has unleashed political relativism across contemporary theory. This is a poor solution to liberal humanism's uncritical collapse into the abstractions of capitalism. For we cannot do without a transhistorical sense of the needs we have and the capacities that are available to us if we are to critique what exists and hope for something better. That this transhistorical dimension of what it is to be human never manifests itself except through a great variety of historical and social forms, goes without saying. Humanism also has the merit of providing a bridge to a wider public at a time when getting a hearing for socialism, let alone Marxism, has been difficult. Why burn that bridge when it is also a necessary part of our philosophy?

Why retreat into a discourse intelligible only to the initiated? Socialism and Marxism provide the resources to reconstruct the problematic abstractions of liberal humanism, and as with capitalism in general, the coming great change must build on and refunction what it inherits from the past. Humanism has been the victim of the rise of identity politics, in which the solidarities and politics of transformation have splintered into discrete oppressions and the claims of recognition have all but eclipsed the politics of wealth redistribution, let alone the ownership, control and production of wealth. We must be *for humanism* indeed.

Mike Wayne and Esther Leslie
Series editors

# Introduction:
# Humanism's Other Story

## *Timothy Brennan*

Once clearly on the side of the renegades, humanism now seems confused, its protagonists and antagonists passing each other in the night. It is important, then, to begin with a clarification so that one knows what being for or against it means. Humanism has to do above all – and non-negotiably – with secularity. Value belongs first with the only world humans really know, the one not given by nature or ruled by God, the one humans have fashioned by skill and effort. This is quite rightly called a 'materialist' view, but matter is not conceived here as inert objects or things; if one dwells only on matter they are not 'materialists' from a humanist's point of view. That must entail a dwelling on sensuous labour and social interaction – the substrate, in other words, of all that binds experience to matter. Not against religion necessarily, humanists are secular only in the sense of being drawn to what transcendence pretends to supersede, viewing the metaphysical – in its classical sense – as reliant on the physical: a conceptual rendering of it.

To say that humans create is, of course, to say they *can*. And that means that they are free, have agency and can do what they have not done in the past regardless of, or rather because of, *their nature*. Logically, then, transformation is possible and the future open. Humanists do not believe humans are the only species that matters, only that it is impossible for any species to think outside the limits of its own being – a view that does not preclude ethical behaviour towards other species or respect for the natural environment. As Ludwig Feuerbach puts it in *The Essence of Christianity* (1841), 'If God were an object to the bird, he would be an object to it only as a winged being – the bird knows nothing higher, nothing more blissful than the state of being winged.'[1] Following from this, the humanist contends that every human, *qua* human, shares universal attributes – a vital tenet so that no one can be relegated to a subspecies or denied membership in humanity on the grounds of his or her particularities.

The body of ideas called humanism was never just a set of beliefs but a collection of contrarian intellectual practices. We are talking not only of positions but methods and habits of thinking. This aspect has been largely lost in the post-war flight from humanism so vigorously adduced in the pages of the present volume. It grew out of a body of study we today call the humanities, and the current attacks on the humanities can, to that degree, be seen as evidence of our culture's mainstream antihumanism.

We should remember that humanism's early exponents – in China and the Arabic world, not only Europe – all expressed their view in the form of a project of training in the liberal arts (expressed in the West as *humanitas* or *paideia*), and so we are talking about a revolution in learning based on the study of books, especially the forgotten wisdom of the past, just as the present volume (we might notice) – *For Humanism* – is involved in a similar recovery. Despite my just quoting Latin and Greek, the contributions to humanism are universal – a view that is frequently denied today. They can be found in the agnosticism, scepticism towards the supernatural, and emphasis on human choice and agency found within strains of Hinduism, Buddhism, Taoism, Confucianism and Zoroastrianism.

As I have just laid them out, these foundations are obscured today for a number of reasons, and they contribute greatly to the confusion. For one thing, our historical moment is a uniquely disorienting one. Biotechnology obviates the long-standing debate over human nature by threatening to invent a new one according to a managerial plan. Venture capitalists declare openly that if yesterday's economic game-changer was 0's and 1's, today's are A's, G's, T's and C's – the bases of DNA. The classic question of what the human being *is*, then, has been gamed by forces that seek to control it to a degree unknown in any other historical period – picking up where the twentieth century's innovations in this regard left off: the manipulation of libidinal drives by the commercial media and the merciless incantation of official 'news' in the major Western countries which has, many argue, short-circuited mental capacities. Between the managed emotions of overprescribed antidepressants and social media fixations (Twitter, Facebook) that blur the distinction between free time and advertising, how could it be otherwise than that coercion would be widely mistaken for freedom, and submission for resistance? What is

Right and what is Left is no longer clear – and that more than any other point defines the current humanism debate.

*For Humanism* is for that reason very well timed, and also for that reason apparently untimely – as though holding on to ideas with a warm heart and unstifled hopes to prolong a dead (if sorely missed) historical moment of socialist internationalism. Again, our moment is unique. For it is only in the last four decades that attacks on humanism – until then, the standard-issue views of apologists of religious absolutism, Church censors and the reactionary wings of modernism – have been thought politically progressive. In fact, the lineages of antihumanist thought have always been aligned with aristocratic or theocratic privileges; or they assumed the form of apocalyptic amoralism for which the (equally aristocratic) Marquis de Sade is usually the emblem. It was de Sade, in fact, who by way of Georges Bataille helped bring antihumanism into post-war theory and made it a model of failed gods, sexual desire and a mockery of progress.[2] It made people associate radical opposition with transgression and the non-normative rather than with social trans-formation – a realm explored in the illuminatingly revisionist chapter on the politics of gender and sexual desire by David Alderson in the present volume.

What *For Humanism* returns to, by contrast – these rich if now neglected mid-twentieth-century narratives of dissident humanism in figures like Karel Kosík, Jean-Paul Sartre, Raya Dunayevaska and the Yugoslavian Praxis group – is part of a wider historical arc than the recent form of the debate would have us think. This volume's genealogies remind us just how much theory in recent decades represents an idiosyncratic detour. It is true, as theory had charged, that humanism may have been enlisted as a slogan of capital in its nineteenth-century colonial form – the technocratic fetish of managerial progress whose 'dialectic' Theodor W. Adorno and Max Horkheimer sceptically diagnosed mid-century – but this was overall a co-optation. More typically it was the groundwork of antinomians, visionaries and iconoclasts.[3] In this volume, Kevin Anderson describes how on the very heels of proclaiming existential-ism a humanism, Jean-Paul Sartre distinguished himself from the 'liberal and republican humanism' that was theory's real and only target. The ledgers of humanism abound, Anderson implies, with just the opposite: struggles against religious dogma, ideas imported from other cultures in order to curb ethnocentrism, and intellectual life brought face to face with politics so that reality might be thought something less to observe than make.

The case against humanism in the post-war period would have us think of humanism in terms of an exclusivist rhetoric of innate qualities and character found in figures like David Hume, Jeremy Bentham and Napoleon III. Historically, though, humanism belongs much more to the maverick secularity of Thales and Anaxagoras, the philological study of Roman law in Varro, the preservation of Oriental learning in the Islamic Golden age (Averroes, Avicenna), the great rediscovery of Egypt in Neoplatonism, the creation by scholasticism of the first European universities, the madrasas of the Maghreb and the Levant, and the triumph of reading in the Italian renaissance of Poggio Bracciolini and Erasmus, the great philological sociologies of ibn Khaldun and later, in an identical spirit, Giambattista Vico. The humanism of the French Revolution and, in its wake, the young-Hegelians, especially Ludwig Feuerbach and Marx, is usually staged as a radical fissure in history or a lamentable march down a dead end historical lane. And yet, left Hegelianism (including Marx) is only the continuation of a spirit of learning, of vernacular inclusiveness and political renovation that had preceded them in Eastern and Western antiquity.

It may be even more of a challenge to the idiosyncratic reigning story of recent decades to recall that the intellectual leaders of anticolonialism after World War II deployed humanist motifs consistently and very consciously. Edward Said's well-known rallying to the cause of humanism (against the stream of theory) grew out of a broader understanding of the scholarship of George Makdisi on the Arabic contributions to humanism and to the revolutionary solidarities of his close friends Eqbal Ahmad and Mahmoud Darwish. He often illustrates those commitments, in fact, by quoting Aimé Césaire's *Notebook on a Return to my Native Land*, where the poet reclaims the essential humanity of actors, black and white, on either side of the colonial divide at the 'rendezvous of victory', and bitterly satirises the antihumanist doctrines guiding a colonial enterprise propped up, as he puts it in *Discourse on Colonialism*, by 'chattering intellectuals born stinking out of the thigh of Nietzsche'.[4]

John Dewey's pragmatism took shape as an effort to reverse the nativism and racial panic of early twentieth-century anti-immigration trends, just as the Brahmo Samaj of Tagore and others in West Bengal set out to secularise the Hindu Right at the dawn of the Indian independence movements. M. N. Roy, the co-founder of the Mexican Communist

Party, and a Bengali revolutionary who collaborated with Lenin on the writing of his 'Theses on the National Question', spent the final decades of his life building a movement tied to an Institute at Dehradun on behalf of what he called 'a cultural-educational organization founded with the object of re-educating the educators and young intellectuals of India in spirit and with the ideas of Radical (or Integral) Humanism'.[5] By the 1950s, humanism was for Roy the logical, secular, extra-party version of interwar Marxism.

So the very point of departure of antihumanism is politically vexed. To join its forces is to reject much more than hypocritical Eurocentric philosophies of 'progress' or imperious universals moulded in the image of Western males. It is rather to assault a centuries-long heritage of resistance and renovation. The symbolism, then, of the appearance of the *locus classicus* of post-war antihumanist thought, Heidegger's 'Letter on Humanism' (1947), is notable, since it coincided almost exactly with the Universal Declaration of Human Rights (1948) – the most far-reaching practical statement of humanist convictions published in the century, and not coincidentally composed by UN delegates from Egypt, Chile, India and other former colonies. The two texts stand as mid-century antipodes – the former arguing that 'Man [*sic*]' cannot attain his proper 'dignity' under humanism since the latter relies on a system of logic and values that prove powerless to capture the plenitude of being; the latter, codifying the universal protections necessary to safeguard human subjects whose particularities vis-à-vis European and American norms had deprived them of the right to well-being, freedom and autonomy.

The nature of antihumanism's complaint, though, is not exhausted by these examples, and becomes more evident in the observation that humanism defined itself as an embrace of learning, literature and the book traditionally associated with philology.[6] Since the 'theory' invoked in the subtitle of this volume grew out of an extreme position on language as grammatically fixed – to written as opposed to spoken language – we can begin to appreciate the motives of this peculiar philosophical demarche. Heidegger's representative move in 'Letter on Humanism', in another flipping of the script, only appears to protest this tyranny when he appeals to 'the liberation of language from grammar into a more original essential framework ... reserved for thought and poetic creation'. The freedom he has in mind is not the inventiveness of a vernacular speech making new rules but a freedom from 'the dictatorship of the public realm', returning language to 'the house of being' – that is, to see the communicative and expressive means on which all debate, discussion and sociality depends as being not about meaning or intention but a kind of medium within which the artist-thinker dwells.[7]

Heidegger's famous declaration that language speaks Man rather than the other way around was one of the many ideas interwar phenomenology derived from Nietzsche, although, as Barbara Epstein crucially observes in this volume, figures like Maurice Merleau-Ponty (an important early influence on Said) and Sartre reappropriated aspects of phenomenology for humanist thought. And yet, in the end all modern antihumanism is Nietzschean, expanding on or adapting his philosophy's central principles that free choice is an illusion; that knowledge, even if it were possible, has no 'use'; that ethics constrain Man's life-enhancing instincts; and that 'truth' is rhetorical, language a means of artful deception. Lying, states Nietzsche unequivocally, gives humans their evolutionary advantage over other animals. A professional philologist, Nietzsche's revolt was precisely aimed at his own earlier training in the humanist tradition of letters with which he had grown disaffected. Not learning but art, creative illusion, are the dignity of Man for him; not making life anew but coming to admit what we are: unequal, visceral.

It is not going too far to say that understanding the contemporary recoil from humanism is impossible without becoming familiar with Nietzsche's thought. Antihumanism derives from him more than from any other source – idea for idea, word for word. It is Bataille who in the late 1940s enshrines Nietzsche, announcing that 'Nietzsche's position is the only one apart from communism',[8] and whose fealty goes so far that he considers himself 'the same as he'. Foucault's and Deleuze's later efforts to claim Nietzsche for the radical Left are taken very directly, although without acknowledgement, from Bataille's earlier experiments in appropriating the language of the Hegelian Left for the purpose of destroying it from within. Bataille redeploys Hegelian terms like 'totality', 'sovereignty' and 'negation' on behalf of a human subject forced to reckon with its instinctive cruelty, its amoralism and its illusory subjectivity. Foucault's 'death of the subject' and Deleuze's 'pure immanence' are both echoes of Bataille's already perfected gestures.

Antihumanism, nevertheless, passed through various phases.[9] Anthropological antihumanism, to take a fascinating and little-known example, was a dominant aspect of culture in the late nineteenth and early twentieth centuries, harmonising with aspects of Nietzsche's critique. Loudly charging academic humanism with enshrining the 'positivist, ratiocinating West' and excluding Africans and Asians from the human as such, an insurgent anthropology arose with a counter-method that was both intellectually appealing and commercially viable. It appeared radical to many at first, producing a large number of popular museum exhibitions and pamphlets: 'Rather than excluding the colonised other, anthropology would focus explicitly on societies that, all agreed, were radically separate from narratives of Western civilisation. Instead of studying European "cultural peoples" (Kulturvölker), societies defined by their history and civilisation, anthropologists studied the colonised "natural peoples" (Naturvölker).'[10]

As a populist discourse with the aim of displacing academic mandarins, anthropology promised Germans that they could reinvent themselves along the lines of the country's new imperial ambitions. The conquest of foreign territories provided antihumanism with its 'ethnographic performers, artifacts, body parts, and field sites that provided the empirical data' and so linked the imperial, the natural, and the German in a style of thought that led directly to theories of 'racial hygiene'.[11] One particularly well-known anthropologist, Leo Frobenius, argued that 'Germans like Africans were people of emotion, intuitive reason, art, poetry, image, and myth', thereby establishing an antihumanist affinity with the peripheral subaltern that had the great merit of making Germanness unique within the family of Europe.[12] A neo-Orientalist theory of absolute cultural and mental otherness, then, could portray itself as an insurrectionary ideology – a minority tendency reclaiming 'difference' for use against the establishment.

Evident in this reversal, phenomenology – as Stefanos Geroulanos points out – turned the tables on older terminologies, claiming for itself an 'atheism' that it counterposed to the 'religion' of humanism.[13] Alexandre Koyré, Alexandre Kojève, Bataille and Heidegger all declared provocatively in the 1930s that secularism was a form of religious belief, an idea recycled later by Raymond Aron in 1944 on the eve of his fame as a nouveau philosophe in the rightward shift of French intellectual life after the 1960s. It is not humanism's overestimation of human capacities that troubles them, they assert, but the degradation of 'Man'; when the gods of social utopia fail. They are not merely anti-Communists, they insist (although they were that); they only wish to free us of the myths of 'secular, egalitarian, and transformative commitments'.[14] These views, we recall, were being refined and promoted at the height of mainstream

Communist acceptance just as anticolonial sentiments were gathering momentum in Europe under the influence of the Third International.

This interwar 'reactionary modernism', in Domenico Losurdo's phrase, had cleverly co-opted the lexicons of the traditional Left.[15] The result was a kind of genre flipping – a series of feints that had the effect of disrupting the usual polarities, making them no longer operative. Phenomenology's summoning of the terms 'being' and 'existence', for instance, made a bid to address material life in a new way, casting Marxists in the camp of the metaphysical – the merely speculative or quasi-religious. In one of his earliest essays, 'The Idea of Natural History', Adorno, recognising this conundrum, launches a life-long philosophical crusade against the Heideggerian challenge, a project that reached its culmination in one of his last books, *Negative Dialectics*, in a long chapter on 'The Ontological Need' where he concedes that 'the ontologies of Germany, Heidegger's in particular, remain effective to this day' (that is, 1966).[16] At issue centrally was the familiar problem of human nature. For Adorno, the only way around the nature/history dichotomy was 'to comprehend historical being in its most extreme historical determinacy, where it is most historical, as natural being, or if it were possible to comprehend nature as an historical being where it seems to rest most deeply in itself as nature'.[17] In other words, it is the nature of humans to effect change, to create newness out of inherited conditions. The human finds a way out of what it has been forced to confront as a prior determination, and to find solutions to it. Ernst Bloch's way of putting it is to sum up the entire movement of phenomenology in an epigram titled 'In Itself.' It reads: 'One is. But this is not enough; indeed, it is the very least.'[18]

We need to distinguish, though, between critiques of humanism's excesses or misuses (Adorno, Frantz Fanon), antihumanism (Schopenhauer, Nietzsche, Heidegger and their epigones – for example, Giorgio Agamben) and post-humanism (Deleuze, Foucault, Donna Haraway, Bruno Latour, Levi Bryant and others). Unlike antihumanism's political distaste with the unwarranted privileging of subjectivity and historical progress, post-humanism moves in the direction of a subordination of human prerogatives to an indifferent nature (as we see, for instance, in the current fixations on the 'anthropocene'). It speaks in terms of an anthropological mutation. Scientism, we could say, is the most pronounced form today of post-humanism. Its lineages of thought appear at first markedly different from that of Nietzsche, and yet even in

Nietzsche's rhetorical and artistic devotions there is a social Darwinism and biologism.

Here however is where we find one reason for the widespread return to Spinoza in recent decades – as well as to other mechanistic rationalists of the seventeenth-century scientific Enlightenment, including Descartes, Leibniz, Pierre Bayle and Nicolas Malebranche. Theory now embraces them from the other side, as it were, replacing its earlier culturalism with a purported materialism without abandoning its lexicon of the 1980s and 1990s: the multiple, the contingent, the particular and the molecular (the basis of theory's one-sided protest that Robert Spencer here cleverly calls 'crimes against hybridity'). One can see this very clearly, for example, in the speculative realism of Quentin Meillasoux and Graham Harman and in the neo-ontologies of Jane Bennett.

The inter-reliance of humanism and the humanities is especially clear at this juncture. For what separates the humanist from his or her antagonists (anti- and post-) is as much methodological as political. The sciences isolate manageable parts of matter in order to control observation; the humanities consider the social whole. The sciences pursue certainty within defined parameters; the humanities have no such limits, exploring the ensemble of relations, above all the human being in his or her environment as a complex, interactive totality. The sciences see reality as matter; the humanities as matter reflected upon (the perception and evaluation of matter). The sciences quantify; the humanities qualify. For the sciences, there is nothing outside material existence; for the humanities, nothing is itself an existence. In the sciences, competing and mutually incompatible theories (as in contemporary physics, for example) are not seen as undermining their claims to science, or casting doubt on their ability to offer a persuasive account of reality; in the humanities, the conflict of incompatible theories (greeted by the public as a sign of the humanities' unscientific nature) is seen as a conflict over motives, opposed interests and philosophical positions that are ultimately political. In the sciences, when an earlier consensus collapses because it has been disproved, it signifies the threshold of a final breakthrough in which a unified-field theory of reality is imminent – always-already imminent, in fact (since it never seems to be reached); in the humanities, it signifies the victory of new philosophical choice based on perceived social needs. The sciences prove their methods by material results – where social benefit, preferable alternatives or adverse future effects are strictly corollary considerations; the humanities, by contrast, interrogate their own methods, subjecting themselves to a constant self-criticism. The sciences ask what; the humanities why and how.

This in some ways – not all – antipathetic set of coordinates is not common knowledge in the public discourse on science, especially in the genre of newspaper article – familiar since at least the late 1980s – in which the irrelevance of the humanities is contemptuously announced. Even more striking is the fact that the good-hearted efforts to defend the humanities tend to neglect the history of the development of the sciences *out of* the humanities, their relative indistinction in antiquity, and their fatal separation in the seventeenth century: a move that is analogous to the turn in economics from political economy to the neoclassical revolution of the mid-nineteenth century – which is to say, from human actors and values to mathematical projections, and from profitable needs to questions of 'equilibrium' and 'marginal utility'.

Why, one wonders, with a rich history to draw on, would one pass up the chance of highlighting thinkers from the past who demonstrated that the sciences as we know the term today are not scientific in important ways that the humanities are? Here I am not referring to those moves across the spectrum of theory to adopt aspects of perceived scientific method, to mimic its procedures, or to appropriate some of its gestures in an attempt to acquire authority. It is of course not simply opportunism that motivates these trends, but serious convictions; all the same, it is striking to note this repeated pattern of tailing the sciences in Saussurean linguistics, structuralism and semiotics, logical positivism, analytic philosophy, Althusserian Marxism, Gilles Deleuze's attractions to Leibniz and Spinoza, and his mimicking of the language of fractals, lines of force and modal spatialities – all of the terms taken wholesale from the virtual universes of theoretical mathematics. Today in the humanities, this trend of metaphorically adopting the trappings of science continues with a kind of inexorable momentum in wings of animal studies, political ecology, the digital humanities and distant reading. Despite their immense variety, they share an antipathy towards – or perhaps only an inability to witness or digest – the traditions of political philology I associated above with Khaldun and Vico, a strain of thinking consciously taken up and elaborated by critical theory, Georg Lukács, Gramsci and contemporary Left philologists like Said.

Again, the methodological import of humanism comes to the fore. These new currents do not simply challenge a vision of the human being, or question his or her nature, but wish to erase the very idea of critical thought, and by those means provide a revolutionary solution in the *dis*solution of the human as such. The proleptic force of Vico and Hegel, by contrast, was to have provided an anthropological-political economy of the species. The human, they persuasively show, is the being beyond which we cannot think –the creature who, we might say in the present context, is so utterly free as to invent the 'post-human' for ethical reasons, wilfully pretending thereby to have demonstrated its lack of will.

Vico, more than anyone, counterposes to the natural sciences a comprehensive theory of poetic interpretation, and a theory of language and literary figure whose complexity, interconnectedness and sweep constituted for him, and for many others after him, a science all of its own. His ripostes against Descartes and Spinoza are explicit, angry and sustained. He thus created a tradition of literary worldliness and sociological awareness that informed early-century political struggle and has been for the century's latter half an absent presence.

What Max Horkheimer effectively argues in 'Traditional and Critical Theory' (1937) to be the unjustified assumptions regarding the superiority of the methods of the natural sciences when compared to dialectical thought[19] – and he cites Vico openly – are assumptions very much in evidence in non-mainstream, oppositional theories like Althusserian Marxism, the new ecological criticism and the digital humanities – one of whose principal contributors, Franco Moretti, writes very consciously in the vein of the scientistic, explicitly anti-Gramscian Marxism of Galvano Della Volpe. Each of these rather dissimilar figures is brought together by an anxiety over philology's emphasis on will, spirit and belief. In this case, though, 'spirit' refers to the relation of theoretical frameworks to truth and to the interpretability of textual facts.

The debate over humanism, in other words, is a debate over the possibility of knowing – of learning from historical experience, and of recovering that experience of the past through the study of texts – a position specifically mocked by Nietzsche and by the Spinozist traditions of Althusser and Deleuze (although, importantly, not in Spinoza himself). For Moretti and the digital humanities, the process of reading does not preclude truth as it does for the others. However, it is a truth that must be stalked, or got around, by detaching the process of interpretation from the meddling of the human mind with recourse to machines for the purpose of unearthing data or combining elements divorced from any plan or synthetic intelligence.

Vichian lineages have been lively and influential for centuries even if they have gone unregistered in the debate over humanism, where they settle for a shadow existence. Individual humanists may well have been invoked from time to time, but an actual constellation of counter-scientistic thought within the humanities has gone more or less unrecognised. Vico's direct descendants include J.-G. Herder, Hegel, Jules Michelet, Francesco de Sanctis, Gramsci, Georges Sorel, V. N. Voloshinov, Nikolai Marr, Lukács, Simone de Beauvoir, Jose Carlos Mariátegui, Cornelius Castoriadis, Horkheimer, Said and many others. As a tendency, they moved the humanities away from a narrow science of the literary text known as 'philology' in the positivistic turns of the nineteenth century (Said's target in *Orientalism*) to the more expansive, sociological sense of the philological as Khaldun and Vico had originally conceived it – a conception captured well by Erich Auerbach in his 1924 German translation of Vico's study: 'anything that we now call the humanities: the whole story in the strict sense, sociology, national economy, the history of religion, language, law and art'.[20]

Post-humanism today, quite apart from its enthusiasm for what the Cartesian philosopher Julien de la Mettrie – a contemporary of Vico – called 'Machine Man', poses itself as an antagonist of this generalist, integrated approach to knowledge. Hence Bruno Latour (setting out from the brave new world of Alan Turing) posits that since computers have become capable of solving tasks of which humans are individually incapable, that they have themselves become subject-objects divorced from their human interlocutors, possessing an independent culture, no longer dependent on the humans that built them, programme them or interpret their findings. The performative contradiction escapes their proponents – that until computers programme humans, grow their own hardware or contest their programmers' instructions, nothing like independence can be claimed for them.

Whatever its intentions, post-humanism – to the humanist, at least – gives alienation a philosophical and scientific respectability: to disembody human skill and intelligence, to de-realise human will and effort, to unthink the human. This is, importantly, not a sober observation but a desire. The human subject alienated from its powers of cognition, divorced from its body, descaled from its species, and deprived of its will, is the form of its sublime. It is a massively willed and historically determined effort to be done with will and history. Scientism in the humanities, to this degree, indiscriminately harmonises with a market sublime. Ignoring philological sociology, it yields the stage to the latest inanities of *New York Times* or *Nature* stories, reported with servile enthusiasm, about physicists discussing the Big Bang in language taken, more or less unchanged, from Lucretius' *On the Nature of Things* and Plato's *Timaeus*.

In 'Systems and Things', for example, Jane Bennett latches on to a 'materialism' represented by Spinoza, Latour and neuroscience to affirm 'a vitality or creative power of bodies and forces at all ranges or scales' to 'cut against the hubris of human exceptionalism'.[21] Just as things are endowed with creative force, so are humans now, in this conception, undifferentiated things (except perhaps in the obvious sense overlooked by Bennett, that none of them, as she has, are involved in theorising their own non-exceptional materiality). Not unlike the logic of Spinoza, Bennett dissolves the rift that divides the human and things to create an atmosphere or environment of non-differentiated heterogeneities. In this way the multiple expresses itself, and has in reality become by sleight of hand, the unitary, just as a purely subjective wilfulness learns to express itself through a philosophy of impersonality.

Very much in this spirit, Deleuze (one of Bennett's inspirations) had earlier written that he is not a will who makes, but a conduit for larger energies – that the supposed insight offered by the question 'What does it matter who writes?' is a boast rather than what it appears to be – namely, rendering fame unimportant in a modesty that projects a collective vision. For he is telling us that to challenge his words is not simply to disagree with his idiosyncrasies, invented concepts, neologisms or dubious interpretations but to be against nature itself. He is, after all, only its spokesman, only a conduit for the modalities of perception that flow through him. A radically immodest individualism in this way presents itself as a decentring.

But this sort of point would only be evident to those who gave quarter to the dialectical reason both thinkers scorn. Bennett and Deleuze, like many others within the broad reach of post-humanist thought, are rebellious spirits who would be mortified to think they had given comfort to corporate life. But this is why the subject of humanism is confusing, as I said at the beginning, and why its antagonists look past one another. Left and Right have exchanged roles, and each side sees the other as complicit. From the vantage point of humanism, the post-human position uncomfortably resembles bourgeois thought without, of course, intending to.[22] In that arena, objective reality is the only subjectivity, relying on an authorship impersonally mediated. Trickery, now as a spiritual principle of neither-nor-ness, is demanded to establish the right to irresponsibility. This relationship of convenience – now you see it, now you don't –replicates itself across capitalism's symbolic terrain. Apart from the few indictments associated with the 2008 mortgage collapse and Wall Street speculative fraud, financial markets for the most part are widely perceived as operating (in Bruno Latour's pernicious phrase) as 'human fabrications no human has made'.[23]

This concept of the 'imperson' (we might say) is much more than legal evasion in a contemporary capitalism that officially sees corporations as individuals. The chameleon-like shift between two incompatible public faces finds its pattern in the bourgeois as an unsentimental and efficient cog in the machine of capital, on the one hand, and on the other, the bourgeois as poet, rebel and *avant* philosopher (as in Steve Jobs's widely quoted phrase of being among 'the crazy ones, the misfits, the rebels, the troublemakers, the round pegs in the square holes ... they push the human race forward').[24] So speak today's monopolists, sweatshop owners and tax dodgers. Is this not a parody that has found its form? Are these not definite features of the bourgeois today, as tangible as images of the top hat and moneybags of yesterday? As a more than convenient or merely flippant symbol, military drones are very apt for capturing this slippage – this ideological centrepiece of capitalism in its contemporary, anarchist phase. Intensely mercenary and subjectivist appetites demand the symbolic sacrifice of the subject. The person must be killed so that the capitalist might live; the historical actor must be paralysed so that his or her unconscionable acts can proceed without reprisal, keeping its illicit money in the no-man's land of offshore accounts, or promoting a virtual reality meant to obscure the computer banks riveted to the floor in an air-conditioned underground warehouse in Nevada. Why else would there be such confusion among those who, subjectively at any rate, want nothing to do with capitalism, who express their hatred of capitalism and yet who subversively share this same evacuation of spirit's ethical will as a protest against capital?[25]

Sharing this anarchist spirit, post-humanism finds its foe in only one side of capitalism: its Enlightenment arrogance entrepreneurially setting out to master nature. But here it misses what accompanies these gestures dialectically: the negation of nature (in the form of corporate ecological devastation) and the erasure of persons – the unnamed and underpaid ones who make the product, the consumers coerced to buy it, the spiritual impoverishment of owning it, the state surveillance it complicitly enables, and by means of the product, the equation of persons with pilfered sales data. It neglects entirely what Left philology brings out into the open: the *counter*-Enlightenment directives of capitalism, where all responsibility is necessarily ambiguated, testimony selectively forgotten, information privatised and intellectual skills apotheosised as market genius (that is, reified, made objective).

*For Humanism* offers us a vital prolegomenon to this contemporary setting, laying out a field of thought and action that pre-empts the appeal of post-humanism by offering us another, and earlier, story of language and sensibility. There is so much still to learn about a body of work unfairly consigned to the past, waiting to be rediscovered like Lucretius' Epicurean masterpiece from the first century BCE languishing in a German monastery until Bracciolini stumbled upon it fifteen centuries later. Only sixty years or so, even less, separates us from the masterpieces under review in this volume. Acquainting ourselves with them is not simply a studious act but a political one – a reassertion of a modernity made by and for human beings who might have done otherwise. We still can. The alternative is there, and is waiting to be read and acted upon.

## NOTES

1. Ludwig Feuerbach, *The Essence of Christianity*, trans. Marian Evans, London: John Chapman, 1854, p. 15.
2. Georges Bataille, *The Accursed Share*, vols. 2 and 3, New York: Zone, 1993, pp. 173–84.
3. An invaluable study in this context is Sankar Muthu's *Enlightenment Against Empire*, Princeton, NJ: Princeton University Press, 2003, which in close readings of Montaigne, Diderot, Kant and Herder traces the depths of anticolonial thought in these central thinkers, while exploring their principle of 'humanity as a moral ideal'.
4. Aimé Césaire, *Discourse on Colonialism*, trans. Joan Pinkham, New York: Monthly Review Press, 1972, p. 33.
5. Dr. Ramendra and Dr. Kawaljeet, *Rationalism, Humanism and Atheism in Twentieth-Century Indian Thought*, Patna: Buddhiwadi Foundation, 2007, no page number. See http://bihar.humanists.net/Roy.htm.
6. The discussion here on the role of philology in Marxism, anticolonialism and the Left, and on Nietzsche's relationship to antihumanism, is explored more fully in Timothy Brennan, *Borrowed Light: Vico, Hegel and the Colonies*, Stanford, CA: Stanford University Press, 2014.
7. Martin Heidegger, *Basic Writings*, David Farrell Krell (ed.), San Francisco: HarperSanFrancisco, 1993, pp. 218, 237.

8. Bataille, *The Accursed Share* vols. 2 and 3, p. 318.

9. Brennan, *Borrowed Light*, p. 162.

10. Andrew Zimmerman, *Anthropology and Antihumanism in Imperial Germany*, Chicago: University of Chicago Press, 2001, p. 3.

11. Ibid., p. 241.

12. Ibid., pp. 7, 246.

13. Stefanos Geroulanos, *An Atheism that is Not Humanist Emerges in French Thought*, Stanford, CA: Stanford University Press, 2010, pp. 2–15.

14. Ibid., p. 6.

15. Domenico Losurdo, *Heidegger and the Ideology of War: Community, Death and the West*, Amherst, NY: Humanity Books, 2001 [1991], p. 101.

16. Theodor W. Adorno, *Negative Dialectics*, trans. E. B. Ashton, London: Routledge, 1990 [1966], p. 61.

17. Theodor W. Adorno, 'The Idea of Natural History', trans. Robert Hullot-Kentor, *Telos*, 60 (1984), pp. 111–24.

18. Ernst Bloch, *Literary Essays*, trans. Andrew Joron and others, Stanford, CA: Stanford University Press, 1998, p. 1.

19. Max Horkheimer, 'Traditional and Critical Theory', in *Critical Theory: Selected Essays*, trans. Matthew J. O'Connell and others, New York: Continuum, 1982.

20. Vorrede des Übersetzers and Giambattista Vico, *Die Neue Wissenschaft: Über die gemeinshaftliche Natur der Völker*, Nach der Ausgabe von 1744, trans. and intro. Erich Auerbach, Munich: Allgemeine Verlagsanstalt, 1924, p. 23 (my translation).

21. Jane Bennett, 'Systems and Things: A Response to Graham Harman and Timothy Morton', *New Literary History*, No. 43 (2012), pp. 230–2.

22. The following two paragraphs are taken, with modifications, from Timothy Brennan, 'The Free Impersonality of Bourgeois Spirit', *Biography*, Vol. 37, No. 1 (2014), p. 11.

23. Bruno Latour, *We Have Never Been Modern*, trans. Catherine Porter, London: Harvester Wheatsheaf, 1993 [1991], p. 70.

24. The words open Apple's 1997 'Think Different' campaign, a commercial ('Steve Jobs').

25. Finding in consumer culture's production of 'new subjectivities' an ontological resistance to capitalism characterises post-humanism, as we find in the representative collection by Chris Kraus and Sylvère Lotringer, *Hatred of Capitalism: A Semiotext(e) Reader*, Cambridge, MA: MIT Press, 2002.

# 1

# The Rise, Decline and Possible Revival of Socialist Humanism

*Barbara Epstein*

Socialist humanism was an international current, in some instances expressed in political activism as well as in intellectual work, that appeared in the 1940s and 1950s and reached its point of greatest influence in the late 1950s and early 1960s. Of the two terms, socialism and humanism, the meaning of socialism is reasonably clear: socialists are those who are in favour of a society based on cooperation and the common good, rather than competition and profit for the few. What humanism means is less clear. Some use it to describe the outlook of the irreligious. This somewhat old-fashioned usage of the term suggests that the basic division within the intellectual world is between those who believe in God and those who do not. Others use it in a more contemporary way to refer to those who place humans at the centre of their intellectual universe; often the term antihumanism is used in this way to cast the same sort of doubt on a human-centred perspective that the Enlightenment cast on a God-centred perspective. Yet others use humanism to refer to those who are ideologically committed to a sunny view of humanity, according to which humans have only good impulses, no evil ones, and social progress is inevitable. In this view, humanists are naïve optimists.

None of the above definitions accurately describes the outlook of Left intellectuals and activists who identified with socialist humanism in the 1940s, 1950s and 1960s. Socialist humanism was not equivalent to atheism, agnosticism or secularism: there were some socialist humanists who were religious, and many whose thought was strongly influenced by religious traditions. Socialist humanism asked what human nature consists of and what sort of society would be most conducive to human thriving. Though this was a discussion about humans and their capabilities, it was not an assertion that nature exists to serve human needs or that humans should dominate other species and the natural environment. Some socialist humanists saw God or spirit of some sort as the centre, and some criticised the pursuit of human mastery over nature. None of the leading socialist humanist writers of the mid-twentieth-century thought that progress was inevitable or that humans were either devoid of socially destructive impulses, or perfectable. What socialist humanists did (and do) believe is that there is such a thing as human nature, that is, that humans, like other animal species, have characteristics, including specific needs, abilities, and limits to those abilities. Socialist humanism is based on the view that humans require social cooperation and support, are capable of collective effort and individual creativity, and are most likely to thrive in egalitarian communities dedicated to the common welfare rather than to the pursuit of private profit. Socialist humanists also believe that humans are capable of empathy, rational thought and effective planning, and that a better society, and world, is therefore possible. The socialist humanist perspective, as it was developed in the late 1950s and early 1960s, did not focus on the welfare of non-human animals or of the natural environment. But in the intervening years it has become clear that the welfare of the human race is linked to the health of the environment. An expansion of human concern to include the welfare of other living creatures, and of the planet, is clearly compatible with socialist humanism.

\*   \*   \*

Socialist humanism flourished as a set of international networks of intellectuals, and as an outlook with influence in peace and to some degree other social movements, from 1956 to the late 1960s. Socialist humanism drew upon Marx's concept of alienation, developed in his *Economic and Philosophic Manuscripts of 1844*, unknown before being published in Moscow in 1932 in the original German. Over the following decades, selections were published in French and then in English.[1] Marx's analysis of alienation as the result of a form of production based on private profit created the basis for a critique of capitalism based on capitalism's impact on the human spirit. Marx argued that the alienation of the worker from her/his product led to the alienation of the worker from other humans, and even to self-alienation. Marx's concept of alienation is humanist both in the sense that it points to the dehumanising character of capitalist relations, and also in its implication that humans must be the authors of their own liberation. Marx continued to employ the concept of alienation in his subsequent work, but it is possible to read his later analysis of capitalist political economy as suggesting that the structural contradictions within capitalism are the system's greatest weakness and the most likely source of capitalism's demise, and that human experience and action are secondary.

*    *    *

The 'scientific socialism' of the first half of the twentieth century emphasised the structural side of Marx's analysis; the Soviets used this perspective to downplay the role of collective action in social change, and to justify substituting party rule for democracy. The *Economic and Philosophic Manuscripts* provided the basis for a challenge to this perspective within the context of Marxism, and gave Marxist and socialist humanists a common theoretical reference point. Even socialist humanists who did not regard themselves as Marxists, such as Martin Buber, appreciated Marx's writings on alienation. Many Marxists, philosophers and others, who were drawn to this perspective, called themselves Marxist humanists, but Erich Fromm and others used the term socialist humanism instead, so as to include socialists who did not consider themselves Marxists. In this chapter I use the term 'socialist humanism' to refer not only to those who so described themselves but also those who preferred the term 'Marxist humanism'. In some respects, though, the humanist tradition I trace here becomes visible through its differentiation from the dogmatisms of both 'scientific' Marxism and subsequent antihumanism.

The publication of Marx's early work on alienation provided the intellectual background for the development of socialist humanism, but it took the succession of shocks to the Stalinist version of socialism that occurred during 1956 to turn what had been a trickle in Marxist thought into a current with intellectual and political influence. The first and most important of these shocks was the 20th Congress of the Communist Party of the Soviet Union in February, at which Khrushchev denounced and enumerated Stalin's crimes and later officially announced his policy of peaceful coexistence with the capitalist West. The second shock was the Hungarian Uprising and the Soviet repression of it, in October and November. Khrushchev's acknowledgement and description of Stalin's crimes threw the international Communist movement into crisis, leading many to leave Communist parties to which they had devoted their lives, suggesting that there might be an opening for a more democratic form of socialism in the Soviet Union, or if not that at least a more democratic form of socialism might become the goal of a newly configured world Left. Khrushchev's promulgation of his policy of peaceful coexistence suggested the possibility of a break in the Cold War. The Hungarian Uprising later the same year led to hopes that Eastern European peoples might be ready to challenge Soviet control; the harsh Soviet response to the uprising reinforced the opposition of many who had left the Communist parties, and other socialists and Marxists, to Soviet repression of democratic initiatives.

The purpose of this chapter is to indicate the main themes of socialist humanist thought in the 1950s and 1960s, to explain why socialist humanism disappeared from the intellectual and political agenda of the Left in the US and Western Europe in the late 1960s and early 1970s, and to argue that its core insights remain valid, and would still be of use to the Left. This is not to suggest that socialist humanism is the solution to all or even most of the problems of the contemporary Left. Socialist and Marxist humanism were products of a particular period. Neither had a great deal to say about issues that have since become priorities for movements for social change: environmental crisis, race, gender, sexuality, technology and its social impact. Neither had much to say about strategy for the Left or about organisational questions.

Socialist humanists of the late 1950s and early 1960s opposed the Cold War and hoped that an end to it would open up space for movements for democratic forms of socialism in both East and West, based on decentralised communities and popular participation rather than bureaucratic control, and that should also involve workers' control of their labour. They defended utopian thinking as a necessary intellectual framework for efforts to bring about change, arguing that even if the future society that we imagine will never be achieved, formulating the goal is a precondition of any advance towards it. In these respects socialist humanism shared a good deal with anarchism; in its orientation towards nonviolent means of change, it came close to pacifism. Socialist humanism made the question of what kind of society we want to live in central. It criticised any form of socialism that would set social solidarity against freedom of expression and the right to dissent, and more broadly it stressed the need to create the conditions under which individual creativity could flourish. Socialist humanism challenged dogmatism by insisting that the future remains open and that no theory can predict it with certainty.

I begin this chapter with a more or less historical survey of the main contributions to socialist humanist thought, emphasising their common themes. Some socialist humanist writers, such as E. P. Thompson, were and remain well known, but primarily for work other than their writings directly addressing socialist humanism. Others, well known on the Left at that time, are no longer widely read. I divide my survey between those for whom socialist humanism was a political as well as an intellectual project, and those whose engagement with it was primarily intellectual. Whose work fell into which of these categories was mostly a question of where they lived: in the West the themes of socialist humanism aligned most easily with the concerns of the peace movements of the late 1950s and the early 1960s, while for the dissident movements in Eastern Europe sustained activity beyond writing and speaking was often difficult. The Praxis School, a group of dissident Yugoslavian philosophers, were able to use the relative openness of Yugoslavian society under Tito to challenge Soviet Marxism and to criticise elements of the Soviet bureaucratic mindset in Yugoslavia itself, but their work took place largely on the plane of philosophical debates. A number of Left theorists in continental Western Europe, especially in France and Germany, aligned themselves with and contributed to socialist humanism, but in the absence of active peace movements their views were expressed through their written work and not through activism.

In Britain and the US, socialist humanists who were activists as well as intellectuals brought their perspectives to their political activity as well as to their intellectual work. In Britain, socialist humanism had influence within the peace movement. In the US, currents of thought among peace and civil rights activists overlapped with socialist humanism. In both Britain and the US, many of the tens of thousands who left the Communist parties in the wake of Khrushchev's disclosures continued to engage in political activity and remained socialists while rejecting the authoritarian version of socialism that held sway in the Soviet Union. In Britain many former Communists explicitly identified with socialist humanism, as did others in the early New Left.[2] In the United States McCarthyism made it difficult openly to criticise the Soviet Union without appearing to align oneself with the repression of leftists. But many of the Left projects that emerged as McCarthyism receded were influenced by former Communists for whom the Soviet Union was an embarrassment and whose major point of political reference was the 1930s, with the Popular Front at home and the anti-fascist struggle abroad. The New Left that emerged in the US in the early 1960s shared socialist humanism's orientation towards utopian thinking and its vision of participatory politics in a decentralised society without necessarily being in favour of socialism.

In the late 1960s and early 1970s the American Left and much of the European Left lost interest in socialist humanism. The Cold War had abated and the danger of nuclear war had ceased to be a major focus of protest. By 1968 the Vietnam War had become the central issue for the Left, especially in the US. In the context of the war the New Left grew and anger and militancy escalated. The Sino-Soviet split, the Chinese critique of the Soviet Union, and the rise of Third World revolutionary movements, especially the Chinese Cultural Revolution, offered a new conception of Left politics to young radicals in the US and elsewhere in the West. According to the Maoist, or more broadly Third Worldist, perspective, the central struggle in the world was between the imperialist West and the anti-imperialist movements of the East, and the task of leftists, now more often calling themselves radicals, in the West, was to support Third World revolutionary movements and look forward to following their example. The critique of the Soviet Union no longer focused on its undemocratic character and its repression of dissent but rather on the charge that it was too compromising in its stance towards the US. From this perspective, the Soviet policy of peaceful coexistence was an obstacle to the struggle against imperialism, and liberal reform was an obstacle to revolution in the capitalist West. Third Worldism swept the US Left and movements of the Left in Europe, especially those on the continent. Against the background of the hyper-militancy and revolutionary expectations of the Left in the late 1960s and early 1970s, socialist humanism seemed tepid.

\*   \*   \*

Many of the issues of the Vietnam era are still with us, along with others that have appeared since then, or have become more urgent. The US continues to engage in foreign wars despite the repeated experience of seeing its intervention only make things worse for the peoples of the affected countries. The gap in wealth and power between the US, and the advanced capitalist countries of the West generally, on the one hand, and the rest of the world on the other, has grown. In the US we face a widening gap in wealth and power and a political arena that is increasingly detached from and unresponsive to the public. Along with the rest of the planet we face looming environmental catastrophes. But the exuberant, ultra-leftist politics that appealed to so many young people during the Vietnam era now seem like quaint memories of a very different moment. Perhaps a return to the legacy of socialist humanism may provide suggestions for a Left politics appropriate for a more sober time.

## SOCIALIST HUMANISM AS A POLITICAL PROJECT

In 1956, E. P. Thompson and John Saville, both labour historians and both then members of the Communist Party of Great Britain, launched *The Reasoner*, a dissident inner-party journal focused on the critique of Stalinism and Soviet Marxism. In the wake of the Soviet repression of the Hungarian Uprising, Thompson and Saville, among many others, left the Communist Party. *The Reasoner*, renamed *The New Reasoner*, became the vehicle for a politics that combined opposition to the Cold War and to both great powers, with advocacy of participatory democracy as the basis for a democratic socialist society. It expressed and helped to shape the perspective of many of those who had left the Communist Party of Great Britain in the wake of Khrushchev's revelations about Stalinism, and it also influenced the thinking of young people just entering the political arena, drawn to the socialist Left but uninterested in aligning themselves with the Soviet Union.

In 1957 *The New Reasoner* published an article by E. P. Thompson entitled 'Socialist Humanism: An Epistle to the Philistines',[3] a call for a revolt against Stalinism within the international Left in the name of a socialist humanism which, Thompson argued, replaced the abstractions of official Soviet Marxist theory with the needs, struggles and outlook of real men and women. Thompson argued that the entire Communist movement had been infected with the dogmatism inherent in the official brand of Marxist theory, and that even Western Marxism, despite having moved away from structural analysis through its focus on culture and ideology, had failed to challenge the prevailing dogmatism. Marxist theory must begin with the needs, thoughts and actions of real human beings. Socialism must have a moral basis and Soviet socialism must not be regarded as a model in any way. Thompson argued that the Cold War and the arms race sustained ruling groups in both the Soviet Union and the US, and enabled political repression in both East and West. He pointed out that revolt against the Cold War, and against the repressive regimes that sustained it, was brewing among young people not only in the West, where mass peace movements were beginning to appear, but also in Eastern Europe; he hoped that resistance might spread to the Soviet Union itself. Such a revolt, Thompson argued, could develop into an international movement for a version of democratic socialism based on humanist principles.

The New Reasoner, along with Universities and Left Review, a journal initiated and run by young academic leftists, became the centre of the early British New Left, which consisted of circles of students, intellectuals and other young people. The New Left brought them together in discussions of new directions in politics and culture, and also introduced them to the emergent British peace movement. Virtually the entire New Left became actively involved in what was rapidly becoming a mass movement for a British policy of non-alignment in the Cold War, and for the dismantling of NATO missile sites in Britain. The New Left gained considerable intellectual credibility, and influence, in the British peace movement. Socialist humanism had a lasting impact on intellectual currents in the British Left.

Though both The New Reasoner and Universities and Left Review described themselves as journals of socialist humanism, their orientations differed somewhat: the editors of The New Reasoner were grounded in the British labour movement and in the history of class struggle in Britain, while their counterparts at University and Left Review were more interested in the cultural changes then underway, and more attentive to issues of racial and ethnic difference. Nevertheless, the broad political compatibility of the two led to a merger in 1959 and the creation of New Left Review. In 1962, the founding editors of The New Reasoner, including E. P. Thompson, were dropped from the editorial committee of New Left Review, now headed by Perry Anderson, and the journal ceased to identify itself with socialist humanism.[4] In 1964, a new journal, Socialist Register, was founded, continuing the legacy of socialist humanist intellectual work.

Over time differing responses to international events and to emerging theoretical currents, along with continuing bitterness over the split itself, widened and hardened the differences between the two currents that had worked together to form the early New Left. E. P. Thompson's growing fame was based primarily on his magisterial historical work, The Making *of the English Working Class*, which inspired a generation of young historians to embark on the study of 'history from below'. Along with his directly historical writings Thompson continued to engage in theoretical debate, and also in political activity: in the 1980s he played a central role in the movement against the Second Cold War. His critique of Althusser, *The Poverty of Theory: Or, an Orrery of Errors*, was a passionate defence of a version of Marxism that placed the experiences and efforts of people, rather than theoretical categories, at its centre, and that was informed by history and by a moral sensibility.[5] Thompson's essay was criticised for his tendency to assume that experience, and morality, were self-evident categories that could be taken at face value. Critics also pointed out that Thompson's judgement was at times distorted by his rage at Althusser's stance, leading him to mistake Althusser's intent, as in assuming that Althusser's critique of humanism was an expression of Stalinism, when in fact Althusser's sympathies lay not with Stalinism but with Maoism.[6] But even if Thompson overshot the mark at times, the theoretical difference between him and Althusser was real and important. The human subject, as conceived by Althusser, was merely a carrier of class relations. In Althusser's view theory took precedence over history and structure over human experience, decision and action. Althusser's human subject was in effect a puppet, incapable of resistance to the forces driving his/her actions. In his view capitalist society (and in fact, every society) exuded a fog of ideology that engulfed all members of the society except the theorist, who could rise above the fog and criticise the social relations laid out before him. For Thompson, it was the human subject, shaped by history and by the experience of class and class conflict, that drove history, and it was human subjects collectively, in particular members of the working class, who had the capacity to lead the way to a socialist society. Althusser regarded history as very nearly irrelevant: all one needed to understand capitalism, in his view, was the Marxist theory of class structure, correctly understood. Marx's early humanism, in Althusser's view, was superseded and cancelled by his later structural analysis of capitalism. In Thompson's view classes, class relations and class conflict were constructed historically and could not be understood apart from history.

Thompson was enraged by a version of Marxism that disregarded human agency and its historical context. He was also dismayed by the influence of Althusser's antihumanism and his structuralist and anti-historical version of Marxism. Thompson, writing in the late 1970s, still in the early days of post-structuralism, may have sensed that he was battling the wave of the future. Althusser's antihumanism appealed mostly to Marxist intellectuals, particularly young political economists; their influence was considerable within Left intellectual circles, but these circles had their limits. Althusser's influence was soon eclipsed by that of Michel Foucault, who especially in his early work showed little interest in class or political economy, disdained Marxism, and turned antihumanism into a kind of common sense, an assumed basis for social criticism. Through Foucault's influence, a generation of young intellectuals came to regard antihumanism as the ground not so much of Marxism as of intellectual life as a whole. Thompson's rage was prescient.

In the US, the main current of socialist humanism developed in the context of the Frankfurt School, relocated, after Hitler's rise to power, in New York City and later in California. Most members of the school regarded the concept of alienation as central to social criticism, rejected the Soviet version of Marxism, and subscribed to a democratic socialist politics, and thus in some broad sense could be described as socialist humanists. But the work of most members of the Frankfurt School was focused on the analysis of authoritarian trends and on the critique of culture rather than on more directly political questions, and many held a dim view of the prospects of human civilisation that set them apart from the more hopeful stance associated with socialist humanism. Two members of the Frankfurt School, Erich Fromm and Herbert Marcuse, were engaged in intellectual work that was directly concerned with a critique of contemporary capitalist society and the prospects for moving beyond it. Both were also involved in movements for social change, in Fromm's case the peace movement, and in Marcuse's the New Left. Both gained a public association with socialist humanism.

Fromm became the most influential proponent of socialist humanism in the United States and, arguably, internationally as well. His edited collection, *Socialist Humanism: An International Symposium*, published in 1965,[7] was an attempt to solidify international networks of socialist and Marxist humanists and to give socialist humanism a new degree of public visibility and influence, as Kevin Anderson highlights in detail in Chapter 2. Marcuse later came to be widely regarded as a socialist humanist due to the centrality of liberation, individual and collective, in his conception of Left politics, and the importance of his work, especially his book, *One-Dimensional Man*, for the New Left.[8] But in fact he was quite ambivalent about socialist humanism. In his essay in Fromm's collection, 'Socialist Humanism?', Marcuse expressed scepticism about the possibility of a humanist form of socialism in the age of advanced technology. He wrote that a humanist society may have been possible in an age when 'the mind and the soul were not yet taken over by scientific management ... where there could still be a realm of freedom not correlated with that of necessity' but that given the colonisation of life by organised business and organised leisure he could not envision such an outcome. 'Marxist theory,' Marcuse wrote, 'retains an idea of man which now appears as too optimistic and idealistic.'[9]

Fromm has gained a reputation as a liberal or social democrat, perhaps because he avoided left-wing and Marxist terminology in his writing, or because his political activity, in the peace movement, was not explicitly revolutionary. But in fact Fromm was a socialist and a Marxist. The question of alienation was a central focus of Fromm's work; his analysis was framed by a critique of capitalism. In his book *The Sane Society*, published in 1955, Fromm argued that separation from nature is the basic human trauma, creating a sense of emptiness that is often addressed negatively – through the pursuit of power, wealth and fame, or through engagement in relations of dominance and subordination – but that can also be addressed positively, through the pursuit of human solidarity and through love and care for others.[10] Fromm argued that love and solidarity are basic human needs that are frustrated by capitalism, and he called for a decentralised socialist society based on cooperation and workers' participation in management. Fromm pointed out that this was consonant with Marx's vision of a future communist society as decentralised, stateless and egalitarian. In his 1961 book, *Marx's Concept of Man*, Fromm argued that the concept of alienation was central to the mature as well as to the young Marx.[11] Fromm also pointed to the discrepancy between Marx's vision of communism as a decentralised social order and the reality of Soviet authoritarianism. Though he acknowledged that Marx could not be held responsible for Stalin's actions, Fromm argued that Marx's view that the decentralised society could arrive only in the far-off future encouraged authoritarian conceptions of socialism, and that his habit of denouncing other socialists who disagreed with him on minor points opened the door to authoritarian practices within the socialist movement.[12]

Over the same period during which Thompson, Fromm and others were developing a conception of socialism as a democratic and humane society in which the alienation of the capitalist system would be overcome. So too was Raya Dunayevskaya, an activist, intellectual and former Trotskyist leader whose work is considered in more detail by Anderson in Chapter 2. Marx, Dunayevskaya pointed out, first called the philosophy governing the transcendence of capitalist alienation 'humanism', later substituting the term 'communism'.[13] Thompson, Fromm and Dunayevskaya were each part of a larger effort to reorient the Left, in their countries and internationally, to a humanist version of Marxist theory and socialist politics, and each of these, along with others in their circles, considered their practical political work part of a broader effort to build a socialist/Marxist humanist Left. Fromm's arena was the US peace movement, in particular the Committee for a Sane Nuclear Policy, of which he was a founder and in which he played an active role. Dunayevskaya's arena was labour organising. Thompson's was the early British New Left and the British peace movement, in particular the Committee for Nuclear Disarmament, and later the movement against the Second Cold War of the 1980s. In the late 1950s and through the first half of the 1960s, many activists in the peace movements in Britain and the US, and some in the US civil rights movement, were critical of capitalism, open to or in support of socialism, and rejected the Soviet model of socialism due to its authoritarianism. This was to some degree a result of the influence of Fromm, Thompson, Dunayevskaya and others with similar views, but it was probably to a much greater extent due to the lasting influence of Communism and other forms of socialism in the 1930s. For many in these movements the goal of socialism remained valid even if the Soviet Union could no longer serve as a model.

## C. L. R. James

Cyril Lionel Robert James, an Afro-Trinidadian intellectual, activist and comrade of Dunayevskaya's, like her sought an alternative to the Soviet model of socialism. His book *Facing Reality: The New Society: Where to Look For It and How to Bring It Closer*, co-authored by Grace C. Lee, addressed the immediate problems of the socialist movement as well as longer standing problems of Marxism. James, an autodidact, wrote widely respected works of history, literature and Marxist theory, and he became an influential leader within the international arena of socialist/anti-Stalinist activism. Born in Trinidad in 1901, where he became a teacher and participated in the anti-colonial struggle, he moved to Britain in 1932, joined the Trotskyist movement, advocated Pan-Africanism, and played an active role in the international anti-colonial/anti-fascist movement. In 1938 he moved to the US. In Britain he had been an active member of the Socialist Workers' Party (SWP), the leading international Trotskyist organisation, which regarded the Soviet Union as a degenerated workers' state, identified itself with Leninism while vigorously opposing Stalinism, and endorsed the concept of a vanguard party. In the US, James became critical of vanguardism. James left the SWP, joined the further-left Workers' Party, and, with Raya Dunayevskaya and Grace Lee (later Grace Lee Boggs), both of whom shared his Trotskyist critique of the Soviet Union and his rejection of vanguardism, he formed the Johnson–Forest Tendency, the name referring to James' party pseudonym, Johnson, and Dunayevskaya's, Forest.

Later both James and Dunayevskaya rejected Trotsky's understanding of the Soviet Union as a degenerated workers' state and came to regard it instead as a state-capitalist system. (The phrase 'degenerated workers' state' indicated a view of the Soviet Union as socialist, despite its flaws, and thus worthy of critical support; the phrase 'state capitalist' indicated a shift to a view of the Soviet Union as not socialist and not warranting even critical support.) James and Dunayevskaya left the Trotskyist movement and formed the Correspondence Publishing Committee. Lee, a Chinese-American activist and intellectual oriented towards African-American and Third World struggles was, like Dunayevskaya, deeply influenced by her reading of Hegel and of Marx, especially Marx's *Economic and Philosophic Manuscripts*. Marxist humanism became a major current within the Johnson–Forest Tendency, and influenced the perspectives of James as well as Lee and Dunayevskaya. Nevertheless, in 1955, when James left for England, James and Dunayevskaya split. Dunayevskaya and her supporters left the Correspondence Publishing Committee, which James continued to lead from abroad, and formed the Marxist humanist News and Letters Committee. James and Lee's book *Facing Reality*, like Raya Dunayevskaya's writings, reflected the intellectual and political debates and the political activism of the Trotskyist and Marxist humanist arena. It rejected utopianism in the sense of a fantasised conception of the future, unconnected to present realities. But their conviction that those who lacked a conception of a better society would not be able to advance towards it, and their efforts to outline such a vision, aligned them with others who called their own visions utopian.

*Facing Reality*, first published in 1958, was inspired by the Hungarian Uprising of 1956, and also by its authors' view that the socialist and anti-totalitarian impulses that informed this uprising were widespread among the working classes of other nations as well, and their hope that similar uprisings would take place in the West. James and Lee's book was informed by their extensive experience as organisers and Left activists, and contributed a fine-grained knowledge of these arenas that was less noticeable in the work of those whose daily experience revolved around intellectual circles and institutions. They described the workers' councils formed during the Hungarian Uprising, and the role that they assumed of organising production and managing local affairs, as the model for a new civilisation, a socialist society based on the self-management of workers and of allied members of the middle class. They described the Hungarian Uprising as an instance of the rejection of not only the vanguard model of revolutionary parties, espoused by both Communists and Trotskyists, but of political parties in general.

James and Lee asked, rhetorically, 'Is the Government of Workers Councils ... only a historical accident, peculiar to totalitarianism, or is it the road of the future for all society?' They saw evidence of a turn in this direction on the part of the American workers, who, they argued, were much more interested in shop-floor struggles with management and union bureaucracy than with the programmes of political parties. They wrote scornfully of the tendency of leftists to scan the horizon for signs of working class support for a socialist party or a Left-leaning union movement. 'They find none,' James and Lee wrote, 'because the American workers are looking for none. The struggle in America is between management, supervision, and the union bureaucrats on the one side and the shop-floor organizations on the other. If any one national struggle can be pinpointed as the one on which the future fate of the world depends, it is this struggle, and the American workers hold all the cards.'[14]

James's and Lee's confidence that shop-floor struggles would lead to socialist uprising reflected an exaggerated view of the readiness of American workers to reject capitalism – a version of myopia widespread at the time among activists and intellectuals who hoped for a socialist revolution. Their more lasting contributions were to point to the centrality of the issue of race, the importance of automation (or more broadly technological change) as a threat to employment and to the balance of power between workers and management, and the many failures of what they called 'the Marxist organisation' (meaning the Communist Party) on these and other issues. In regard to race, they wrote that 'the fear of offending one race and then the other ... the capitulation to the prejudices of official society and to the prejudices of particular workers or groups of workers, the blunders, stupidities and confusion the Marxist organizations have been guilty of on this question are by themselves sufficient to condemn them on all other questions. In the US who fails on the Negro question is weak on all.'[15] They called for strong support for the then emergent civil rights movement regardless of its lack of socialist politics, and also for a willingness to welcome what they called 'Negro aggressiveness' on the race question. 'It is here that the Marxist organization has to show firmness, not in defense of its own abstract principles, but in its determination that the Negro worker shall say what he wants to say and how he wants to say it.'[16]

James's and Lee's insistence on the centrality of race and on the need for support of black protest, whether it took the form of a demand for the right to vote and an end to all forms of discrimination, or of black nationalism, showed a rare degree of insight. Their criticisms of the Left of that time, focused on the Communist Left, were equally insightful:

> It is absolutely imperative to put an end to the legend of 'the vanguard' which has dominated the revolutionary movement for so many decades and with such catastrophic results ... The idea is inherent in ... the majority of present-day groups that there must be a body of sharply differentiated individuals who must separate themselves from the working class and so form a permanent organization which is more conscious, more militant, more coherent in its actions than the great mass of the workers. This is pure and simple delirium. The people who consider themselves 'the vanguard' are not in general more conscious than the 'backward' working class except from one point of view ... in that they know (generally very badly) the history of the workers' movement and the elements of Marxism reduced to their most simple formulae; they are interested in international politics ... But they are in general unconscious of what constitute the most profound realities of capitalist society, the realities of production.[17]

James and Lee were insightful in their critique not only of the Communist Party but of the existing organised Left as a whole for its insularity, its tendency to cling to outmoded theories and its reluctance to acknowledge new developments and to engage with people who did not speak the vocabulary familiar to the Marxist Left. Their hopes for a Left movement based on workers' councils turned out to be misplaced, and their rejection of the political arena as a whole was ungrounded. But their call for a socialist movement that would avoid theoretical dogmatism and organisational elitism coincided with currents of thought among young people just beginning to form what would take shape as the New Left.

### The Praxis School

During the years in which socialist humanism was being promoted in the US and Britain by politically active intellectuals, it was also taking hold among dissident Left intellectuals in Eastern Europe. This current took its most organised and politically engaged form in Yugoslavia, among a group of dissident Marxist philosophers. Members of what became the Praxis School based their approach on Marx's *Economic and Philosophic Manuscripts of 1844* and his subsequent writings on alienation, and upon their opposition to Stalinism and to the Cold War, as well as their conviction that Soviet Marxism provided the basis for Soviet authoritarianism. The circles out of which the Praxis School was formed consisted initially of students and young professors critical of Soviet socialism and drawn to the work of the early Marx. Over time many of the students obtained positions in the philosophy departments of the University of Belgrade, the University of Zagreb and elsewhere. By the early 1960s Marxist humanism had become the dominant trend in philosophy in Yugoslavia and the centre of opposition to Stalinism.

In 1964, members of the group founded the journal *Praxis*, publishing two versions of it. One of these, in Serbo-Croatian, was directed at a domestic audience; the other, intended for an international audience, included articles in English, French and German as well as in Serbo-Croatian. The Praxis School emphasised the critique of bureaucracy, which its members regarded as a major source of alienation and an impediment to a truly democratic form of socialism. The Praxis School held a summer school on the island of Korcula, off the Croatian coast, almost every year from 1963 to 1974, attended by international scholars with similar political and theoretical orientations, as well as by Yugoslavians, students and others. The Korcula Summer School fostered ties among like-minded socialist intellectuals as well as introducing their perspective to dissident Yugoslavian students.[18]

The rise of the Praxis School had been made possible by Tito's 1948 break from the Soviet Union and the subsequent anti-Stalinist tilt of the Yugoslavian Communist Party, which promoted an independent path to socialism for Yugoslavia based on 'self-management' – a conception of workers' control of their workplaces. Members of the Praxis School supported this effort and the Yugoslavian Communist Party's critique of Soviet socialism. But over the course of the 1960s members of the Praxis School began to perceive problems of bureaucracy in Yugoslavian society as well, and they extended their critique to the Yugoslavian government. Tensions between the Yugoslavian Communist Party and the Praxis School steadily increased, and in 1974 the Yugoslavian government banned the publication of both editions of *Praxis*. Eight members of the Praxis School were dismissed from their university departments. All were ultimately able to find academic positions elsewhere, in other universities, but neither the journal *Praxis* nor the Korcula Summer School were ever resumed.[19] Despite these projects, the Praxis School had relatively little influence on the development of socialist humanism in the West. Most publications by members of the Praxis School were in Serbo-Croatian, and thus inaccessible to a Western audience. Furthermore, the concerns that drove the Western version of socialist humanism were not quite the same as those that drove its Yugoslavian counterpart. Soviet authoritarianism and its milder version in Yugoslavia was a pressing, immediate concern for the Praxis School. Their Western counterparts were more focused on the questions of how to move beyond the Cold War, frame opposition to capitalism, and move towards a socialist society that would avoid the pitfalls exhibited by the Soviet Union. These discussions took shape differently.

## SOCIALIST HUMANISM AS A THEORETICAL PROJECT

For Fromm, Thompson and Dunayevskaya, socialist or Marxist humanism was a political project, grounded in a perspective that was philosophical, social and historical. All three were, throughout their adult lives, actively involved in the project of building a viable movement of the Left, responsive to the demands of their time, as they saw them; there could be no division between their intellectual efforts and their political aims and activity. There were many other intellectuals, many of them philosophers, who shared the vision of a democratic and humane socialist society, but whose contributions to the development of socialist or Marxist humanism were more in the realm of theory than of activism. *History and Class Consciousness*, by Georg Lukács, the Hungarian Communist and Marxist philosopher, was published in 1923. Though Marx's *Economic and Philosophic Manuscripts* were yet to be discovered and published, Lukács' careful reading of Marx's discussion of alienation and commodity fetishism in *Capital* enabled him to elaborate on Marx's understanding of these concepts in a way that turned out to be remarkably close to Marx's own discussion in the 1844 manuscripts. Lukács' work was the foundation to the development of socialist humanism, though that was to take place decades after the publication of his book.

### Georg Lukács

Lukács did not see himself as a founder of socialist or Marxist humanism, but rather as a disciple and interpreter of Marx who was presenting Marx's own ideas as Marx himself had understood them. Lukács' reliance on a Hegelian vocabulary, or frame of reference, was a product of his intellectual training and commitments before he encountered Marxism and adopted its perspective. But Lukács' use of Hegel also mirrored Marx's grounding in Hegel, in addition to Marx's extensive use of Hegel's conception of the dialectic and of his commitment to the idea of totality, of the ultimate reality of the connectedness of all things, despite the appearance that the world consists of a plethora of discrete and unrelated phenomena. Along with the concept of totality, Lukács absorbed Hegel's view of history as the framework within which the problem of division would be resolved. As Lukács used these concepts, via his reading of Marx, history was the terrain on which the division between subject and object could be overcome, through the proletariat's recognition of itself as the object not only of oppression – slaves, too, had been oppressed – but of a process of production in which workers were alienated not only from their products, and from other humans, for whom their labour was a commodity, but also from themselves, because their creative capacities and their relations with others were driven by a logic incompatible with human nature. The working class, unlike all previous oppressed classes, was both object and potential subject: its rejection of its own status as commodity would subvert a social order in which humans related to one another as commodities, and would lead to the creation of a society in which, for the first time, humans would recognise one another as fellow human beings, engaged in the common project of creating a society in which all could flourish. This process of the proletariat's recognition of itself as object and subject, which was at the same time a revolutionary project, could only take place in an unfolding historical context.

Thus far Lukács was expounding Marx's writings, brilliantly, especially considering he had not had the opportunity to read the *Economic and Philosophic Manuscripts*, but nevertheless without going beyond Marx in any major way. Lukács' originality lay in his concept of reification, developed in his essay, 'Reification and the Consciousness of the Proletariat', which can be seen as the heart of his book, *History and Class Consciousness*.[20] The Bolshevik Revolution had been conducted in the expectation that a socialist revolution, in one country, would be followed by revolutions elsewhere in the capitalist world. In Germany such a revolution was attempted, with disastrous consequences. Lukács participated in the founding of the Hungarian Communist Party, in 1918, and in the government of the Hungarian Soviet Republic, founded in 1918 and defeated in 1919. He fled to Vienna where he remained for a decade.

In his prison writings Antonio Gramsci, the Italian Communist leader arrested and imprisoned in 1926 for his revolutionary activity, addressed the larger problem of which the defeat of the attempted Hungarian revolution was an instance: the expected socialist revolutions were not taking place. Marx had suggested that the contradictory nature of capitalist political economy, and the place of the working class within that system, would lead to revolution, but other than in Russia – hardly a typical capitalist nation – this had not happened. Gramsci asked what the Left should do when capitalism turned out to be more resilient than expected, the revolution was delayed, and the Right was ascendant. It was in this context that Gramsci introduced his distinction between a war of manoeuvre and a war of position. A war of manoeuvre, in Gramsci's vocabulary, meant an attempt on the part of the Left to displace those in power so as to create a socialist society. A war of position was the strategy that he recommended for a Left attempting to strengthen itself in a society not on the verge of revolution. This involved entering the institutions that constituted the fabric of society, gaining the respect and support of the working class, forming coalitions with other classes, and through educational, institutional and political work, creating an understanding of the need for socialism and building a basis for its achievement. Gramsci's recognition of the importance of achieving cultural hegemony implicitly challenged the Soviet view that the contradictions inherent in capitalism would themselves lead to a transition to socialism. Gramsci cannot be described as a socialist humanist because his concerns revolved around the question of how to lay the groundwork for a socialist revolution, not what form the revolutionary society would take. But the problem that Gramsci addressed was nevertheless relevant to socialist humanism. The failure of revolution to have taken place in the West suggested to Western socialists that something was wrong with Marxist theory as it stood – beyond disappointment with Soviet socialism – and reinforced the impetus to question the orthodox, or Soviet, version of Marxism.

Though Lukács did not describe his concept of reification as a response to the failure of socialist revolution to take place, it is possible to see it as addressing the same problem that concerned Gramsci, but through an analysis of capitalist culture. Lukács argued that the alienation inherent in a system of production that revolved around the fetishisation of commodities led to a society in which things were regarded as the measure of value, and humans and human relations treated as things. In such a society, he argued, the human role in producing and determining value disappeared from sight. Science, he argued, became formalistic and consciousness of totality was lost: society came to be understood as a mass of discrete, unrelated facts, and the actual complex totality of intertwined, historically unfolding processes became invisible. Lukács argued that because the working class, unlike other classes, aimed to obliterate itself as a class, it could and would rise above the limitations of bourgeois thought, understand the totality, and transform it.

Lukács' genius was to point to the commodification of a widening circle of phenomena when that process was in its infancy, at a time when neither he nor anyone else could have imagined the heights that it has since attained. Lukács developed this theory more than two decades before the appearance of socialist or Marxist humanism as an explicit current within Marxism and the intellectual Left. By the time that current appeared, Lukács no longer associated himself with it. In 1930, Lukács was called to Moscow and was prevented from leaving until the conclusion of World War II, presumably because the Soviet leadership regarded his views as contrary to theirs. His 'Blum theses', of 1928, called for a revolutionary strategy for Hungary similar to that of the People's Front in France and elsewhere in Western Europe, and *History and Class Consciousness* presented a theory in which consciousness played much more of a role than it did in the Soviet version of

Marxism. Lukács remained something of a dissident, perhaps as much of one as was possible under the circumstances. In 1938 he published *The Young Hegel*, an act of defiance given the Soviet rejection of Hegel's perspective. Returning to Hungary after the war, as a member of the Communist government, he supported government repression of dissidence and distanced himself from his earlier work. During the last stage of the Hungarian Uprising of 1956, however, he threw his support behind the rebels. In 1960 he published a critique of *History and Class Consciousness*, describing it as overly influenced by Hegelian concepts such as the totality and subject-object identity. It is easy to understand Lukács' cautiousness and his intellectual shifts; his position as a leading member of the Hungarian Communist Party, under Stalin and beyond, was extremely difficult, and he was lucky to survive. Despite Lukács' individual trajectory, *History and Class Consciousness* continued to be seen as foundational by a growing cohort of socialist/Marxist humanist philosophers.

Lukács' extension of Marx's concept of alienation, from the relations of production to the social relations and culture of capitalist societies, does not solve what might be described as the central problem of Marxism. The contradictions of capitalist political economy, and the exploitation of the working class, do not necessarily lead to socialist revolution. The same can be said of reification. Despite the intensification of commodification and of the alienation associated with it, there is no sign of anti-capitalist revolution on the horizon. But Lukács' analysis does provide the basis for a conception of socialism as a social order in which alienation will be transcended, not only in relations of production but in social relations and culture generally.

Despite Lukács' efforts to develop an alternative view, the version of dialectical materialism endorsed by the Comintern continued to be widely accepted by Communists and others. The Soviet understanding of dialectical materialism posited a direct relationship between the contradictions of capitalism, located within productive relations, and the emergence of class conflict and revolutionary struggle, with human consciousness playing little role in this equation. Likewise, the relationship between matter and consciousness was understood to be that between two discrete entities: consciousness reflected matter, and Marxism represented the correct, scientific form of consciousness. The seeds for the later development of a different view were laid in the 1930s and 1940s, first by the translation of selections from Marx's *Economic and Philosophic Manuscripts* into French, by Henri Lefebvre and Norbert Guterman,[21] and then by a revival of interest in Hegel among Parisian philosophers, inspired by a series of lectures by Alexandre Kojève, attended by an impressive array of philosophers and intellectuals.

Socialist humanism emerged earlier in continental Europe, especially in France, than in Britain and the US. During the war the choice between collaboration and opposition to fascism had been posed in a particularly sharp way in France, by the presence of a local collaborationist regime on the one hand and the militant opposition of the Resistance on the other. In the years after the war the possibility that France might come under the sway of either the US or the Soviet Union posed a quite different and much less clear-cut set of ethical choices. On the continent, as elsewhere, the events of 1956 gave socialist humanism a political credibility that it had previously lacked, and wider appeal. In Eastern Europe it was associated with the politics of anti-Stalinism, but in Western Europe, in the absence of social movements with immediately relevant goals, socialist humanism was developed largely through the writings of Left intellectuals.

### Maurice Merleau-Ponty

Among the earliest and most influential of the socialist humanists was Maurice Merleau-Ponty, a phenomenologist concerned with the question of the relationship between humans and the world that surrounds them, and also with the human propensity for violence, and how an egalitarian society in which humans would treat each other as ends rather than means might be achieved. In 1940, during the German occupation of Paris, Merleau-Ponty joined a resistance group, Socialism and Liberty, that tried to chart a course between the Communist and Christian wings of the Resistance; Jean-Paul Sartre was also a member. In 1945, with the war over, Merleau-Ponty and Sartre both publically gave their support to the party, Rassemblement Democratique Revolutionnaire, which like Socialism and Liberty attempted to fashion a politics that was socialist but independent of both the Soviet Union and the French Communist Party. Like Socialism and Liberty, Rassemblement Democratique Revolutionnaire was unable to sustain itself for long. During the same year, 1945, Merleau-Ponty and Sartre founded the journal, *Les Temps modernes*, of which they served as co-editors.

The decision by Sartre and Merleau-Ponty to launch a journal that would explore both philosophical and political issues was a product of their friendship, the closeness of their views during the war, and their joint assumption that both would continue after the war. As the war had drawn to an end the expectation had prevailed among leftists, in Paris as elsewhere, that with fascism defeated the Left would be stronger and more unified than ever before, able to consolidate the social democratic reforms won during the years of depression and war, and perhaps move towards a transition to socialism. The central Soviet role in the defeat of Germany had led to widespread sympathy for the Soviet Union, especially on the Left. Nevertheless, the anticipated shift to the left was envisioned as an expansion of Popular Front politics, driven by domestic concerns, and not as an agenda driven by alignment with the Soviet Union.

In France, as elsewhere in the West, these expectations were shattered in the aftermath of the war, in the context of a US-Soviet struggle for world power and ideological supremacy that became the driving force in national politics, leaving, it seemed, no room for a position independent of both great powers. For a decade or so both Merleau-Ponty and Sartre struggled to define intellectual and political positions responsive to the transformed context in which they found themselves. Growing differences led to a break; in 1952, Merleau-Ponty resigned as co-editor of *Les Tempes modernes*. In the immediate aftermath of the war Merleau-Ponty wrote *Humanism and Terror: An Essay on the Communist Problem*, an expression of his support for a humanist version of Marxism, influenced by the writings of the young Marx, Hegel and Lukács' *History and Class Consciousness*.

In *Humanism and Terror*, Merleau-Ponty presented a view of the working class as the identical subject-object of history, arguing that since the aim of the working class was to abolish itself, it constitutes the one class whose aims align with the interests of humanity: every other class seeks to elevate itself above other classes; only a working class revolution would lead to a classless, and egalitarian, society. Merleau-Ponty also tried, unsuccessfully, to align the policies of the Soviet Union, and in particular the Moscow trials, with the Marxist humanism that he espoused. Merleau-Ponty defended the judgement on Bukharin not on grounds that Bukharin was guilty of conspiring to overthrow the Soviet state, but that his opposition to collectivisation had, even if inadvertently, strengthened the Right, and that the subsequent German attack made it clear that squelching the opposition had been necessary to ensure the unity and strength of the Soviet Union. From a revolutionary point of view, Merleau-Ponty wrote, a person's actions could not be judged by the person's intentions, or by a liberal conception of legality or justice, but rather by what forces they supported and what their result was: 'It is not a question of a judgment on the person but an appraisal of an historical role.'[22] Furthermore, he argued, while our aim is to create a nonviolent society, in the present we cannot condemn all use of violence, because violence is present in all societies and moreover is always an aspect of social change. We must judge a society not by its use of violence but by the ends to which that violence is put. Capitalist society, he argued, is based on the violence inherent in exploitation and poverty, and uses violence to suppress protest; revolutionary politics, including that of the Soviet Union, uses violence towards the end of an egalitarian and nonviolent society. 'All we know is different kinds of violence and we ought to prefer revolutionary violence because it has the face of humanism.'[23]

The logic of these positions was oddly backwards. A legal system allowing convictions based on the later unintended results of otherwise legal actions would leave everyone permanently vulnerable to accusation and conviction. The same is true of historical judgements. On the one hand, everyone, especially those in power, need to consider the likely results of their actions. But what if actions that seemed rational at the time have unexpected results, due to unpredictable later events? Furthermore, judging the repression of dissent by a government in terms of that government's expressed goals not only undermines the basis for a right of dissent; it also naïvely assumes that the government in question is actually motivated by the aim of achieving a nonviolent and egalitarian society, and not by the desire to bolster its own power. In the same book Merleau-Ponty argued that socialists do not judge societies by the universal values employed by liberals, such as justice and nonviolence, because the values that liberals espouse are so often violated in practice. The same critique could, and should, have been applied to the Soviet Union. The best that can be said for this argument is that it was presented at a time when many Left intellectuals felt that one had to choose between the Soviet Union and the US, and that locating oneself on the right side of history required turning a blind eye to the repression taking place in the Soviet Union.

Sartre meanwhile maintained the third-camp position that both he and Merleau-Ponty had espoused during and immediately after the war. But in the years 1950–2, in the context of the Korean War and growing threats of a wider war, likely to involve France, Sartre concluded that it was necessary to ally with one side or the other. Having come to regard the Soviet Union as the force for peace and the French Communist Party as the expression of the aspirations of the working class, he declared himself a fellow traveller, in three articles, published in *Les Temps modernes*, entitled 'The Communists and Peace'. Meanwhile Merleau-Ponty had come to the opposite conclusion: he regarded the Soviets as the aggressor in the Korean War, and had become convinced that the French working class was on the whole uninterested in dismantling capitalism and creating a socialist society. He moved away from political engagement.

In 1955 Merleau-Ponty, in *The Adventures of the Dialectic*, reversed his former view of the Soviet Union as the embodiment of Marxist humanism and expressed scepticism about the likelihood that the working class would fulfil what Marx had described as its historic role of bringing about a classless, egalitarian and humane society. He argued that since the course of history involves human conscious- ness and action, which are open-ended, there are no guarantees of any particular outcome. He opposed versions of Marxism, whether found in the writings of Marx himself, or in interpretations on the part of Marx's followers, which exclude human subjectivity and deny the openness of history. Despite his unwillingness to regard either the Soviet Union or the working class as preordained vehicles for the attainment of an egalitarian and nonviolent society, Merleau-Ponty maintained hope that such a society could be achieved. Despite his scepticism he continued to work within the framework of socialist humanism, or Marxist humanism, in the sense of a version of Marxism strongly inflected by Marx's discussion of alienation. Merleau-Ponty's philosophical/political project could be described as an attempt to assert, and maintain, the hope for an egalitarian and nonviolent society, in which humans would treat each other as ends rather than means, in the face of uncertainty that such a society will ever be achieved.

Merleau-Ponty's contributions to a socialist or Marxist humanist perspective lay in his development of a philosophical perspective that stressed human mutuality and the ways in which it is thwarted, as well as the openness of the future, and the inability of theory, Marxist or any other, to chart historical development with any certainty. Despite the weaknesses of *Humanism and Terror*, it presented the useful argument that human society entails a constant danger of violence, because humans are, by necessity, embedded in relations with one another, and in a society based on inequality human relations easily become violent, either in the overt form of physical conflict, or in the more subtle form of the denial of recognition that is built into any class society. Merleau-Ponty argued that the most important task of society is to find a way of holding the pull towards violence at bay. The solution, he argued, is the creation of an egalitarian and humane society, one in which people accord one another recognition, including not only the recognition of needs but of individual human value.

Merleau-Ponty was engaged in an effort to reconcile Marxism and existentialism, and to bring the perspective of a Marxist version of existentialism to phenomenology, his earliest and perhaps most fundamental philosophical commitment. His phenomenology revolved around the effort to understand human experience in and perception of the world, a world consisting of other humans and institutions and cultures constructed by humans, as well as non-human beings, objects and phenomena. He insisted that humans experience the world through the body, and that this embodied experience of the world is always grounded in relations with beings and objects outside the self, in particular with other humans.

Merleau-Ponty was also an existentialist. As an existentialist, he saw human consciousness as constrained by material resources, class relations, history and culture, but rejected determinism, whether in relation to society as a whole or individuals. He was concerned with the question of individual and social responsibility in the face of the fact that humans, to a much greater degree than other species, enjoy a limited but nevertheless real freedom. In *The Phenomenology of Perception* as well as other works, Merleau-Ponty sharply criticised Sartre's version of existentialism, though most often without explicitly mentioning Sartre. His difference with Sartre revolved around his insistence on the fundamental engagement of humans with others, in contrast to Sartre's conception of the individual as radically alone. In a public lecture that he gave in 1945, 'Existentialism is a Humanism', later published as an article by the same title, Sartre argued that existentialism, or at least his version of it, fits the category of humanism because it reminds humans that they are responsible for their own choices, and that they must transcend themselves – pursue goals outside of themselves – in order to realise themselves and become truly human. As Sartre describes the responsibility to choose, it is entirely individual: each human must define him or herself by his or her actions. This is, as Sartre argues, a humanist perspective, but it is not socialist.[24] Merleau-Ponty's focus on the mutuality inherent to human experience, and the need for a society that will allow it full expression, contributes much more than Sartre's to a discussion of what a socialist society should look like.

Merleau-Ponty would have agreed that even limited freedom brings responsibility, and that people create themselves through their choices and their action. But the centre of his conception of socialist humanism was the contingency of human history, the recognition that there are no guarantees. In *Humanism and Terror*, Merleau-Ponty wrote that 'to be a Marxist is to believe that economic problems and cultural or human problems are a single problem and that the proletariat as history has shaped it holds the solution to that problem.'[25] But this does not mean that socialist revolution will necessarily come about. 'Perhaps no proletariat will arise to play the historical role accorded to the proletariat in the Marxist system. Perhaps a universal class will never emerge, but *it is clear that no other class can replace the proletariat in this task.*'[26] Finally, it is precisely this absence of guarantees that gives us a basis for hope:

> The human world is an open or unfinished system and the same radical contingency which threatens it with discord also rescues it from the inevitability of disorder and prevents us from despairing of it, providing only that one remembers its various machineries are actually men and tries to maintain and expand man's relations to man. Such a philosophy cannot tell us *that* humanity will be realized ... But it awakens us to the importance of daily events and actions ... It is a view which like the most fragile object of perception – a soap bubble, or a wave – or like the most simple dialogue, embraces indivisibly all the order and all the disorder of the world.[27]

During the late 1940s and early 1950s many leftists outside the Soviet Union were troubled by the same questions that Sartre and Merleau-Ponty faced, and that led to their break: were the problems that were becoming apparent in the Soviet Union merely the result of Western encirclement, or was something going fundamentally wrong? Did the Soviet Union continue to warrant the support of the Left? Before 1956, Communists, and Communist sympathisers, tended to address these questions individually: some dropped out of Left politics, some remained involved in local struggles and did their best not to think about the Soviet Union, some insisted that the rumours of Soviet repression were bourgeois propaganda. The events of 1956 focused these issues and brought together networks of leftists who believed that a different and better form of socialism was possible. Even after 1956, such discussion remained virtually impossible within the Soviet Union, but in Poland and elsewhere within the Soviet bloc dissent began to be openly expressed. Leszek Kolakowski was a leading figure in this regard.

### Leszek Kolakowski

The Polish philosopher, Leszek Kolakowski, joined the Polish Communist Party (the Polish Workers' Party) in 1947, at the age of twenty. Three years later, on a trip to Moscow, he became disillusioned with the Soviet version of socialism. Over the following years he explored the ideas of the early Marx and began to write in the vein of Marxist humanism. In the wake of the Polish October, the thaw in Polish politics that took place, under Gomulka, during the second half of 1956, Kolakowski wrote a number of articles exploring a Marxist humanist position, and addressing the problem of political engagement given, on the one hand, the responsibility of the individual for his or her actions, and on the other, the uncertain results of one's actions. In an article clearly meant as a critique of orthodox Marxism, 'The Priest and the Jester', Kolakowski argued for the indeterminacy of history:

> Every system of thought begins with an absolute starting point of all thinking – which implies an end, a final point, and suggests that everything in between is obvious. Inherent in this is the conviction that the essence of movement is its opposite, immobility ... The absolute point of departure predetermines all the rest, and he who stands on the absolute simply stands still. Any further motion on his part is illusory, like the course of a squirrel in a revolving drum.[28]

And yet, Kolakowski argued, a quest for truth, the pursuit of a principle that will enable us to see the world and our experience clearly, is at the heart of philosophy and cannot be denied. Kolakowski described the priest as the guardian of the absolute and the jester as the critic.[29] Despite recognising the need for both doctrines and critiques of those doctrines, he declared himself on the side of the jester.

In his essay 'Responsibility and History', Kolakowski addressed the tension between the principle of individual responsibility for one's actions and the fact that human actions are socially determined. He maintained that both are simultaneously valid. He argued that although conceptions of good and evil are shaped by society, including history and tradition, individuals are responsible for their actions and subject to moral judgement. Despite social determinism, he wrote, individuals have to make choices, and they are, and should be, judged by their actions. If given norms become widely accepted, they become factors in history; the world of values becomes 'not merely an imaginary sky over the real world of existence but also a part of it, a part that exists not only in social consciousness but that is rooted in the material conditions of social life.'[30]

Kolakowski's insistence on what he called these 'antirealist propositions' led him to a discussion of the role of utopian thinking for the Left, which he defined as a 'movement of negation toward the existent world', a quest for change. But, he pointed out, 'the act of negation does not in itself define the Left, for there are movements with retrogressive goals. The Left is defined by its negation, but not only by this; it is also defined by the direction of its negation, in fact, by the nature of its utopia.'[31] Kolakowski described the aims of the Left in terms applicable to the Soviet bloc as well as the Western capitalist nations: a quest for the abolition of social privileges, racism, colonialism, for freedom of speech and expression, and for the victory of secularism and rational thought. He pointed out that utopias are, by definition, aims that cannot be achieved, at least not at the time when they are conceived:

By utopia I mean a state of social consciousness, a mental counterpart to the social movement striving for radical change in the world – it endows the real movement with a sense of realizing an ideal born in the realm of pure spirit and not in current historical experience. Utopia is, therefore, a mysterious consciousness of an actual historical tendency. As long as this tendency lives only a clandestine existence, without finding expression in mass social movements, it gives birth to utopias in the narrower sense, that is, to individually constructed models of the world, as it should be. But in time utopia becomes actual social consciousness; it invades the consciousness of a mass movement and becomes one of its essential driving forces. Utopia, then, crosses over from the domain of theoretical and moral thought into the field of practical thinking, and itself begins to govern human action.[32]

Kolakowski argued that utopias are indispensable to the Left because they identify a movement's long-run goals. 'Much historical experience,' he wrote, 'tells us that goals unattainable now will never be reached unless they are articulated when they are still unattainable. It may well be that the impossible at a given moment can become possible only by being stated at a time when it is impossible.'[33]

The hopes inspired by the Polish October were not realised, and Kolakowski found himself increasingly vulnerable to retaliation by the Polish authorities. A short critique of Stalinism was forbidden publication, though it circulated widely among students. It was published in English translation, in the US, in 1969.[34] In 1966, on the occasion of the tenth anniversary of the Polish October, Kolakowski delivered a speech that led to his expulsion from the Polish Workers' Party. In 1968 he lost his professorship at the University of Warsaw. Meanwhile a revival of Polish anti-Semitism was leading to threats against Kolakowski's Jewish wife, Tamara. Kolakowski and his family left Poland. Kolakowski then taught at McGill University, in Montreal, then at the University of California, Berkeley, and then settled at All Souls College, Oxford.

In the wake of the collapse of the hopes inspired by the Polish October, and more generally by the events of 1956, Kolakowski began to distance himself from Marxism and to express increasing scepticism about the Left, at least in the form in which he encountered it in the US and Britain in the late 1960s and 1970s. In 1973, E. P. Thompson published 'An Open Letter to Leszek Kolakowski', running to ninety-nine pages, in *The Socialist Register*, in which he recalled the admiration with which he and those in his circle had regarded Kolakowski's writings of the late 1950s and 1960s, and their respect for Kolakowski's courage in openly criticising Stalinism. 'Your voice was the clearest voice out of Eastern Europe in those years', Thompson wrote.[35] He reminded Kolakowski that he had remained a member of the Polish Workers' Party until 1966. It was partly due to Kolakowski's example, Thompson wrote, that he and his comrades had maintained their allegiance to the Communist movement, though not to the Communist parties or their ideology. Thompson reprimanded Kolakowski for having abandoned the struggle. He expressed his deep disappointment with Kolakowski's scathing comments on the New Left in the years since had left Poland, and with Kolakowski's expressions of scepticism about the possibility that alienation could be transcended under socialism. He appealed to Kolakowski to engage in dialogue with him on these issues as a relative of sorts, a fellow descendant of the Marxist tradition.

In a rejoinder, also published in *Socialist Register*, entitled 'My Correct Views on Everything', Kolakowski rejected any sort of kinship based on a common connection to the Marxist tradition. 'You and I,' he wrote, 'we were both active in our respective Communist Parties in the 40s and 50s which means that, whatever our noble intentions and our charming ignorance (or refusal to get rid of ignorance) were, we supported, within our modest means, a regime based on mass slave labour and police terror of the worst kind in human history.'[36] He described Thompson's hope for the emergence of a more democratic form of socialism as another instance of the same naïvety. He accused Thompson, and the Western Left in general, of following a double standard according to which violations of democratic and human rights in the West were inherent in capitalism whereas examples of the same in the East were deviations from socialist principles and therefore more easily reversible. He wrote that since leaving Poland in 1968 he had been struck by the excesses of the Western Left, especially the student Left, with its readiness to substitute political dogma for intellectual reasoning, and its confidence of having all the answers. He ridiculed the easy use of the term 'fascist' to describe authorities inside and outside the universities, as well as critics of the Left. It is difficult not to conclude, on the basis of this exchange of letters, that Thompson and Kolakowski were both right. Thompson was right that Kolakowski had abandoned hope for any positive socialist future, and had become so embittered in his view of the existing Left that he could barely acknowledge anything good about it. Kolakowski was right that Thompson's hopes for a democratic transformation of Soviet socialism were overly optimistic. Kolakowski's criticisms of the Western student Left in the late 1960s were also quite accurate.

In 1978, Kolakowski published his three-volume work, *Main Currents of Marxism: Its Rise, Growth, and Dissolution*, an extensively researched, thoughtful and critical account of Marx's thought and of the development of Marxism as a philosophy and political ideology.[37] Kolakowski maintained his preference for the humanist version of Marxism based on Marx's early work; in his introduction he mentioned the continuing impact of Lukács on his thought. But he nevertheless saw a line of development from Marx to Lenin to Stalin. He had meanwhile come to regard utopian thinking as dangerous. In 1982 Kolakowski delivered a lecture, 'The Death of Utopia Reconsidered', later published in a collection of his essays, *Modernity on Endless Trial*.[38] In it he argued that since difference and conflict are endemic to human relations, left-wing utopias that envision societies based on brotherhood and equality merely serve as justifications for conformity imposed by repressive tyrannies.

## *Lucien Goldmann*

The pessimistic view of human nature that Kolakowski held in his later years, according to which conflict and aggression are dominant and mutuality and equality only likely to appear when imposed from above, differentiated him sharply from those who sustained a socialist/Marxist humanist perspective. Lucien Goldmann, a philosopher who taught Marxism at the School for Advanced Studies in the Social Sciences, in Paris, during the post-war decades, addressed the question of what sort of society would best accommodate human needs, and encourage the expression of the most socially constructive human potentialities. Goldmann, a Romanian Jew, as a teenager had participated in a circle of young people who read radical literature, including Marx. He was also active in Hashomer Hatzair, a socialist Zionist organisation critical of capitalism for its propensity to isolate humans from one another, convinced that the individual could flourish only in community, and devoted to the creation of such communities, by building a youth movement in the diaspora and by training young Jews for life on kibbutzim in Palestine.[39]

Hashomer Hatzair, founded in Galicia in the years before World War I, was imbued with an intense dedication to the moral life in community, and to the goal of fostering a connection with nature. It drew intellectually oriented young Jews whose reading ranged from the Prophets, the New Testament and the Hasidim, to the writings of Martin Buber and his friend Gustav Landauer, a German Jewish socialist-anarchist intellectual who participated in the abortive Bavarian revolution of 1918–19 and was murdered in its aftermath. In the late 1920s, the years in which Goldmann was active in Hashomer, and also the onset of the Great Depression, Hashomer turned to the writings of Ber Borochov, the Marxist Zionist theorist, for an understanding of the place of Jews within capitalism and of the Jewish path to socialism. Goldmann was no doubt influenced by the utopianism of Hashomer Hatzair, its view of community as the basis for individual self-realisation, and by the humanist version of Marxism that was becoming a major element in its outlook. Goldmann did not emigrate to Palestine; after leaving Hashomer he joined the small and persecuted Romanian Communist Party, where his tendency towards dissidence, in particular his critical view of Stalinism, made him something of a problem for an organisation most concerned with its own survival. When he left for Paris in 1935, having earned a law degree at the University of Bucharest, Goldmann retained his Marxism, strongly influenced by his reading of Lukács' *History and Class Consciousness*, but not his Communist Party membership.

Goldmann fled to Switzerland during the war, thus escaping the German occupation, and returned to Paris to participate in intellectual circles in which there was much discussion about the conflict between the US and the Soviet Union, and about whether it was necessary to ally with one or the other or if an independent socialist politics was possible. Existentialism and Marxism were major philosophical currents, and Sartre had wide influence on both philosophical and political issues. By the late 1950s, Goldmann was criticising Sartre for his focus on the individual and for his failure to acknowledge the deep connection between the individual and the community. He also criticised orthodox Marxists for focusing on social forces while failing to acknowledge the importance of the individual. 'For Sartre,' Goldmann wrote, 'consciousness is in the final instance an individual phenomenon and the collective can only be the result of a sum of mutual contacts among a certain number of individual consciousnesses.'[40] For Goldmann, individual consciousness was from the beginning shaped by history, community and class; there was no such thing as an isolated, primordial individual consciousness. At the same time, Goldmann criticised Marxists who left the individual out of their accounts of social change and their discussions of socialism. Although recognising his intellectual debt to Lukács, Goldmann criticised him for failing to address the relationship between individual and class consciousness. Goldmann disagreed with the way in which Sartre was attempting to reconcile existentialism and Marxism, but in his own way he was doing the same by insisting on the inclusion of the individual in Marxist analysis.

Goldmann was also critical of both structuralism, in the form that it took in French philosophy, and post-structuralism; his distaste for these trends separated him from his contemporaries in French philosophical circles, and left him somewhat intellectually isolated. Goldmann regarded the structuralism of Lévi-Strauss as an uncritical reflection of post-war 'organised' consumer capitalism, based on large, impersonal and apparently stable organisations, and on extensive, managed consumption. Goldmann found Lévi-Strauss's analogy between language and society, each governed by inherent laws of communication, ahistorical and therefore theoretically antihumanist. Goldmann endorsed the structural analysis of capitalism, but Lévi-Strauss's structuralism extracted society from history and thereby denied the role of human beings in its construction, and in shaping the future. Goldmann's critique of French structuralism and its corollary, antihumanism, set him at odds with Althusser, with his reduction of the subject to the role of carrier of social forces, and his attempt to separate Marx, the author of *Capital*, from the young Marx, concerned with the problem of alienation. It also separated Goldmann from Foucault, who while rejecting Althusser's Marxist structuralism absorbed the antihumanism of Althusser and others and took it to even greater extremes.

## Martin Buber

Though Martin Buber was only distantly connected to the circles of continental philosophers mentioned above, and his view of Marxism was more negative than theirs, he shared their view of human efforts as the key to the creation of an egalitarian society, and he saw utopian thought as necessary to this process. Buber was a socialist and a humanist; like other socialist humanists, he was influenced by Marx's conception of alienation, and he was appalled by the Soviet version of socialism. His writings made important contributions on topics addressed by other socialist humanists, such as the human need for community and for relations of mutuality, and the role of utopian thinking in creating a more just and humane society. Much of Buber's writing predated the flowering of socialist humanist thought by many years. His most famous book, *I and Thou*, appeared in 1923, the same year as Lukács' *History and Class Consciousness*. Buber's *Paths in Utopia*, which also addressed issues central to socialist humanism, appeared in 1947.

Buber was still writing when socialist humanism emerged as a coherent tendency among European philosophers, but he did not become part of their circle. This was probably due to his intellectual, political and geographical differences with other socialist humanists. Buber, who was raised by grandparents living in L'vov (Lemberg), Poland, grew up in an atmosphere saturated with Jewish learning. As a teenager he was drawn to the writings of Kant, Kierkegaard and Nietzsche, and in the university he studied philosophy, but the Hebrew Bible and Jewish traditional thought remained fundamental to his outlook. He joined the Zionist movement when it was formed, in 1898. Within the Zionist movement Buber was from the outset, and remained, a dissident.

In the early stages of Zionism, Buber opposed Herzl's focus on creating a Jewish state and supported the approach of Ahad Ha'am, who believed that the aim of Zionism should be the renewal of Jewish culture and spirituality through the establishment of a Jewish community in Palestine that would follow Jewish moral precepts, including the admonition to treat the stranger as oneself. Buber pressed for recognition of and negotiation with the Arabs, for a binational state, and, after the establishment of Israel, for equal rights for Arabs and other non-Jews in Israel. In 1933, when Hitler gained power in Germany and began to enact the laws that excluded Jews from public life, Buber resigned from his position at Frankfurt University in protest. Buber was a founder of the Hebrew University in Jerusalem, and a member of its board; he visited Palestine frequently. On 9 November 1938, when the *Kristallnacht* rampages took place, Buber and his family were in Palestine. That night the Buber home in a town outside Frankfurt was ransacked and Buber's library was destroyed. It was clear that they could not return to Germany. Buber and his family settled in Jerusalem. Buber's Zionism was entirely consonant with socialist humanism, but his concern with Palestine/Israel drew him into different circles, and different discussions, than those in which most other socialist humanists were engaged.

Another point of difference between Buber and at least the main current of socialist humanism was religion. Buber was not conventionally observant, but he did believe in God. One of his major projects was the study of Hasidic tales, through which he explored traditional Hasidism as a model of a community united by a project of moral and spiritual renewal. With his friend and colleague Franz Rosenzweig, Buber spent many years translating the Hebrew Bible into German; his method of translation was intended to highlight the meaning of the original texts, and thus bring German Jews back into contact with the sources of Judaism. Buber was not the only socialist humanist who was deeply influenced by the Jewish tradition; this was also true of Fromm. Nor was he the only socialist humanist who was religious; Paul Tillich was the most prominent of a number of Christian socialist humanists. But Buber's view of dialogue between humans as an opening to dialogue between humans and God set him apart from the emphatic secularism of the majority of socialist humanists.

Buber's main contributions to socialist humanism lay in his philosophy of dialogue and mutuality, especially as developed in his book *I and Thou*, but also permeating his work as a whole, and in his discussion of utopian thinking, what form it should take, and why he regarded it as a necessary aspect of a movement for a better, more humane society. Buber famously contrasted the I–Thou relation, in which two humans recognise each other in an unmediated way, and in which what matters is the presence of the other, to the I–It relation, in which the other is seen as an object and the relationship is based on what the other can do for one. Buber argued that I–Thou relations, or moments, are transitory; every Thou, even the most beloved, becomes an It at times. He added that we all have to live in the 'World of It' most of the time: it is in the World of It that we make a living, engage in trade or commerce, and develop the technologies that make it possible for humans to survive the elements and live more or less comfortably. But, he argued, it is the I–Thou relation that constitutes the self; without it there is no I. He described the relationship between the infant and its mother as the primal experience of an I–Thou relationship and argued that while that relationship cannot be repeated, there remains a deep human need for recognition, for the affirmative presence of another human. Meanwhile, Buber argued, society has become increasingly It-centred, and experiences of unconditional, affirmative presence have become increasingly scarce. For Buber, social and economic justice were important components of the good society, but his main concern was with maximising the possibility of I–Thou relations.

Buber's discussion of I–Thou and I–It relations makes it clear that he was not a Marxist. For Marx alienation is rooted in the relations of production; for Buber something very close to alienation is rooted in the nature of human existence, which requires that the World of Thou must be interrupted and undermined by the World of It. 'It is the sublime melancholy of our lot,' he wrote, 'that every Thou must become an It.'[41] But Buber also believed that society affects the balance between the two. Under capitalism, Buber argued, the World of It had expanded to an unprecedented degree. Humans, Buber believed, could create a socialist society in which there would be greater room for the World of Thou. In Buber's view such a society would consist of small, decentralised communities. Though those who made up these communities would seek a decent standard of living for all, their greatest concern would be with the character of human relations.

Buber's conception of community, discussed in his book *Paths in Utopia*, is framed by a critique of the Marxist rejection of utopian thinking. Engels, Buber points out, wrote in *The Peasant War in Germany* that the German socialist movement stood on the shoulders of the pre-industrial utopian thinkers 'who ... anticipated with genius countless truths whose validity we can now prove scientifically'. Marx and Engels, however, dismissed utopian writing that appeared after the advent of industrialism as obscurantist and an obstacle to scientific socialism. Buber challenged this view. 'If socialism is to emerge from the blind-alley into which it has strayed,' he wrote, 'among other things the catchword "Utopian" must be cracked open and examined for its true content.'[42]

Buber argued, first, that while the crises of capitalist society demand resolution, there is nothing given about the form that that resolution will take, but that if we want a form of socialism that will address the human need for both solidarity and independence, we must construct a socialist society based on small, relatively autonomous communities committed to providing for the common welfare while at the same time creating the greatest possible leeway for experimentation and self-management. Only in such a society, he argued, will it be possible for I–Thou relationships to flourish. Second, Buber argued that utopian thinking is key to both a critique of existing society and to the possibility of creating a better one. 'The vision of "what should be",' he wrote, is 'inseparable from a critical and fundamental relationship to the existing condition of humanity. All suffering under a social order that is senseless prepares the soul for vision, and what the soul receives in this vision strengthens and deepens its insight into the perversity of what is perverted.' Furthermore, he wrote, a better society will not come into being of its own accord, but requires human effort. We need to imagine it collectively if we are to create it collectively. Buber wrote that in modern society it had become impossible to believe that 'an act from above [would] redeem human society', but that God had been replaced, in much of contemporary utopian thinking, with technology, which, it was widely assumed, could fix anything.[43]

In advocating utopian thinking, Buber did not mean to open the door to flights of fancy without grounding in the world; his aim was to encourage realistic discussion of what a better society might look like and how it might evolve. He argued that a successful socialist restructuring of human society could only take place from within, 'by a regeneration of [society's] cell tissue', on the basis of a growing network of producer and consumer cooperatives. He imagined 'a network of settlements, territorially based and federally constructed, without dogmatic rigidity, allowing the most diverse social forms to exist side by side, but always aiming at the new organic whole'.[44] Buber criticised the expansion of the state and the centralisation of power, and he advocated direct democracy, by which he meant that communities should manage themselves to the greatest extent possible, and that the delegation of decisions to higher representatives should be kept to a minimum. But he did not imagine that the state or representative democracy would cease to exist. He expressed scepticism about the 'withering away of the state' and the 'leap of humanity out of the realm of necessity into the realm of freedom'.[45] Both conceptions, he thought, were based more on dialectics than on any objective assessment of real possibilities. He warned against the contamination of the idea of community by sentimentality or emotionalism: community, he argued, must not be about itself but must be formed in response to concrete problems. 'Community is the inner disposition or constitution of a life in common ... It is community of tribulation and only because of that community of spirit; community of toil and only because of that community of salvation.' Community, he wrote, should never be made into a principle; 'it ... should always satisfy a situation rather than an abstraction. The realization of community, like the realization of any idea, cannot occur once and for all time; always it must be the moment's answer to the moment's question, and nothing more.'[46]

## The Eclipse of Socialist Humanism

In the latter half of the 1960s, student and youth movements for social change grew and took on a more radical character, in the US and elsewhere, in response to the war in Vietnam and also to widespread frustration with bureaucratic controls in a period in which growing prosperity seemed to provide the basis for freer and more self-determined lives. The movements of this period brought about changes in popular attitudes and public policy. In the early 1960s the civil rights movement in the US had won formal equality of rights and the end of legal segregation in the South; in the late 1960s and early 1970s movements of people of colour, in the US and elsewhere, attacked racism as a whole. The feminist movement re-emerged in the late 1960s, after decades of dormancy, and became a powerful force for changes in culture and in public policy. Movements for gay and lesbian rights spread, and their forthright stance put homophobia on the defensive. A new, radical environmentalism went beyond earlier protests on behalf of protection of the wilderness to criticise a culture built on dominance and exploitation of the natural environment. The movement against the war in Vietnam played an important role in bringing that war to an end.

The war in Vietnam, and international protest against it, led to a heightened awareness of developments in the international Left. Since the late 1950s, the Chinese had been seeking to displace the Soviets as the leadership of the international Communist movement. In the context of the Vietnam War, the Chinese critique of the Soviet policy of peaceful coexistence and their call for a more confrontational stance towards the US resonated with many activists in the anti-war movement and in other increasingly radical movements that overlapped with it. The Chinese argued that the central contradiction, or main struggle, in the world, was between Third World anti-imperialist movements and US imperialism, and not, as Marxists had traditionally maintained, between socialism and capitalism. This made sense to young people in the US for whom the main problem was the war in Vietnam, and to activists around the world who shared the goal of ending the war and preventing future US interventions. Sympathy for Chinese Communism was also bolstered by the inadequacy of the Soviet Union as a revolutionary model. There were many on the Left who admired the Bolshevik Revolution, but hardly any who were sympathetic to what the Soviet Union became in the years thereafter. Even young people who joined the Communist Party did so mostly out of an identification with the Communist and labour struggles of the 1930s, and the Popular Front; many regarded the Soviet Union as an embarrassment.

During the latter half of the 1960s and the early 1970s the radicalism and militancy of the anti-war movement, and the plethora of movements allied with it, escalated rapidly. Anger over the war, over the role of mainstream liberals in directing it, and over the reluctance of liberals to support movement actions, drove many to conclude that nothing could be accomplished within the system and that revolution was necessary. Though not everyone in the movement shared this view, the core activists in each of the intertwined movements of the time constituted the movement's most radical constituency, and the movement as a whole tended to follow. By the late 1960s talk of revolution was widespread among movement activists, though there were many different conceptions of what revolution meant, and few were thinking about how to bring it about. By this time liberalism was widely disparaged. Third World revolutionary movements, especially the Chinese Cultural Revolution, were regarded through a romantic haze. Though movement activists engaged in very little violence (most violence was initiated by the police), a willingness to use violent rhetoric or to make a public show of possessing arms was regarded by many as a sign of revolutionary dedication.

The Maoist/Third Worldist tendency that, following the Chinese, described itself as Marxist-Leninist was not the only radical tendency in the movements of the Vietnam era. Trotskyist organisations also played important roles in the US and in Western Europe, and a politics that was in effect anarchist but rarely used that term to describe itself was also widespread, especially in feminist movements and in the Left counterculture. Trotskyists did not share the Maoist enthusiasm for Communist China, and many proto-anarchists, especially feminists, rejected the hierarchical structure and authoritarianism of Third World revolutionary movements, as well as the strategy of armed struggle and seizure of the state. Maoists and other Third Worldists spoke of armed struggle and of seizing the state at some point in the future, but in the meantime most focused on organising among workers and others whom they hoped would be receptive to revolution. Weatherman and a host of small underground groups believed that spectacular acts of violence would awaken the masses and lead to revolution. Feminists and countercultural leftists rejected hierarchical forms of organisation and authoritarian governments; their strategy for transforming society was to create institutions and communities governed by the values of a cooperative, egalitarian society.

Despite sharp differences of outlook, the various radical currents within the movement, which together constituted its leading edge, shared an ultra-leftist set of assumptions. It was assumed throughout the movement that revolution was coming, and that promoting it required radical actions. Revolution carried different meanings in different sectors of the movement: it could mean an armed seizure of power leading to a socialist economy, or the dismantling of patriarchy, or a transition to a society free of racism. But radical action generally meant an uncompromising stance, strident rhetoric, and, often, an effort to shock one's audience. To some extent this made sense. The movement as a whole aimed to expose US imperialism and to challenge racism, sexism, and, ultimately, homophobia; shock could help in the effort to drive these messages home. But the view that the revolution was on the way was an illusion, and strident rhetoric and an uncompromising stance could get in the way of forming alliances and winning support. The formation of separate and autonomous movements of people of colour and women, necessary for solidarity within these groups and for effective mobilisation, led to a widespread view of separatism as a rule of Left organisation. In the heat of movement activity, tactics and organisational forms prompted by immediate circumstances often acquired the status of basic principles of the new form of radicalism.

Socialist humanism was not compatible with the radicalism of the late 1960s and early 1970s because of the association of humanism with the wrong side of the Sino-Soviet split, because anti-imperialism seemed to call for the rejection of peaceful coexistence in favour of more militant opposition to the US and the West generally, and because it seemed too close to liberalism, which radical movements in the US and elsewhere had come to regard as the enemy. Furthermore, the universalism of socialist humanism, its emphasis on the common social needs of humans and their capacities for mutually beneficial cooperation, seemed to go against the movement's increasing orientation towards difference. In this context radical activists did not reject socialist humanism; they simply ignored it.

In the decades that followed, interest in socialist humanism failed to revive on the Left, partly because the conception of radicalism that had been forged at the high point of movement activity retained its hold among those who had participated in or identified with movement politics, and because the longing to revive that movement, as it had been at its height, was much stronger than any impulse to evaluate those politics critically and forge something different for a moment in which revolution was clearly not happening. In the early 1970s some on the Left turned to the *Prison Notebooks* of Italian Communist Antonio Gramsci, who addressed the question of strategies of the Left in a period when revolution is not forthcoming and a direct challenge to capitalism is not possible, and for his analysis of the role of civil society and of the institutions that comprise it in supporting capitalist hegemony and also as potential vehicles for Left engagement and influence, and for the development of an oppositional culture. In the US, writers associated with the journal *Socialist Revolution* (later renamed *Socialist Review*) attempted to develop a Gramscian approach to the problems of the Left in a period of Left stagnation. But Gramsci's work was not conducive to being turned into a new doctrine of the Left. His writing, difficult at best, was made more obscure by the necessity of evading prison censors. His analysis of the development of capitalist society and of the problems that it posed for theory, and for the Left, was highly nuanced, more exploratory than hortatory. It was not intended as a new doctrine and was not taken as such.

Meanwhile, thinking among Left intellectuals generally was going in a somewhat different direction. By the late 1960s, *New Left Review* had taken on the task of communicating Left trends in Marxist theory on the continent to an English-speaking audience. The editors of *New Left Review* were particularly drawn to the work of Althusser, professor of philosophy at the prestigious École Normale, prominent Communist theorist, and a supporter of the position of the Chinese Communist Party within the strongly Soviet-aligned French Communist Party. In the early 1960s a group of students who were involved in the rapidly growing world of French Maoism convinced Althusser to give a seminar on Marxism. The seminar and others that followed were wildly successful, and Althusser became a magnet for students on the Left. As Anderson highlights in Chapter 2, Althusser sharply distinguished Marx's later work, primarily concerned with a structural analysis of capitalism, from the *Economic and Philosophic Manuscripts* and other writings in which a humanist perspective and an analysis of alienation were prominent. He rejected the earlier work and in defining the latter, tweaked it a bit in his account of it, removed Marx's continuing humanism and concern with alienation. Althusser thus developed a rigorously structuralist version of Marxism, which he described as genuine Marxism.

Althusser's work ultimately also bridged Marxism and post-structuralism, which took hold among young Parisian intellectuals in the late 1960s. Many young French intellectuals were at least on the sidelines of the spontaneous student rebellion that took place in May 1968, which led to massive working class protest and nearly turned into a revolution, but instead subsided leaving relatively little changed. The French Communist Party denounced the mobilisations of May 1968. Trotskyists played a role in the uprising; the Maoist students associated with Althusser missed its significance and sat it out. Despite the participation of Trotskyists, who tried to give the movement organised structure, it remained spontaneous and faded without bringing about major changes in French society. In the years following May 1968 and its collapse, both Trotskyist and Maoist organisations attracted many thousands. In each of these camps, organisations with hierarchical structures remained small. Organisations that sought to blend traditional perspectives and styles with anarchism, by rejecting internal hierarchies, emphasising the role of young people, and developing campaigns around gender, sexuality and race, grew rapidly. The Maoist organisation, Gauche Proletarienne, became the dominant influence in the protests that swept Paris in the late 1960s and early 1970s.

Many French intellectuals were drawn into the orbit of the Gauche Proletarienne. Alain Badiou, a leading figure in a smaller Maoist organisation of the same period, described the Gauche Proletarienne, in a much later interview, as marked by 'a kind of impatient megalomania with regard to the course of history, a conviction that the Maoists were in a position to take power ... which led them to launch a series of absurd campaigns, completely detached from reality, out of pure ideologism, with a radicalism that was vehement and imaginary in equal measure'.[47] He commented that the Gauche Proletarienne attracted many intellectuals because of its aura of activism and radicalism. He said he had been put off by what he called 'a kind of hystericization of activism' and described the Gauche Proletarienne's approach as 'an adventurist and fallacious style of action, but one that was exciting at the same time, a politics that was also a fashion'.[48]

During the same years, post-structuralism was taking hold among French intellectuals; Jean-Paul Sartre and Michel Foucault, among others, became involved in the Gauche Proletarienne and were enthusiastic supporters of its politics. Just as the anti-war movement and the radical currents surrounding it had a formative influence on the thinking of a generation of Left academics in the US, the Maoist/revolutionary movement had the same impact on French post-structuralism, many of whose adherents thought of their outlook as radical, and whose concept of radicalism was similarly shaped by the movement in which they had participated. Not all of the intellectuals who were caught up in the Maoist movement of the late 1960s and early 1970s were on their way towards post-structuralism: Sartre's intellectual trajectory took a different course. But it was post-structuralism that was to become the dominant intellectual influence on the Left, and the Maoist experience of Foucault and others had a profound impact on the way in which post-structuralism was to approach issues of social change, and the political culture that was to develop around it.[49]

In the late 1970s and early 1980s post-structuralism crossed the Atlantic and was taken up by Left academics in the United States, in particular by feminists and others in the humanities. By the mid-1980s it had become a kind of crusade for intellectual hegemony in elite universities or at least in their humanities divisions, and also for a particular variety of radicalism. To many of its adherents it became not a particular theoretical perspective intertwined with a particular conception of radical politics, but the only valid theoretical perspective, in effect theory itself, and similarly the only valid conception of radicalism. Its crusading and polemical style was reminiscent of the ideological cast of debates within the Left in the late 1960s and early 1970s, in which adherents of particular perspectives undercut competing arguments by subtly distorting them, and each side claimed to be the sole possessor of the correct approach.

Especially in its early years, post-structuralism was intertwined with social constructionism, and radical intellectual practice was taken to consist largely of demonstrating the socially constructed character of institutions and attitudes taken to be natural and unchangeable. This kind of critique was a major element of many of the movements of the time: feminists pointed out that the nuclear family was not the only possible form of family life, and criticising racist, sexist and homophobic attitudes was an important component of radical movements of the time generally. The effort to show that what might seem to be based in nature was actually not was also linked to a conception of radical politics as critique (without, necessarily, any concrete positive alternative) and to the widespread conception of post-structuralism, on the part of its adherents, as a stance of pure critique, capable of unmasking and criticising the assumptions of other perspectives while itself remaining free of assumptions that might be similarly open to criticism.

The problem with equating radicalism with social constructionism was that this created a lopsided version of radicalism. Some institutions and attitudes are entirely socially constructed, and it is useful to point out that alternatives are possible. But many are partially based in nature. The fact that women can become pregnant and can nurse their babies, while men cannot do either, has consequences for everyone concerned, and an effort to deny this amounts to tilting at windmills for the sake of sustaining an ideological commitment. The post-structuralist view of radicalism as a campaign to attribute as much as possible to the influence of human discourse and as little as possible to nature recalled the 'anything is possible' attitude that permeated the movements of the late 1960s and early 1970s, expressed in the May 1968 slogan, 'all power to the imagination'. The problem with this view is that everything is not, in fact, possible, and that in order to be effective, movements for social change have to take limits as well as possibilities into account. In this regard the post-structuralist conception of radicalism was more about assuming a posture than about accomplishing social change.

And in fact, the post-structuralist conception of radicalism came to be much more about resistance, without any clear aim, than bringing about social change. In the 1960s Althusser had introduced structuralism to the Left intellectual world by developing a structuralist version of Marxism that rejected the humanist element in Marx's thought. Over the course of the 1960s and 1970s, Foucault wrote a series of institutional studies of the functioning of power, and a study of the changing epistemes, or frames of understanding, that shape discourse, the human sciences and the exercise of power. Through the influence of these and other works Foucault became the dominant influence within post-structuralism, and reshaped it. He was interested in how power functions in the context of institutions, and through discourse and culture. Althusser's audience consisted largely of young Marxists, especially political economists. At this point in his career, Foucault had little interest in Marx, class or political economy. In the context of the movements of the late 1960s and early 1970s, Foucault's focus on issues of power and culture gave him a much wider audience.

Foucault's article 'Governmentality'[50] made more explicit his opposition to the modern democratic state and the liberal agenda of social welfare that prevailed when he was writing. His view of the modern state as a vehicle for repression and of liberal reform as a means of making this repression more sophisticated and effective coincided with the views of many in and around the movements of the late 1960s and early 1970s. Foucault's writings captured the trend towards increasing state surveillance that accompanied the growth of the welfare state. But he failed to address the urgent need for government-provided social services and also the need for government regulation and intervention to limit exploitation and dis-crimination, and to keep a complex society functioning.

Foucault supported resistance, and had himself participated in it, but he never developed a concept of what a better society should be like, and he resisted the suggestion that this should be a topic of discussion on the Left. In a 1971 debate between Noam Chomsky and Foucault, Chomsky argued that a desire to engage in creative work, free of coercion, is fundamental to human nature, that a good society would encourage such activity, and that in technologically developed Western societies, drudgery could be reduced to a minimum and creative work could become the norm. He advocated 'a federated, decentralized system of free associations, incorporating economic as well as other institutions ... in which human beings do not have to be forced into the position of tools, of cogs in the machine'. Foucault responded, 'I admit to not being able to define, nor for even stronger reasons propose, an ideal social model for the functioning of our scientific or technological society'. He argued that the immediate task was to uncover and describe the relationships of power that control and oppress society. Chomsky agreed that the nature of oppression, repression and coercion should be studied and, he added, opposed, but he argued that this was not sufficient:

> I think it would be a great shame to put aside entirely the somewhat more abstract and philosophical task of trying to draw the connections between a concept of human nature that gives full scope to freedom and dignity and creativity and other fundamental human characteristics, and to relate that to some notion of social structure in which these properties could be realized and in which meaningful human action would take place.

Foucault objected that Chomsky's recommendation required defining a human nature 'which is at the same time ideal and real, and has been hidden and repressed until now, in terms borrowed from our society, from our civilization, from our culture ... Isn't there a risk that we will be led into error? Mao Tse-Tung spoke of bourgeois human nature and proletarian human nature, and he considers that they are not the same thing'. Chomsky agreed that our knowledge of human nature is limited and in some respects socially conditioned. Nevertheless, he said:

> It is of critical importance that we know what impossible goals we're trying to achieve, if we hope to achieve some of the possible goals. And that means we have to be bold enough to speculate and create social theories on the basis of partial knowledge, while remaining very

open to the strong possibility, and in fact overwhelming probability, that at least in some respects we're very far off the mark.[51]

### The Possible Revival of Socialist Humanism

In some respects the US and the Western world generally have become more congruent with Foucault's description of the modern world than was the case when he wrote. Government surveillance is now vastly more extensive and sophisticated than it was in the 1960s and 1970s; the political arena is more remote and less accessible to public pressure. But in other respects Foucault's vision, and more generally the outlook associated with post-structuralism, appear increasingly dated. The widening gap in wealth and power between the very wealthy and everyone else, and parallel global inequalities, make the issue of class unavoidable. A politics, or an analysis, that sees the liberal state as the main problem, is no longer viable.

In the very early stages of protest against the Vietnam War, Carl Oglesby, then president of Students for a Democratic Society, distinguished between two kinds of liberalism: the mainstream politics sustaining the war in Vietnam, and exploitation and discrimination at home, which he called corporate liberalism, and the tradition of democratic reform, which he called humanitarian liberalism. The movement, Oglesby said, opposed the first but supported the latter. This distinction became lost in the rising protest against the war and the escalating radicalism associated with it.[52] The Foucaultian perspective, and to a large extent post-structuralism generally, lost not only the distinction between these two forms of liberalism but the link between the more repressive form of liberalism and corporate power, thus promoting a radical politics focused on the liberal state and suspicious of liberal social programmes. In the intervening years corporate wealth and power has expanded to the point that the state often appears to be a ward of the corporations.

The mainstream liberalism of the post-war decades, which involved a regulatory state committed to sustaining a basic level of social welfare and also to social control, has been replaced by a neoliberal perspective that rejects regulation and is committed to sustaining profits. In accord with this project the income gap has widened, social services have been undermined and the public sphere has been largely destroyed. To the extent that state-funded social services still exist, they still involve social control as well as social support, but in an era in which public education is under attack and government support is being withdrawn from public services generally, it is hard to see such programmes as the source of our problems. Humanitarian liberalism is not enough, but those engaged in such efforts are not the enemy. The politics of suspicion promoted by post-structuralism was all too often focused on the closest allies of the Left.

The politics of resistance associated with post-structuralism, like the politics of suspicion, is also no longer adequate. A movement that knows what it is against but has no clear conception of what it is in favour of cannot be sustained for long; social movements need concrete victories, or at least reasonable prospects of such victories, and conceptions of their overall aims. Alternative communities can thrive and exert influence when they are part of a broader movement for social change. In the absence of such a movement they tend to lose their appeal, especially in a society that undermines and starves them. A politics that revolves around resistance lacking clear goals encourages spontaneous protest rather than sustained organisation.

Socialist humanism does not provide any answers to the questions of organisation and strategy, but it encourages attention to the question of what sort of society we want, and how the Left can prefigure that society. It also contributes a conception of human nature, and of the kinds of relations that human nature calls for, that points to the positive capacities of humans, individually and collectively. The environmental crisis, human responsibility for it, and the narrowing chances of reversing it make it much more difficult than it once was to sustain a positive view of the human race or hope for the future. But it remains the case that humans are capable of constructive behaviour. Socialist humanism builds on this possibility.

## NOTES

1. *The Economic and Philosophic Manuscripts* were first published in full by the Marx–Engels Institute, later the Institute of Marxism-Leninism, Moscow, prepared by D. Riazanov, in Karl Marx and Friedrich Engels, *Historisch-kritische Gesamtausgabe*, Berlin: Marx-Engels Verlag, 1932, Abt. 1, Band 111. In 1961 Erich Fromm published a translation by T. B. Bottomore of the greater part of *The Economic and Philosophic Manuscripts* in his *Marx's Concept of Man*, New York: Frederick Ungar, 1961.
2. Interview with Sheila Rowbotham, London, July 2011.

3. E. P. Thompson, 'Socialist Humanism: An Epistle to the Philistines', *The New Reasoner*, No. 1 (Summer 1957), pp. 105–43.

4. Perry Anderson's *Arguments Within English Marxism*, London: Verso, 1980, provides an account of this split that is remarkable for its objectivity.

5. E.P. Thompson, *The Poverty of Theory: or an Orrery of Errors*, London: Merlin Press, 1995 [1978].

6. For critical assessments of E. P. Thompson's *The Poverty of Theory*, from readers sympathetic to his perspective, see Kate Soper's 'Socialist Humanism' and William H. Sewell, Jr's 'How Classes are Made: Critical Reflections on E. P. Thompson's Theory of Working-Class Formation', in Harvey J. Kaye and Keith McLelland (eds), *E. P. Thompson, Critical Perspectives*, Philadelphia: Temple University Press, 1990, pp. 204–32 and pp. 50–77.

7. Erich Fromm, ed., *Socialist Humanism: An International Symposium*, New York: Doubleday, 1965.

8. Marcuse and Fromm disagreed sharply about Freudian drive theory, which Marcuse supported, and used as the basis for his view of the revolutionary potential of marginalised sectors of the population, and which Fromm rejected, both in theory and also as an explanation for revolutionary action. The bitterness of this debate and resulting bad feelings on both sides may have widened the differences between the two over the larger question of socialist humanism.

9. Herbert Marcuse, 'Socialist Humanism?', in Erich Fromm (ed.), *Socialist Humanism: An International Symposium*, New York: Doubleday, 1965, pp. 100–1.

10. Erich Fromm, *The Sane Society*, New York: Holt, Rinehart and Winston, 1955, pp. 22–7.

11. Fromm, *Marx's Concept of Man*, p. 7.

12. Fromm, *The Sane Society*, p. 258.

13. Raya Dunayevskaya, *Marxism and Freedom: From 1776 until Today*, New York: Twayne Publishers, 1958, p. 58.

14. C. L. R. James and Grace C. Boggs, *Facing Reality: The New Society, Where to Look For It and How to Bring It Closer*, Chicago: Charles H. Kerr, 2005 [1958], p. 24.

15. Ibid., p. 155.

16. Ibid., p. 156.

17. Ibid., pp. 95–6.

18. See Gerson S. Sher, *Praxis: Marxist Criticism and Dissent in Socialist Yugoslavia*, Bloomington: Indiana University Press, 1977, especially chapter 1, 'The Genealogy of Praxis', pp. 3–56.

19. See Ibid., chapter 5, 'The Praxis of *Praxis*', pp. 104–241.

20. Georg Lukács, 'Reification and the Consciousness of the Proletariat', in *History and Class Consciousness: Studies in Marxist Dialectics*, trans. by Rodney Livingstone, London: The Merlin Press, 1971, pp. 83–222.

21. Henri Lefebvre and Norbert Guterman's early translation of key sections of the *Economic and Philosophic Manuscripts* into French is mentioned by

Edward M. Soja, *Postmodern Geography: The Reassertion of Space in Critical Social Theory*, London: Verso, 1989, p. 47.

22. Maurice Merleau-Ponty, *Humanism and Terror*, Boston: Beacon Press, 1969, p. 60. Originally published in French as *Humanisme et Terreur, Essai sur le Probleme Communiste*, Paris: Editions Gallimard, 1947.

23. Merleau-Ponty, *Humanism and Terror*, p. 7.

24. Jean-Paul Sartre, *L'existentialisme est un Humanisme*, Paris: Editions Nagel, 1946.

25. Merleau-Ponty, *Humanism and Terror*, p. 130.

26. Ibid., p. 156, emphasis in the original.

27. Ibid., pp. 188–9.

28. Leszek Kolakowski, *Toward a Marxist Humanism: Essays on the Left Today*, trans. Jane Zielonko Peel, New York: Grove Press, 1968, p. 20.

29. Ibid., p. 27.

30. Ibid., p. 144.

31. Ibid., p. 69.

32. Ibid., p. 69.

33. Ibid., pp. 70–1.

34. Leszek Kolakowski, *The New Leader*, 18 February 1959.

35. E. P. Thompson, 'An Open Letter to Leszek Kolakowski', in *The Poverty of Theory*, p. 94. Thompson's 'Open Letter' appeared first in *The Socialist Register*, vol. 10 (1973).

36. Leszek Kolakowski, 'My Correct Views on Everything', in Ralph Miliband and John Saville (eds), *The Socialist Register 1974*, London: The Merlin Press, 1974, pp. 1–20, p. 2.

37. Leszek Kolakowski, *Main Currents of Marxism: Its Origins, Growth and Dissolution*, trans. P. S. Falla, Oxford: Oxford University Press, 1978. The three volumes are entitled 'The Founders', 'The Golden Age' and 'The Breakdown'.

38. Leszek Kolakowski, 'The Death of Utopia Reconsidered', *Modernity on Endless Trial*, Chicago: Chicago University Press, 1997 [1990], pp. 131–45.

39. My account of Lucien Goldmann's work is based largely on secondary sources, in particular Mitchell Cohen, *The Wager of Lucien Goldmann: Tragedy, Dialectics and a Hidden God*, Princeton, NJ: Princeton University Press, 1994.

40. Quoted in Ibid., p. 226.

41. Martin Buber, *I and Thou*, trans. Walter Kaufmann, New York: Charles Scribner's, 1970, p. 68.

42. Martin Buber, *Paths in Utopia*, London: Macmillan, 1949, p. 6. First published in Hebrew as *Netuvot b'Utopia*, 1946.

43. Ibid., pp. 7–8.

44. Ibid., p. 78.

45. Ibid., p. 11.

46. Ibid., p. 134.

47. Alain Badiou, 'Roads to Renegacy', interview by Eric Hazan, *New Left Review*, 53 (2008), p. 129. Badiou's organisation was the Groupe pour la

Fondation de l'Union des Communistes de France Marxistes-Leninistes, a highly intellectual grouping that attempted to make realistic evaluations of Chinese Communist policy and of the possibilities of imminent revolution in France, and to develop a sober version of Maoist principles.

48. Ibid., p. 133.

49. For an extended account of the involvement of Foucault, Sartre and other young French intellectuals in Maoism, and of the impact of this involvement on post-structuralism, see Richard Wolin, *The Wind from the East: French Intellectuals, The Cultural Revolution, and the Legacy of the 1960s*, Princeton, NJ: Princeton University Press, 2010.

50. Michel Foucault, 'Governmentality', *The Essential Foucault: Selections from the Essential Work of Foucault*, Paul Rabinow and Nikolas Rose (eds), New York: New Press, 2003, pp. 229–45.

51. *The Chomsky–Foucault Debate on Human Nature*, New York: The New Press, 2006, pp. 39–44.

52. Carl Oglesby, 'Trapped in a System', in Massimo Teodori (ed.), in *The New Left: A Documentary History*, Indianapolis: Bobbs-Merrill, 1969, pp. 182–3.

# 2

# Marxist Humanism after Structuralism and Post-structuralism: The Case for Renewal

## *Kevin Anderson*

PROLOGUE: THE EMERGENCE OF
RADICAL HUMANISM AFTER WORLD WAR II

Outrage at the barbarism of Nazism, Stalinism and nuclear weapons sparked a period of radical activism in the post-World War II era. A new peace movement directed against nuclear weapons, national liberation movements against colonialism, and rank-and-file labour struggles against both capital and the labour bureaucracy, as well as an array of newer social movements – of racial and ethnic minorities, women, youth and, later, sexual minorities – emerged rapidly in the post-war era, culminating in the upheavals of the 1960s. To be sure, the East–West rivalry between liberalism/social democracy on the one hand, and Stalinism on the other, continued to dominate political and social discourse, especially during the early years of the Cold War. Nonetheless, new and sometimes revolutionary forms of activism continued to develop during this period, based upon alternative forms of politics that often tried to transcend the Cold War divide.

New radical sensibilities also emerged at the level of philosophy and culture. The post-1945 world saw a renewal of humanist thought, often on a radical, even revolutionary basis. Older forms of progressive humanism like pragmatism, which counterposed science to religion, had been undermined by the ways in which science had been harnessed by capital and the state to perpetuate mass murder. Liberal humanism, which had tolerated and engaged in dialogue with everything, including fascism, had been discredited too, for its failure to stop Hitler during the 1930s.

To take one prominent example, in post-war France, the existentialist philosopher Jean-Paul Sartre gained a following among the new generation of youth when he attacked the older liberal 'republican humanism, which was taught in the schools' and 'made tolerance the primary virtue' in 'a sort of moral relativism'. Sartre held that this made liberal and republican humanism powerless in the face of the radical 'Evil' of Nazism, which 'aimed expressly at destroying' that very humanism.[1] The older humanism had died, Sartre wrote, replaced by a newer, more radical form of humanism that 'reaffirmed the human' in the face of torture and at the same time rediscovered 'the absolute at the heart of relativity itself'.[2]

Another strand of newly emergent radical humanism arose, as Barbara Epstein notes in Chapter 1, during the 1940s and 1950s, when Marx's *1844 Manuscripts*, with their stress on alienation and humanism, came to the fore as a challenge to an oppressive social order, both East and West. Among those writing in this vein were the former Frankfurt School psychologist Erich Fromm and the erstwhile secretary of Leon Trotsky, Raya Dunayevskaya. The stakes of this new humanism included motifs that went beyond even those of the Hegelian Marxism of the post-World War I era, as exemplified by the writings of Georg Lukács, Karl Korsch, and somewhat later, Herbert Marcuse. The noted philosopher Louis Dupré put his finger on this in terms of Dunayevskaya's work: 'Dunayevskaya aims at total liberation of the human person – not only from the ills of capitalist society but also from the equally oppressive State capitalism of established communist governments.' Dupré contrasted Dunayevskaya not only to orthodox Marxism but also to Hegelian Marxists like Lukács and Korsch, who had limited their critique of capitalism 'to the social and political order'.[3] The two points underlined by Dupré – (1) the liberation of the human being as a whole, not only from class domination; and (2) an equivalence between statist communism and capitalism – distinguished this specific and self-conscious Marxist humanism, which will be my principal focus.

Before turning to this, however, I shall examine the implications for the Left of the theoretical exclusion of humanism in the work of Bourdieu, Althusser, Foucault and some of their followers.

## THE POST-1960S REJECTION OF SUBJECTIVITY AND HUMANISM: BOURDIEU'S ATTACK ON SARTRE

Since the 1970s, other forms of radicalism have largely displaced existential or Marxist forms of humanism. While radical thought has not for the most part returned to pre-1945 scientific rationalism, structuralist and post-structuralist theories that attack humanism and subjectivity as well as Hegel have become dominant among critical philosophers and social theorists. As an illustration of the pervasiveness of these trends, let us consider the 1972 attack on Sartre by the prominent sociologist Pierre Bourdieu, a thinker with only loose affinities to structuralism. Bourdieu's point of attack was a passage in Sartre's *Being and Nothingness* of 1943, where he had written, in what I consider to be a fine dialectical passage:

> For it is necessary to reverse the common opinion and acknowledge that it is not the harshness of a situation or the sufferings it imposes that lead people to conceive of another state of affairs [*état de choses*] in which things would be better for everybody; instead, it is from the day that we are able to conceive of another state of affairs, that a new light is cast on our troubles and our suffering and we *decide* they are unbearable.[4]

Here, Sartre is arguing for the crucial importance of the idea of freedom, and of thinking differently about the 'given' world of capitalism – with its commodity fetishism, notion that there is no alternative, etc. – in order to overcome those conceptual barriers. In this very unusual passage of *Being and Nothingness*, the rest of which centres almost entirely on the human subject as a hyper-isolated individual, Sartre is writing not so much of the individual subject as of one involving 'people' and 'everybody'. Sartre sees this kind of rethinking as the precondition for a genuinely revolutionary transformation, or even for a movement that is attempting to move in that direction.

Sartre continues, connecting the above directly to working class praxis, in a discussion of the early, pre-Marxian French workers movement:

> The worker of 1830 is able to revolt if his salary is lowered, for he easily conceives of a situation in which his wretched standard of living would not be as low as the one they are trying to impose on him. But he does not view [*se representer*] his suffering as unbearable; he adapts himself, not due to resignation, but because he lacks the culture and the reflection needed to allow him to conceive of social conditions [*état social*] under which this suffering would not exist. Consequently *he does not act*. Having become the masters of Lyon following a riot, the workers at Croix-Rousse do not know what to do with their

victory; they return home, and the regular army has no trouble taking them by surprise.[5]

Slightly off in his chronology, Sartre is probably referring to the silk workers riot of 1831, the harbinger of a much larger social movement in 1834 that constituted the first major French labour uprising, during which the military massacred some 300 workers. He is also somewhat imprecise conceptually, but he appears to be groping towards the notion that without a positive vision of a new, post-capitalist social order, the workers can neither generalise about their social conditions nor develop an effective, sustainable form of resistance to capital: 'Therefore suffering by itself cannot in itself be a motive for his actions. To the contrary, it is after he has created the project of changing the situation that it seems to him intolerable.'[6] What is clear, however, is that for Sartre in this passage, the problem is not solely one of how many workers are participating in the movement, if they are well organised, etc. What is of greater import is what kinds of ideas constitute the workers' intellectual and cultural arsenal in their battle against capital and the state.

Upon a first reading, these passages from Sartre seem to show some remarkable insights, which is surprising for a philosopher who up to then had had little contact with the Left, let alone labour. It is therefore somewhat surprising that in his *Outline of a Theory of Practice* of 1972, Bourdieu launches his unremittingly harsh attack on Sartre, based upon the first of the passages quoted above.

At a general level, Bourdieu notes – correctly in my view – the problematic nature of Sartre's one-sided and subjectivist concept of 'choice', which often tended to minimise objectivity, whether in philosophy or in society. He also critiques cogently Sartre's notion – elsewhere in *Being and Nothingness* – of the social as a collection of individuals who are by default separate and isolated. Finally, Bourdieu attacks effectively Sartre's later efforts – in *Critique of Dialectical Reason* (1960) and other writings – to get his readers to 'entrust to the absolute initiative of individual or collective "historical agents" such as the Party' the job of representing the workers' consciousness and forming them into a class rather than a collection of individuals.[7] The last point referred to Sartre's long-time embrace of the Stalinist French Communist Party, and by the time of Bourdieu's writing, of Maoist groups.

But rather than leaving it at that general level, Bourdieu wades into the above-cited passage from *Being and Nothingness*, a passage where Sartre, as we have seen, speaks of collective, not individual subjects, and which concentrates not on what is going on in the head of an intellectual, but on the world of French labour activism and working class consciousness. Instead of grappling with these issues, Bourdieu simply dismisses Sartre's entire discussion of working class subjectivity as a form of idealism 'devoid of objectivity':

> If the world of action is nothing other than this universe of inter-changeable possibilities, entirely dependent upon the decrees of the consciousness which creates it, and hence totally devoid of objectivity, if it is moving because the subject chooses to be revolted, then emotions, passions, and actions are merely games of bad faith, sad farces in which one is both bad actor and good audience.[8]

In carrying out this critique, Bourdieu proceeds to cite one of the most deterministic and positivistic texts of sociologist Émile Durkheim, *The Rules of Sociological Method*.[9]

Bourdieu extolls Durkheim's book as a prime source for critiquing what he regards as Sartre's complete and utter subjectivism and idealism, citing a passage attacking idealism from Durkheim's book: 'It is because the imaginary offers the mind no resistance that the mind, conscious of no restraint, gives itself up to boundless ambitions and believes it possible to construct, or rather reconstruct the world by virtue of its own strength at the whim of its desires.'[10] Bourdieu refrains from citing the blatantly positivist sentence that precedes Durkheim's attack on idealism, in which he merges the natural and the social sciences, provocatively comparing the 'beginnings of the physical sciences' in 'alchemy' and 'astrology' to the origins of the social sciences in critical idealism.[11] Here and elsewhere, Durkheim rejects the dialectical tradition altogether.[12]

Bourdieu, perhaps sensing elements of an errant subjectivity even in Marx, never declared himself a Marxist, unlike Sartre who by 1957 had written that as long as capitalism exists, philosophy would be living in the 'moment' of Marx.[13] While he would have accepted some of Marx's conclusions, Bourdieu would not have felt very comfortable with Marx's acknowledgement of both the subjective and the objective sides of human social practice. Take, for example, Marx's statement – in the 'Alienated Labour' essay of 1844 – that 'free, conscious activity is the species-characteristic of human beings'.[14]

Nor is it very likely that Bourdieu would have been entirely comfortable even with the Marx of *Capital* who wrote famously, continuing this theme, albeit in a more precisely worked out form:

> We pre-suppose labour in a form that stamps it as exclusively human. A spider conducts operations that resemble those of a weaver, and a bee puts to shame many an architect in the construction of her cells. But what distinguishes the worst architect from the best of bees is this, that the [human] architect raises his structure in imagination before he erects it in reality.[15]

Here Marx makes clear his view of workers as thinking subjects, who are robbed of their humanity in the capitalist workplace. This is the price paid by the worker as set out more concretely in the chapter on 'Accumulation of Capital': 'They distort the worker into a fragment of a human being [*Teilmenschen*]; they degrade him to the level of an appendage of a machine; they destroy the actual content of his labour by turning it into a torment; they alienate from him the intellectual potentialities of the labour process.'[16]

The latter passage is a concretisation of the commodity fetishism section of chapter 1 of *Capital*, where human relations become like relations between things because that is what 'they really are'.[17] In turning the workers into variable capital, the system robs them both of the value created by their labour and of their humanity more generally, as the very process is one of deep dehumanisation that cries out for a humanist response. And as Marx sees it, those same workers, yearning for free and associated labour, seek to shake off those shackles, both mental and manual, and to move towards that society of 'freely associated human beings'.[18] But in order to get there they need to clarify their thinking about their concrete situation and about capitalism as a whole. And doing so necessitates thinking theoretically and philosophically, not just strategically. For these reasons, as Marx saw it, they need Marx's *Capital*, and as later dialectical Marxists added, Hegel as well. The workers also need allies among other social groups, especially revolutionary intellectuals, who can help clarify their thinking while simultaneously clarifying their own thought as intellectuals, for even the most critical intellectuals are themselves necessarily prisoners of commodity fetishism as well.

## THE ALTHUSSERIAN CUL-DE-SAC: ANTIHUMANIST MARXISM

Bourdieu left some room in his theorising for human subjectivity, or agency, as he preferred to call it. However, the possibility of subjectivity in the sense of critique, resistance or revolt on the part of the subjugated, is closed off almost completely in the work of the structuralist Marxist Louis Althusser. This stance mars Althusser's celebrated essay on 'Ideological State Apparatuses' (1970), which was indeed a serious attempt to go beyond reductionist arguments concerning ideology's relationship to its material base, and to theorise its place in late twentieth-century capitalist society in terms of institutions outside value production like religion and education. As Althusser sees it, the notion of subjectivity is an illusion that props up the dominant political form developed under modern capitalism: liberal democracy. In short, if one validates the possibility of human creativity and self-movement within – or even in struggle against – existing society, one is at best an idealist dupe, and at worst a propagandist for the capitalist system.

The fact that these apparatuses interact with individual members of society by engaging in 'the interpellation of these "individuals" as subjects' is simply part of these individuals' 'subjection to the Subject' with a capital 'S', i.e. the capitalist system. This interpellation is part of the system's 'rituals' of domination: 'They must be obedient to God, to their conscience, to the priest, to de Gaulle, to the boss, to the engineer, that "thou shalt love thy neighbor as thyself", etc.'[19] Playing on the ambiguity in the term 'subject', which can refer to either a 'free subject' or a 'subjected being', Althusser forces these two into a single totality, wherein: 'The individual is interpellated as a (free) subject in order that he shall submit freely to the commandments of the Subject, i.e., in order that he shall (freely) accept his subjection.'[20]

Althusser confines his discussion largely to individual rather than collective subjectivities, ignoring the varying forms of collective self-consciousness and resultant collective action for self-liberation that emerges again and again on the part of oppressed classes, genders, nations, ethno-racial groups and sexual minorities. This is a most problematic omission indeed for a Marxist. But even if one remains on Althusser's ground, that of the individual subject who is a mere subject of domination, isn't he creating a false totality here? Where is the possibility of contradictions between these individual subjects and their subjugation? Althusser acknowledges that such a situation may occur, but passes this off as a 'bad' subject who is then dealt with by the openly 'repressive' state apparatus, i.e. police, prisons, etc.[21]

But what about a rebellious individual subject whose rebellion touches off wide support within an entire subjected group? Consider Rosa Parks getting herself arrested for violating the racial segregation laws on that bus in Montgomery, Alabama in 1955, for example. Parks' actions, taken in connection with a large support network, which grew rapidly in the days following her arrest, touched off a decade of radical change today termed the Civil Rights Movement. When such an occurrence comes at the right moment, when historical circumstances are aligned towards liberation, and when the organisation of both emancipatory ideas and the means to implement them are present, we have what Dunayevskaya called a 'subjectivity which has absorbed objectivity, that is to say through its struggle for freedom it gets to know and cope with the objectively real'.[22]

Another problem with Althusser's ideological apparatuses is that they seem to float above the economic structures of society. Here, his surprising, albeit muted, affinity to Maoism is important to note – something that is often missed because Althusser remained a member of the pro-Moscow French Communist Party. Such a focus on culture and ideology as opposed to economic base was also a hallmark of Mao's theory of contradiction, as well as the underpinning for his 'Cultural Revolution' of the late 1960s. That 'revolution' was in reality more of a top-down affair in which Mao used Red Guards recruited from among the student youth – supported by one bureaucracy he did not shake up at this time, the military – in order to dislodge some of his fellow leaders, whom he deemed too close to Russia, among other sins. The Maoist Red Guard attacks on forms of 'Western culture', like classical European music or books, supposedly constituted a challenge to global imperialism, this at the very time when Mao was refusing to give much in the way of material aid to Vietnam in its struggle against US imperialism. The whole process ended, not as Mao's international followers had hoped, in the establishment of a new International to the left of the pro-Moscow Communist parties, but instead with a rapprochement with the United States under Richard Nixon, the butcher of Vietnam.

Another problematic feature of Althusser's apparatuses like religion and education is that they are not new or unique to capitalism. Despite this, Althusser does not analyse their specifically capitalist character very much. In this sense, his ideological apparatuses lack historical development or grounding. More problematically still, his focus on the cultural and superstructural realm obviates any real discussion of the working class, a human subject that is both subjected to and at the same time, in the form of a revolutionary subject, able to resist or even revolt against capital. Althusser implies that real changes have to begin at the level of superstructure, of ideology. This ignores the fact that real changes in consciousness often result when changes in the economic structure of society wrench people out of their customary modes of existence, plunging them into new forms of production and property relations.

Althusser also famously attacked both Hegelianism and humanism as bourgeois, if not reactionary. This was a departure even from orthodox, Engelsian Marxism. Although Engels had conceptualised idealism and materialism as a general dividing line between progressive and reactionary forms of philosophy, he made an exception for Hegel's idealism, which he regarded as definitely revolutionary. Thus, Engels had always acknowledged Hegel as an important antecedent of Marx's thought.[23] Nor had Engels explicitly repudiated humanism, although he did not make a core category out of it either.

For his part, Althusser, reacting against both Marxist and existentialist humanism, went on the attack, writing of the 'phantom' or 'shade of Hegel'. He called upon Marxists, as if exorcising a vampire, 'to drive this phantom back into the night'.[24] Althusser was to continue this theme unabated throughout his intellectual career, rallying more orthodox Marxists against the threats posed by Hegelian and humanist versions of Marxism. He carried the debate into Lenin's work as well, attempting to deny Hegel's influence on Lenin, despite clear evidence to the contrary in the latter's 1914–15 Hegel notebooks.[25]

Althusser also attracted not a few younger intellectuals to an antihumanist Marxism that, at least on the surface, did not mark a return to the scientistic and quasi-positivist philosophical orientation of many earlier Marxists. This earlier scientistic orientation, attractive in an age when 'progressive' science fought against religion, had been severely undermined during the post-World War II period, when various forms of radical humanism assailed the ravages that had taken place through the use of modern science, most notably the nuclear bombs dropped on Hiroshima and Nagasaki in 1945. But by the time Althusser came on to the scene, in the 1960s, some at least were ripe for an antihumanist counter-attack, a sentiment that only grew larger in the wake of the defeats of the revolutionary movements of the 1960s. This was especially the case in France, where the near revolution of 1968 had first raised and then dashed hopes for a profoundly radical revolution inside an industrially developed capitalist society.

Beginning in the early 1960s, Althusser famously dismissed the writings of the early Marx as pre-Marxist, imbued with what he saw as liberal and Hegelian notions of alienation and humanism. These writings were simply not Marxist, he held, because they were humanist, but he went further, placing antihumanism at the core of Marx's thought despite the lack of textual evidence on this point: 'One can and must speak openly of Marx's theoretical anti-humanism.'[26] The term 'speak openly' may have been intended to imply that 'real' Marxists 'knew' this, but had de-emphasised it in order to gain broader appeal.

The French Hegel scholar Jacques d'Hondt, who, unlike Althusser, was to resign from the French Communist Party in 1968 to protest the Russian invasion of Czechoslovakia, noted at the time that for generations, Marxists had been at great pains to answer attacks from liberal humanists, who had claimed that Marxism reduced the human being, in dehumanised fashion, to a set of economic categories and forces. Therefore, wrote d'Hondt, the Althusserian attack on humanism amounted to 'a type of provocation' that served to delink Marxism from the democratic and anti-fascist traditions to which it had often been allied. As against Althusser's rejection of the term 'man' or 'human being' as a liberal illusion, d'Hondt noted that Marx had used this term when he wrote that the human being 'makes history'.[27] Moreover, d'Hondt wrote, 'One runs the risk of undermining Marxist methodology if its human basis is ignored.' From a Marxist standpoint, he added, 'the point is [human] liberation.'[28]

Althusser's key Marxological notion, pursued more virulently than others who had only hinted at such a thesis, was that Marx made an 'epistemological break' in 1845 with his earlier writings, especially the *1844 Manuscripts*.[29] Initially, Althusser dismissed attempts to tie *Capital* to Marx's early writings via the psychoanalytic concept of projection: 'The whole, fashionable theory of "reification" depends upon a projection of the theory of alienation found in the early texts, particularly the *1844 Manuscripts*, onto the theory of "fetishism" in *Capital*.'[30] This ignores the fact that it was Lukács who foregrounded the notion of reification while neglecting the concept of alienation, but also distorts what are often held to be the most important pages in *Capital*. Ignoring Marx's own language in the fetishism section to the effect that under capitalism, the 'social relation' between human beings takes on 'the fantastic form of a relation between things,'[31] Althusser declares peremptorily: 'In *Capital* the only social relation that is presented in the form of a thing (this piece of metal) is money.'[32] A few years after these were published in *For Marx*, Althusser asserts in his preface to a widely circulated paperback edition of *Capital* published in French in 1969, that the entire first part of *Capital* is marked by 'a method of presentation' imbued with 'Hegelian prejudice.'[33] For these and other reasons, Althusser now advises the reader to 'leave Part I (Commodities and Money) deliberately on one side in a first reading.'[34]

By now, moreover, Althusser had modified his earlier notion of an 1845 'epistemological break' with Hegel on Marx's part. Here in 1969, he laments 'survivals in Marx's language and even in his thought of the influence of Hegel's thought' in *Capital* itself.[35] Marx, it seems, did not become fully 'Marxist' until nearly a decade after he first published *Capital*, with '*Critique of the Gotha Program* (1875) as well as the *Marginal Notes on Wagner*' of 1881, texts that were finally free of the supposed taint of Hegel and humanism.[36] In other words, Marx was not really a Marxist until eight years before his death!

Here, Althusser's argument flirted with an open anti-Marxism, and in no small way anticipated the post-structuralist rejection by Foucault and others of Marx *tout court*, as a Hegelian humanist whose thought was supposedly marked by the concept of a fixed human essence.

## FOUCAULT'S ANTI-MARXIST ANTIHUMANISM

Michel Foucault's writings had already gained some prominence outside France by the 1960s. For example, *Madness and Civilisation* appeared with a major US publisher in an abridged edition in 1965. But in the 1980s his international fame skyrocketed, as the most notable representative of post-structuralism. This was the time when neoliberal economics and socially conservative politics came to the fore at a global level, as seen in the ascendancy of Margaret Thatcher, Ronald Reagan and Pope John Paul II. During these years, even dissident and revolutionary movements began to distance themselves from Marxism, if not opposing it outright. Such was the case with Soviet dissident Alexandr Solzhenitsyn's avowal of an archconservative, moralising form of Christianity. Elsewhere, a rejection of Marxism could be seen in social revolutions and upheavals as disparate as those in Iran and Poland. Tiny Nicaragua was an exception, but its revolution, inspired by Marxism and

Theology of Liberation, was eventually strangled by the Reagan administration with the open collusion of the Vatican and the complicity of
Western European social democrats.

After having carried out philosophical studies with Althusser in the
1940s and briefly joining the French Communist Party, Foucault had
moved away from Marxism altogether by the 1960s. In 1966, a year
after Althusser's attacks on Marxist humanism in *For Marx*, Foucault
intoned in *The Order of Things* that Marxism itself was a hopelessly dated
perspective: 'Marxism exists in nineteenth-century thought like a fish
in water: that is, it is unable to breathe anywhere else.'[37] This may have
been an oblique answer to Sartre's 1957 declaration, cited earlier, that
one could not go beyond Marx so long as capitalism existed. In any case,
these statements earned Foucault a rebuke from Sartre, who accused him
of a 'rejection of history', of being trapped in a structuralist 'succession of
immobilities'. Escalating the polemic, Sartre termed Foucault's argument
'the last resort the bourgeoisie can enact against Marx'.[38]

Foucault attacked humanism even more forcefully, mocking its preoccupation with 'man', and with the human being in general. This was
because human beings exhibited profound differences from each other
that could not be captured within a humanist framework. Instead of Marx,
it was Friedrich Nietzsche who anticipated the future, who 'indicated
the turning-point' – that of 'the death of man'. In the bleak ending of
*The Order of Things*, Foucault wrote that while the Enlightenment 'made
it possible for the figure of man to appear', the era of humanism was
'nearing its end' and by the 1960s 'one can certainly wager that man
would be erased, like a face drawn in sand at the edge of the sea'.[39]

In *Discipline and Punish*, published nearly a decade later, Foucault
links the oppressive character of the modern apparatuses of surveillance
and domination not to antihumanism but to humanism. He writes, for
example, that the 'rigorous discipline' of Napoleon's military machine,
with its close surveillance over the troops, as the juncture where 'the man
of modern humanism was born'.[40]

Some of Foucault's differences with humanism were generational.
Sartre's type of humanism led him to write of human beings in general,
and he was sometimes leery of the concreteness of race, ethnicity
or gender. At one point he told a black audience that blackness was
the 'minor term of a dialectical progression' towards the universal of
class,[41] for which he received a sharp retort from another revolutionary humanist, the young Frantz Fanon. Two decades later, Sartre found

himself alongside Foucault in the French prisoner rights movement of the 1970s, a movement in which Maoists played a prominent part. As Bernard Harcourt notes, Sartre's idea of public solidarity was to hold a press conference of intellectual notables speaking out in support of the prisoners. Instead, as against what was by now perceived as Sartre's intellectual elitism, what prevailed was Foucault's idea of a press conference where ex-prisoners would speak in their own voices, with the intellectual luminaries present only as a supporting cast.[42]

Foucault rightly contested the straightjacket of Althusserian Marxism, although he kept many of Althusser's – and other structuralists' – notions of antihumanism in his work. Although Foucault repeatedly denied he was a structuralist, he can be viewed nonetheless as having operated generally within the structuralist camp. This can be seen in the tense public exchange between Foucault and the structuralist psychoanalyst Jacques Lacan, on the one hand, and the Marxist humanist and 'genetic structuralist' Lucien Goldmann, on the other. Their exchange followed Foucault's 1969 presentation to the Société Française de Philosophie of his now canonical text, 'What Is an Author?'[43] Below are brief excerpts from that exchange, which included a sharp retort to Goldmann by Lacan:

> Goldmann: The negation of the subject is today the central idea of a whole group of thinkers, or more precisely, of a whole philosophical current ... [This is] the French school of non-genetic structuralism [which] includes notably the names Lévi-Strauss, Roland Barthes, Althusser, Derrida, etc. ... [In May 1968, a student wrote on the blackboard] 'Structures don't go out into the streets.' This means: it is never the structures who make history, but human beings, even though the actions of the latter always has a structured and significant character. ...
>
> Foucault: ... I have never, myself, used the word structure. Look for it in *The Order of Things*; you will never find it. ...
>
> Lacan: I don't think that it was in any way legitimate to have written that structures don't go out into the streets because, if there is one thing demonstrated by the events of May, it is precisely the going out into the streets of structures.[44]

This exchange, in which Goldmann was seen to have been the loser,[45] was a prominent marker in the shift in French intellectual thought towards structuralism and post-structuralism. As Goldmann himself would have noted based upon his other writings, however,[46] this shift away from dialectical humanism came in the wake of the defeat of a revolutionary movement, in 1969 rather than 1968.

Until the mid-1970s, much of Foucault's work stressed the subjugation of the human subject under various institutions of power, developing notions of the decentring of power. In some respects, this decentring of power paralleled Marx's concept of capital, while at the same time diverging sharply from Marx in denying the centrality of the basic forces and relations of production. Like Marx's logic of capital, power for Foucault pervades all social relationships, and these relationships are irreducible to other forms like the economic structure of society. Foucault's world is one where modern forms of power are subtle in similar ways to capital's rule over the worker and society through the commodity fetish rather than the bullwhip or iron chains of old. And as with Althusser, modern power is not primarily repressive, but gentle, often presenting itself in the guise of caring or education. It grows and develops as part of what Foucault terms regimes of truth.

Moreover, as Foucault sees it, modern power brings with it nothing in the way of progress. This is of course at variance with Enlightenment liberalism and even with the Marxian tradition, which articulated, in varying degrees, a dialectical view of what is termed progress, including technological progress. Foucault is particularly interested in critiquing modern apparatuses of power that refer to scientific knowledge and which are marked by the carrying out of scientific research on subject populations: mental institutions and their subject populations, modern penitentiaries with their criminological research projects and reha-bilitation systems, and the modern 'science' of sexuality, especially its preoccupation with 'deviance'.

The modern apparatuses of power penetrate the human subject deeply in a capillary fashion, here described by Foucault through an evocation of the Panopticon design for the nineteenth-century prison as developed by the liberal philosopher Jeremy Bentham:

The Panopticon is a privileged place for experiments on men. ... The Panopticon functions as a kind of laboratory of power. Thanks to its mechanism of observation, it gains in efficiency and in the ability to penetrate into men's behaviour; knowledge follows advances of power, discovering new objects of knowledge over all the surfaces over which power is exercised.[47]

These notions of studying and experimenting upon the subjugated are central to Foucault's notion of modern power, which forms or reforms the human subject, requiring or even inspiring its active participation.

In contrast to both Althusser and Bourdieu, however, there is apparently more scope, especially in Foucault's later writings, for a resistance to power. In 1976, a year after *Discipline and Punish*, Foucault sketches his notion of resistance at a conceptual level for the first time in his *History of Sexuality*, volume 1:

> Where there is power, there is resistance, and yet, or rather consequently, this resistance is never in a position of exteriority in relation to power. ... Their [power relationships'] very existence depends on a multiplicity of points of resistance. ... Hence there is no single locus of Great Refusal, no soul of revolt, source of all rebellions, or pure law of the revolutionary. Instead there are specific cases [*cas d'espèces*] of resistance ... They are the other in the relations of power; they inscribe themselves as irreducible in relation to it.[48]

In the above sense, resistance is everywhere, without a fixed point. However, it seems unable to overcome power.

As has been noted by several of his critics, Foucault's notion of resistance has important limitations: both a certain circularity and the lack of a concept of emancipation. In their introduction to Herbert Marcuse's writings on psychology and philosophy, Douglas Kellner, Clayton Pierce and Tyson Lewis offer a philosophical critique: 'With the rise of post-modernism and the discourse of power – in particular Foucault's critique of the Great Refusal – it has become fashionable to replace revolution with the terms resistance – or even with micro-resistance. Resistance is here internal to power, and ultimately produced by power, thus challenging power from the inside.'[49] Similarly, autonomist Marxist John Holloway notes the absence of a concept of 'emancipation' in Foucault's notion of resistance.[50]

At a more empirical level, one can also critique the types of resistance that preoccupied Foucault. He celebrates resistance among prisoners fighting for their rights in France and the US during the early 1970s. Foucault's participation in the French prisoner rights movement forms the background to *Discipline and Punish*. Here, in what are his finest moments as a thinker-activist, he nonetheless neglects to take up the emancipatory politics that were sometimes present within the Marxist and black liberation frameworks articulated by many of the prisoners at Attica, Soledad and other sites of US prison radicalism in the early 1970s.

More problematically, though, Foucault also supported uncritically the dominant Islamist wing of the Iranian revolution of 1979. He did so without troubling himself very much about the agenda of its clerical leadership, all the while heaping scorn upon liberal and leftist opponents of the regime as incurably Westernised and therefore outdated. Moreover, in his Iran writings, Foucault sees wrathful figures like Khomeini (or earlier, the fifteenth-century Florentine dictator Savonarola) as the very embodiments of revolutionary enthusiasm, which he links in turn to madness. He travelled to Iran twice in 1978, and argued that the Iranian Islamists were expressing the collective will of the Iranian people in a more or less unmediated fashion. Of course, such notions of the sameness of Iranian Muslims illustrated the Orientalist overtones that imbued these writings. Moreover, Foucault extolled the possibilities of a wider Islamic revolution throughout the Middle East in terms of undermining global hegemonies, while also arguing that the secularised West had a lot to learn from Iran's political spirituality. When an Iranian feminist attacked the naïveté of his writings on Iran, he heaped scorn upon her as too Westernised, as hostile to Islam, and therefore unrepresentative of the Iranian people. Foucault's assessment of Iran also came under implicit criticism by France's leading scholar of Islam, the Marxist Maxime Rodinson, who critiqued Foucault's Iran writings as an abstract flight of philosophical fantasy in the pages of *Le Monde*. In the spring of 1979, after Khomeini came to power and immediately began to repress women, leftists and gay men, Foucault experienced even more intense attack and ridicule in France. He accused his critics of misconstruing his writings, made some perfunctory criticisms of the new regime, and then lapsed into silence over Iran until his death five years later.[51]

Many have regarded Foucault's Iran episode as an aberration. They were stunned to see a radical leftist philosopher, who was also a gay man, support uncritically an ideology that justified the brutal repression of homosexuality, feminism and democracy more generally. This notion of Foucault's Iran writings as aberrant could be questioned, however, for his Iran writings continue, albeit in exaggerated form, one of his key flaws:

a one-sided and too sweeping critique of Western modernity. At least in the Iran writings, Foucault's critique of Western modernity reveals as well a surprising sympathy for what he perceives as a pre-modern social order, bathed in an uncompromising, antihumanist form of religious culture that supposedly helped the popular classes to resist or at least endure a harsh state domination. He showed little awareness that the Khomeinists possessed a modern, quasi-Leninist form of organisation, and that their politics was no mere reiteration of 'traditionalism'.

Were these momentary enthusiasms in the heat of the Iranian revolution, or can one read Foucault backwards, looking at his earlier, 'classic' writings through the lens of these very problematic ones on Iran? In fact, the theme of conservative and antihumanist forms of religious subjectivity as loci of resistance to modern apparatuses of power can already be discerned here and there in Foucault's earlier work. It is present, although not that prominently, nearly two decades earlier in his first major work, the *History of Madness* (1961), where he gives examples of passionate religious devotion as instances of resistance to the modern apparatus of the asylum. This occurs as part of his critique of the Enlightenment reformer Philippe Pinel, who played a role in the unchaining of French mental patients in the 1790s, under the impact of the revolution.

Foucault calls particular attention to Pinel's hostility towards religion. For Pinel, he writes, 'Religion was not to be a moral substratum of life in the asylum, but purely and simply an object of medicine.'[52] Foucault finds this objectionable, especially Pinel's Enlightenment notion of 'a neutral asylum, purified of all the images and passions that Christianity had brought into existence, and which led the mind to error, illusion, and ultimately delirium and hallucinations'. Thus, it was not only the critique of religion as such that was the problem for Foucault. His more specific target is the Enlightenment effort 'to reduce the imaginary forms' of religion and preserve in a 'Voltairean' manner only the rational, 'moral content of religion'.[53]

In his stance towards religion, Pinel stood on the ground of Enlightenment humanism. This framework was eloquently articulated by his contemporary Mary Wollstonecraft, who argued against pre-modern strictures on women that were propped up by religious orthodoxy in *A Vindication of the Rights of Woman* (1792). More broadly, Wollstonecraft sought to subject religion to reason, taming its 'wild fanaticism', in order to make room for notions of women's equality and freedom:

If [religion] be merely the refuge of weakness or wild fanaticism, and not a governing principle of conduct, drawn from self-knowledge, and a rational opinion respecting the attributes of God, what can it be expected to produce? The religion which consists in warming the affections, and exalting the imagination, is only the poetical part, and may afford the individual pleasure without rendering it a more moral being. ... Men will not become moral when they only build airy castles in a future world to compensate for the disappointments which they meet with in this; if they turn their thoughts from relative duties to religious reveries.[54]

While it is hard to defend entirely Wollstonecraft's separation of reason from emotion, one can certainly see as laudable her Enlightenment humanist notion that the world's major religions could be seen to possess – and to share – elements of the modern notions of social justice and civic morality, if they could be stripped of their fanatical, irrational and retrograde elements.

But this was exactly the Enlightenment notion of religion that Foucault was attacking in *History of Madness*, and later, in his Iran writings, with his vindication of 'the images and passions' of religion, which, *contra* Wollstonecraft and others, he did not wish to see subjected to reason. This was because, to him, the greater danger was Enlightenment reason and the modern apparatuses of domination he saw it as justifying. Here, in counterposing those forms of modern domination to pre-modern religious ones, Foucault revealed, prefiguring his Iran writings, that his critique of modernity did not exclude the validation of extremely reactionary, antihumanist forms of religious subjectivity when they constituted themselves as forms of resistance to modern power.

Tellingly, at the very time of his Iran writings, Foucault had almost nothing to say about another prominent example of spiritual politics, Theology of Liberation in the Nicaraguan revolution of 1979. Was this because the ferment over Theology of Liberation and Marxism at the time in Latin America looked towards the future, towards the progressive features of religious subjectivity – egalitarianism and self-mobilisation of the poor – and because its notion of social justice, although deeply anti-imperialist, was free of the harsh Puritanical strictures on modern 'Western' culture, especially concerning gender and sexuality, that one found in Khomeinism? Was it simply too Marxist, too humanistic?

## HAS TODAY'S PHILOSOPHICAL IMPASSE CREATED GROUND FOR THE RETURN OF MARXIST HUMANISM?

The period 1979–81 was an era when both Michel Foucault and Edward Said refused to criticise the outcome of the Iranian revolution in a fundamental way, and, as we have seen, Foucault even became a quasi-follower of Khomeinism for a period in 1978–9. One cannot find wild gestures like Foucault's enthusiasm for the Iranian ayatollahs in the more careful but less philosophically rich work of Edward Said. Said is also a more ambiguous figure in terms of socialist humanism, as Robert Spencer's somewhat different take on his work in Chapter 3 demonstrates. Still, Said suggests that 'every European, in what he could say about the Orient, was consequently a racist, an imperialist, and almost totally ethnocentric.'[55] This is surely cultural nationalism dressed up in sophisticated postmodernist language. As Aijaz Ahmad writes, 'only the most obscurantist indigenists and cultural nationalists had previously argued ... that Europeans were ontologically incapable of producing any true knowledge about non-Europe. But Said was emphatic on this point.'[56]

Said's *Orientalism* identified a powerful dynamic – indeed, I have relied on it in my own critique of Foucault – but in its absolutist form it has succeeded in driving a wedge between those whose identities are Asian, Middle Eastern and/or Muslim, on the one hand, and Europeans and Euro-Americans on the other. The entire analysis ignores the class position of those who hold these various identities. It has contributed to a form of identity politics for which diversifying the leadership of the dominant institutions is sufficient, a point made forcefully by Michael Hardt and Antonio Negri in *Empire*,[57] and the limits of which can be seen with even greater clarity after the Obama presidency.

Hardt and Negri try to go beyond these kinds of identity politics, but they develop instead notions of class that minimise social differences like the hierarchies of race and gender among the world's working people, not to speak of their overly peremptory rejection of the nation-state as a global actor. *Empire* also falls short because of its underlying philosophical perspective, an eclectic mix of Deleuze, Foucault, Machiavelli and Spinoza, along with some elements from Marx, particularly the section of the *Grundrisse* on technology and labour. But the elements of Marxism that are soundly rejected are the Hegelian and humanist underpinnings of Marx's thought.

Thus, whether under the influence of structuralists like Althusser, or post-structuralists like Foucault, the 1970s, 1980s and 1990s saw a turn away from humanism, from Hegel, and from the dialectic more generally. In these milieus, Hegel was characterised as a fundamentally reactionary, even racist thinker, and Marx as a pro-colonialist, Eurocentric one. Frequently, a version of Foucault was presented as the alternative. Meanwhile, humanism in the socialist humanist sense was at best ignored and at worst maligned.

Nonetheless, the various post-structuralisms themselves reached an impasse by the beginning of the twenty-first century. Many began to argue that the work of Said and Foucault had been too closely linked to identity politics, while that of Hardt and Negri was seen as a naïve evocation of a global multitude with no real hope of success in its opposition to the global capitalist order.

Recently, many have returned to Marx and some have even advocated a return to Hegel and the dialectic. Very few, however, are returning to any form of radical humanism. This is unfortunate, for it is the humanist element that has helped to ground, at least philosophically, notions of a real alternative to the existing state of affairs, to the domination of capital and the state over the human being.[58] Moreover, the structuralist and post-structuralist philosophies were, as a whole, markers of the defeat of the Left after the 1960s, especially during the long years of Reagan–Thatcher–John Paul II–Khomeini during the 1980s. In addition, with the collapse during the years 1989–91 of the Soviet Union and the Eastern European bloc it dominated, the death of Marxism was proclaimed loudly nearly everywhere, especially since the dissident forms of socialism, some of them Marxist humanist in orientation, that had predominated in the anti-Stalinist revolts of 1956 and 1968 had by this time largely dissipated. At the same time, the Reagan–Thatcher forms of market fundamentalism and authoritarian politics were continued through the 1990s, albeit in slightly softened form under politicians like Tony Blair and Bill Clinton. But this only served to solidify the era of neoliberal capitalism.

The 1990s also saw other developments that pointed in a different direction. In 1994, the Chiapas revolt broke out, challenging not only the dominant classes of Mexico in terms of indigenous rights, but also the entire system of neoliberal capitalism, and the way its form of globalisation was affecting rural populations. This movement paralleled a certain revival of Marxist thought, at least compared to the 1980s. In 1993, the year before Chiapas, one of the chief representatives of postmodern thought, Jacques Derrida, had given a keynote address at a conference in California that had been intended as yet another dismissal of Marx, this time in favour of postmodernist and post-structuralist forms of critique. Instead, and to the chagrin of some of his hosts, Derrida delivered a ringing endorsement of Marx's *Communist Manifesto*, in which he declared that he 'knew of few texts in the philosophical tradition, perhaps none whose lesson appears more urgent today'.[59]

The twenty-first century began in a radically bifurcated manner, with some evidence of new challenges to neoliberalism, if not capital itself. On the one hand, the beginning of the new century was marked by the 1999 upheaval in Seattle, which placed the new alterglobalisation movement on the world stage. This youthful movement, unlike the more identitarian movements of the 1980s and 1990s, had coalesced around a number of issues, from ecology to labour, but always including an opposition to capitalism, if not *in toto*, at least in its neoliberal form.

On the other hand, the 11 September 2001 attacks on the US by reactionary fundamentalists constituted a totally different sort of marker for the new century. These murderous attacks, by men who carried a misogynist, retrogressive social agenda combined with an opposition to global power networks, gave the green light to another and more powerful set of reactionaries in the Bush administration. The latter proceeded to launch what they called a global war against terrorism, engulfing whole regions in imperial violence. At first, the so-called war on terror between the US and reactionary forms of Islam seemed to crowd out everything else, especially the new openings exemplified by Seattle.

By the second decade of the twenty-first century, however, it was clear that the 'war on terror', in addition to its human toll, constituted one of the most disastrous examples in human history of overreaching by an imperialist power. By 2008, the world economy plunged into the second deepest economic crisis in the history of capitalism, with only that of 1929 being a worse example. These twin crises resulted in a whole series of upheavals, most notably the Arab revolutions, but also serious unrest in Greece and in a number of other contexts that were directly influenced by the Arab revolutions, most notably the Occupy movement. These events suggested that the spirit of Seattle 1999 had not only persisted, but also deepened. In the midst of despair, it seemed that a new generation of the Left was dawning, something not seen since the post-war years 1945–70.

Perhaps history teaches us something here. As the Marxist humanist Lucien Goldmann once wrote in terms of Hegelianism, Marxism and periods of revolt and revolution:

> Hegelian categories are all recovered in Marxism; and it is no accident that they were reactualised in Europe around, say, the years 1917–23: first by Lenin in the *Philosophical Notebooks*, secondly by Lukács in *History and Class Consciousness*, and thirdly, I believe, somewhat later in Gramsci's concretely philosophical analyses. ... And if after 1923 this renaissance of dialectical thought subsequently ended, it was because the revolutionary period was clearly over: we know that with the 1923 defeat in Germany, after 1925–26, there was no longer any trace of this.[60]

One could extend Goldmann's point into a more general one about Hegelianism and revolution, also noting the period 1945–70.

But what about radical humanism, so often the companion of Hegelianism, at least in the second half of the twentieth century? Perhaps what Goldmann said of Hegelianism could also be said of the category of humanism, that it comes to the fore only at times when there is a real hope of positive revolutionary change. In that sense, we may be on the eve of a revival of radical humanism at a time when the hopes and aspirations of a new generation are being articulated in a way that brooks no compromise with an utterly dehumanised global capitalist system that has plunged that whole generation into depths of despair out of which revolutionary challenges are beginning to emerge.

Whether or not that is the case, I would argue that the indifference towards or dismissal of radical humanism weighs down the movements for change and revolution of our era. In the remainder of this chapter, I will be calling for a return – albeit on twenty-first-century ground – not only to Marx's humanism as seen in the *1844 Manuscripts*, *Grundrisse* and *Capital* – but also to the writings of the post-World War II socialist humanists in the West, people like Sartre, Erich Fromm and above all Raya Dunayevskaya; Eastern European dissident Marxist humanists like Karel Kosík; and finally, African socialist humanists like Frantz Fanon. I will also be arguing that it was Dunayevskaya who critically appropriated the philosophical contributions of most of these thinkers. In so doing, and in deep – and sometimes very critical – dialogue directly with Marx, Hegel and post-Marx Marxists like Lenin, Trotsky and Luxemburg,

Dunayevskaya developed Marxist humanism as a full body of ideas that covered dialectics, changes in capitalism since Marx's death, the emergence of rank-and-file labour and of the Third World revolutions, and the politics and philosophy of women's liberation/feminism, all the while critiquing other forms of radical thought that did not measure up to the times, from Maoism and Trotskyism to structuralism and the Frankfurt School.[61]

But in order to appreciate Dunayevskaya's achievement, we first need to examine the explicitly Marxist humanist tradition in greater detail.

## ERICH FROMM'S SOCIALIST HUMANISM

Besides Sartre, the best known of the twentieth-century socialist humanist thinkers is Erich Fromm, who is often underestimated today in Left academia as a mere liberal or as a populariser who lacked rigour, in contrast to other members of the Frankfurt School like the melancholy Theodor Adorno. None deny, however, that it was Fromm who first introduced the Frankfurt School to a form of Freudian Marxism that was at the root of all of their subsequent efforts to theorise 'authoritarian personalities'. Drawn frequently from the lower middle classes, these authoritarian personalities combined a masochistic reverence and obedience to higher authority with sadistic urges to dominate the less powerful. The prime point of reference for Fromm and his colleagues was fascism, but their argument could be extended to the guards at Abu Ghraib or those drawn to religious fundamentalist movements, including radical Islamism. Fromm summed up these issues in popular form in *Escape from Freedom* (1941), a pioneering analysis of the appeal of fascism to those living under the uncertainties and the atomisation of modern capitalist society.

By the 1950s, with publications like *The Art of Loving* (1956), Fromm seemed to be entering the American mainstream, perhaps moving from Marxism towards liberalism as so many others were doing in that period. That was what Marcuse suggested in his *Eros and Civilisation* (1955), which led to a sharp exchange with Fromm in the left-liberal journal *Dissent*. However, a closer look at Fromm's published and unpublished work in this period shows a more complex picture. That same year, in *The Sane Society*, Fromm began to put forward a humanist interpretation of Marx's thought, extolling Marx's humanism as one of the major 'answers' to the 'decay and dehumanisation behind the glamour and wealth and political power of Western society'.[62] In that book, Fromm criticised Lenin for having helped to lay the ground for Stalinism. In 1958, however, Fromm recalibrated his position on Lenin and Trotsky as well. In an unpublished review of *Trotsky's Diary in Exile*, issued in 1958 by Harvard University Press, Fromm deplores the 'general habit of considering Stalinism and present-day Communism as identical with, or at least a continuation of revolutionary Marxism', especially the attempt to link 'Marx, Engels, Lenin and Trotsky' to 'the vengeful killer Stalin, and to the opportunistic conservative Khrushchev'. Concerning Lenin and Trotsky, he adds: 'They were men with an uncompromising sense of truth, penetrating to the very essence of reality, and never taken in by the deceptive surface; of an unquenchable courage and integrity; of deep concern and devotion to man and his future; unselfish and with little vanity or lust for power.'[63]

By 1961, in his *Marx's Concept of Man*, Fromm foregrounded his Marxist humanist position, writing that Marx's 'theory does not assume that the main motive of man is one of material gain; ... furthermore, the very aim of Marx is to liberate man from the pressure of economic needs, so that he can be fully human; that Marx is primarily concerned with the emancipation of man as an individual, the overcoming of alienation, the restoration of his capacity to relate himself fully to man and to nature.'[64]

Fromm's (and Marx's) notion of human emancipation is markedly different from the Foucaultian notion of resistance. In this respect, Sartrean existential humanism is also lacking, in the sense that an emancipatory moment is largely absent. For Marx, of course, the key is human emancipation, not only resistance to domination. Resistance to capital is predicated on a vision of a new society: not as a distant or imaginary utopia, but as a real possibility that exists as a tendency inside the very structures of capitalist society itself. For the first time since the neolithic revolution subjected labouring populations to unremitting toil in order to achieve a surplus product that helped to create the first class societies, the vast productive apparatus created by capitalism makes possible – for the future – sharply reduced hours of labour alongside material abundance. This possibility is of course conditioned by the danger that the system might first annihilate humanity in nuclear war or irrevocably damage the global ecological system.

Though Fromm's was not the first effort to launch a discussion of the *1844 Manuscripts* in the US, *Marx's Concept of Man* probably did more than any other publication to introduce them to the English-speaking public, also bringing the notion of socialist humanism to the fore. *Marx's Concept of Man* consists of a ninety-page introductory essay by Fromm, Tom Bottomore's translation of 110 pages from Marx's *1844 Essays*, twenty-three pages from other texts by Marx (primarily *The German Ideology* and *The Critique of Political Economy*), and forty pages of reminiscences from Marx's contemporaries.

Despite the widely repeated legend that Fromm expresses in his introduction a preference for the young Marx over the 'mature' Marx of *Capital*, Fromm makes no such statement anywhere in the book, or later on for that matter. Another critique of Fromm is supported by the facts, however. Unfortunately, in his introduction to *Marx's Concept of Man*, Fromm sometimes imposes his own more eclectic form of religion-tinged humanism on Marx himself. I am not arguing here for an Enlightenment, let alone a positivistic or Darwinian form of atheism, as I recognise that there have been many progressive and radically humanist forms of religion and politics, from Gandhi's *satyagraha*, to Martin Luther King's Christian humanism, or to Latin American Theology of Liberation. To be sure, these forms of radical humanist spirituality share many assumptions and goals with Marxist humanism. However, it is a serious distortion of Marx to argue, as some liberals like Schumpeter have done, that Marx's own perspective is ultimately a form of religious subjectivity or prophecy. I would argue that Fromm falls into this kind of excess – albeit in an attempt to make Marx relevant to the 1960s – when he writes in *Marx's Concept of Man* that 'Marx's philosophy constitutes a spiritual existentialism in secular language' and that Marx's concept of socialism is rooted in 'prophetic Messianism'.[65] He also links it to Zen Buddhism. At the time, some of those on the Left who had chosen the Western camp in the Cold War seized upon these weaknesses to attack not only Fromm, whom they already resented for his critiques of the US nuclear arsenal, but also the whole new view of Marx as a radical humanist that he was presenting. (These critiques were also spurred by the publication the same year of Fromm's searing attack on nuclear weapons, *May Man Prevail?*)

An interesting and sadly still relevant part of Fromm's own contribution to *Marx's Concept of Man* is his critique of what he terms 'the falsification of Marx's concepts' in the mass media and even among intellectuals. He adds that 'this ignorance and distortion of Marx are more to be found in the United States than in any other Western country'.[66] The first falsification, Fromm wrote, involved portraying Marx as a crude materialist who 'neglected the importance of the individual'.[67] Fromm refutes this, holding that 'the very aim of Marx is to liberate man from the pressure of economic needs, so that he can be fully human'.[68]

What Fromm saw as a second 'falsification' of Marx, one carried out by both Western intellectuals and Stalinist ideologues, was the forced identification of Marx with the single-party totalitarianism of the Soviet Union and Maoist China. During the Cold War, this led even leftist intellectuals to take sides with either the West (for example, Albert Camus) or Communism (for example, Sartre) as the lesser evil. Fromm would have none of this, as he sharply differentiates 'Marxist humanist socialism', on the one hand, from 'totalitarian socialism', on the other, with the latter in reality 'a system of conservative state capitalism'.[69] Again, this critique on Fromm's part has relevance for today, in light of the many attempts to tie the collapse of the Soviet Union to the 'death' of Marxism.

Fromm followed up *Marx's Concept of Man* with an edited book, *Socialist Humanism: An International Symposium*. For several years afterwards, this volume was the only widely circulated book on socialism in the US. It comprised essays by some thirty-five noted intellectuals, among them over a dozen from within Eastern Europe, most of them philosophical dissidents, but also a few who hewed more towards the party line. The more dissident Marxist humanists included several who would become prominent in the upheavals of the 1960s in the Eastern bloc, most notably the Prague Spring of 1968. Among the intellectuals from what was then Czechoslovakia were the Marxist humanists Karel Kosík and Ivan Svitak, while Poland was represented by Bronislaw Baczko as well as the more pro-party Adam Schaff, a personal friend of Fromm. What was then Yugoslavia had a particularly large representation, with a number of figures from the dissident philosophers of the Praxis group, among them Mihailo Markovic, Gajo Petrovic and Rudi Supek. From Western Europe, North America and Australia the volume drew upon Marxist philosophers like Marcuse, Dunayevskaya, Goldmann, Ernst Bloch and Eugene Kamenka.[70] As Fromm himself acknowledged in his introduction to the volume, it lacked representation from the Third World, although it did contain essays by the left-wing Gandhian Nirmal Kumar Bose and by Leopold Senghor, the president of newly independent Senegal, who espoused a decidedly non-revolutionary form of socialist humanism.

In his introduction to *Socialist Humanism*, Fromm also spelled out more of his notion of socialist humanism, going to great lengths to show its identity with earlier forms of humanism:

> Humanism has always emerged as a reaction to a threat to mankind: in the Renaissance, to the threat of religious fanaticism; in the Enlightenment, to extreme nationalism and the enslavement of man by the machine and economic interests. The revival of Humanism today is a new reaction to this latter threat in a more intensified form – the fear that man may become the slave of things, the prisoner of circumstances he himself has created – and the wholly new threat to mankind's physical existence posed by nuclear weapons.[71]

But where there was identity there was also difference, and Fromm also stressed the core distinctions between socialist humanism and earlier forms of humanism:

> Although Renaissance Utopians touched upon the need for social changes, the socialist Humanism of Karl Marx was the first to declare that theory cannot be separated from practice, knowledge from action, spiritual aims from the social system. Marx held that free and independent man could exist only in a social and economic system that, by its rationality and abundance, brought to an end the epoch of 'prehistory' and opened the epoch of 'human history', which would make the full development of the individual the condition for the full development of society, and vice versa.[72]

This was not the whole story, however. Marxism also had to be differentiated along a humanist versus crude materialist axis, with the latter not really Marxist in Fromm's eyes:

> Marx was misinterpreted both by those who felt threatened by his program, and by many socialists. The former accused him of caring only for the physical, not the spiritual, needs of man. The latter believed that his goal was exclusively material affluence for all, and that Marxism differed from capitalism only in its methods, which were economically more efficient and could be initiated by the working class. In actuality, Marx's ideal was a man productively related to other men and to nature, who would respond to the world in an alive

manner, and who would be rich not because he had much but because he was much.[73]

To many, then and especially since, even on the Left, such lofty goals, articulated in such a ringing fashion, were at best utopian and at worst completely outdated or even dangerous.

It was while putting together *Marx's Concept of Man* in 1959 that Fromm began his twenty-year correspondence with Dunayevskaya, which contains an interesting Marxist humanist discussion of gender. In 1976, while working on her *Rosa Luxemburg, Women's Liberation, and Marx's Philosophy of Revolution*, Dunayevskaya wrote to Fromm concerning the 'lack of camaraderie between Luxemburg, Lenin, and Trotsky'. Referring to Luxemburg, she asks: 'Could there have been, if not outright male chauvinism, at least some looking down on her theoretical work, because she was a woman?' Fromm responds: 'I feel that the male Social Democrats never could understand Rosa Luxemburg, nor could she acquire the influence for which she had the potential because she was a woman; and the men could not become full revolutionaries because they did not emancipate themselves from their male, patriarchal, and hence dominating, character structure.'[74]

Still, Fromm's socialist humanism had something of an abstract character, often floating above the real social contradictions of modern capitalist society. This could sometimes lead him towards positions indistinguishable from ordinary liberalism, as when, during the revolutionary year 1968, he devoted most of his political energy to reforming the US Democratic Party by backing anti-war candidate Eugene McCarthy. And while he occasionally discussed gender, Fromm gave almost no attention to the searing racial divide that marked the 1960s in the US, as the politics of black liberation came to the fore, espousing a militant revolutionary politics and at times embracing a type of humanism – in Africa and America – that was well to the left of Fromm's. This can be seen in the writings of Frantz Fanon, to be discussed below. It was telling that, although Fromm lamented the lack of African contributors to *Socialist Humanism*, it did not occur to him to include a piece by Fanon.

## KAREL KOSÍK: CAPITALISM'S WORLD OF THE PSEUDOCONCRETE

Karel Kosík (1926–2003) enjoyed a strange kind of fame during his lifetime. Living inside what was then Communist-ruled Czechoslovakia at the height of his intellectual development, he was an original Marxist humanist thinker, which meant that he was harassed and his work suppressed, and yet at the same time he received great admiration among oppositional intellectuals and youth of that tortured land. In the West, his work was greatly acclaimed by varied figures from the more critical parts of the Left, from Jürgen Habermas to Michael Löwy and from Raya Dunayevskaya to Bertell Ollman, yet it never achieved a very wide readership. In the early 1970s, journals like *Telos* ran translations of his work, but when his magnum opus, *Dialectics of the Concrete*, appeared in English in 1978, it seemed almost to end the discussion of Kosík rather than begin it. At the time, much of the intellectual Left was moving towards Adorno's bleak 'negative dialectics', and Foucaultian post-structuralism. In such a context, Kosík's rigorous but nonetheless emancipatory 'dialectics of the concrete' may simply have struck the wrong note, especially since, unlike in 1968, his ideas were no longer connected to a mass movement for socialist humanism inside his own country. At the present juncture, it may be time for another look at Kosík's writings.

Kosík's work is deeply impacted by the phenomenology of Husserl and Heidegger, leading some Western Marxists to see this as the source of his originality. However, one can appreciate his originality very easily by viewing his work in the context of Hegel, Marx, the Frankfurt School and East European Marxist humanism. Kosík's work was the finest flowering of that oppositional form of Marxist philosophy that arose in the 1950s in Eastern Europe, and was associated with the writings of Leszek Kolakowski, Bronislaw Baczko, Mihailo Markovic, Ivan Svitak and others from that region. The Prague Spring of 1968 was the high point, when philosophers united with workers and students in an attempt to forge a socialist humanist society, only to be crushed by Russian tanks. By the time the Eastern European regimes fell in 1989, socialist humanism was more of a memory than an intellectual or political reality. Freed from persecution and censorship and restored to his professorship after two decades, Kosík was soon dismissed again, this time for supposedly economic reasons.

Let me turn to Kosík's greatest work, *Dialectics of the Concrete*, which originally appeared in Czech in the early 1960s. Its first chapter begins with the famous critique of the 'pseudoconcrete' world of 'fetishised praxis'. In the world of the pseudoconcrete, i.e. the everyday world of capitalism, we are made to forget that we have the capacity to alter or even create our world, of course within a set of given historical possibilities: 'Reality can be transformed in a *revolutionary* way only because, and insofar as, we ourselves transform reality.' But to do so, we need to strip away the fetishism of the pseudoconcrete:

> The real world, concealed by the pseudoconcrete, and yet manifesting itself in it, is neither a world of real conditions opposed to unreal ones, nor a world of transcendence opposed to a subjective illusion, but a world of human praxis. It is the comprehension of socio-human reality as the unity of production and products, of subject and object, of genesis and structure.

This means that the world of praxis, which is not only practice, but practice connected to a philosophy of liberation, does not exist outside the given world in some transcendental sphere, nor is it merely the 'real' as opposed to an illusory world of pseudoconcreteness 'as in some naturalistic parallel to Plato's ideas'.[75] Instead, praxis cohabits the world of the pseudoconcrete. Thus, the living negation of the pseudoconcrete exists right inside that pseudoconcrete world of the given social arrangements.

Moreover, the world of the pseudoconcrete cannot be overcome fully with the dominant intellectual Marxist strategies, not even with the concept of totality as developed by Lukács and the early Frankfurt School, whom Kosík critiques without naming them:

> The category of totality has also been well received and broadly recognised in the twentieth century, but it is in constant danger of being grasped one-sidedly, of turning into its very opposite and ceasing to be a *dialectical* concept. The main modification of the concept of totality has been its reduction to a methodological precept; a methodological rule for investigating reality. This degeneration has resulted in two ultimate trivialities: that everything is connected with everything else, and that the whole is more than the sum of its parts. In materialist philosophy, the category of concrete totality answers first and foremost the question, what is reality. Only secondarily, and only after having materialistically answered the first question, can it be an epistemological principle and a methodological precept.[76]

Kosík goes on to critique pre-Marxian atomist-rationalist and organicist concepts of totality, elaborating a Marxian version that implicitly taxes other Marxian versions with falling, at least in part, back into those pre-Marxian ones.[77] A concept of totality remains abstract if the human being 'is intuited primarily or exclusively as an object in the framework of totality'; conversely, a concept of totality becomes 'concrete' when the 'objective-historical praxis' of human beings is recognised as part of the concept.

Kosík's attack on crude Marxist interpretations comes through when he writes that 'even the totality of the base and superstructure is abstract' when it is forgotten that the human being 'is the real historical subject' and actually forms 'both the base and the superstructure' in the human 'process of production and reproduction'.[78] In short, this is a most rigorous philosophical argument for a humanist position within Marxism.

In *Dialectics of the Concrete*, these issues of humanism and dialectic undergird the discussion of Marx's *Capital* that forms the core of the book. Kosík begins by sounding like a Heideggerian, something that has fooled some Western commentators on him, who were perhaps all too willing to be fooled. I would suggest that Heidegger is ultimately a foil, as is seen when his philosophy is termed nothing more than 'an alienated escape from alienation'.[79] Kosík also disputes the notion that *Capital* lacks a philosophical basis, which must therefore be developed outside Marxism. But his main opponents are versions of Marxism that in his view are not fully dialectical. Here he of course sets his sights on positivist and reductionist readings of *Capital* that are too economistic.

Perhaps more surprisingly, Kosík also attacks the Frankfurt School, not for idealism or moving into culture, but for something not usually discussed, what he sees as its attempt to abolish philosophy. Here his target above all is Marcuse, especially his magisterial study of Hegel, *Reason and Revolution*, which includes a brief discussion of Marx under the rubric of 'from philosophy to social theory',[80] summarised by Kosík as follows:

A different way of abolishing philosophy is to transform it into a 'dialectical theory of society' or dissolve it in social science. This form of abolishing philosophy can be traced in two historical phases: the first time during the genesis of Marxism when Marx, compared to Hegel, is shown to be a 'liquidator' of philosophy and the founder of a dialectical theory of society, and the second time in the development of Marx's teachings which his disciples conceive of as social science or sociology.[81]

This is wrong, Kosík maintains, not least because 'the development from Hegel to Marx is not a transition from one philosophical position to another; it does not in any way imply the need to 'abolish philosophy'.[82] In this sense, he highlights the affinities between the Hegelian and the Marxist dialectic.

But the big conclusion comes a few lines later, as the core humanist themes of *Dialectics of the Concrete* come to the fore once again, here in a critique of established – i.e. Stalinist – Marxism. Marxism, Kosík writes, tends to fall back into a simplistic notion of a sociological totality, one that is not dialectical and certainly not infused with the humanist concept of praxis:

> Abolishing philosophy in dialectical social theory transforms the significance of the seminal 19th century discovery into its very opposite: praxis ceases to be the sphere of humanising man, the process of forming a socio-human reality as well as man's openness toward being and toward the truth of objects; it turns into a closedness: socialness is a cave in which man is walled in.

Some brief allusions to Plato's cave are followed by the statements, 'man is *walled in* in his socialness' and 'man is a prisoner of socialness'.[83] This poignant image managed to evoke the Berlin Wall, which had gone up just two years before this book was published. What's more, it showed the possibility of a Marxist dialectical vision that did not fall either into the error of totalising, or into that of reductionism to the social or the economic, while at the same time rooting itself in Marx's humanistic materialism.

In another critique, Kosík takes on the notion of theory and practice, so often abused by crude Marxists:

> The only part of the great discovery of materialist philosophy that uncritical reasoning preserved was the idea that praxis is something immensely important and that the unity of theory and practice holds as a supreme postulate. But the *original philosophical questioning*, in whose light praxis had been discovered, disappeared, and the idea preserved merely the importance of the principle.[84]

Kosík's version of Marxist humanism has a certain lightness of being. Yet it is also firmly materialist, while at the same time a deeply rooted dialectical philosophy that rejects all forms of socio-economic reductionism.

## FRANTZ FANON: THE 'NEW HUMANISM'
## OF AFRICAN LIBERATION

Let us now move outside the sphere of North America and Europe, to the revolutionary African socialist humanism of Frantz Fanon, who was influenced by Hegel, Sartre, the Négritude School and above all Marx. Note Fanon's use, similar to Sartre, of the term 'decide' – this in a declaration about the future of an independent Africa in his *Wretched of the Earth* of 1961, the year so many new nations were being born, in many cases with aspirations towards socialist humanism: 'Let us decide not to imitate Europe; let us combine our muscles and our brains in a new direction. Let us try to create the whole man, whom Europe has been incapable of bringing to triumphant birth.'[85]

While fighting for Algeria's independence from France, Fanon did not dismiss *tout court* the European humanist tradition. He said that the Europeans had not practiced it – whether under Nazism or in the colonies – but predicted that the emerging Third World would be able to do so: 'This new humanity cannot do otherwise than define a new humanism both for itself and for others.'[86] This was, to be sure, a humanism drawing from European revolutionary and democratic traditions, but at the same time it was a 'new humanism'. It not only critically appropriated earlier liberal forms of European humanism, but it also went beyond their limitations. As a theoretician of the newly forming Third World, Fanon also distanced himself from the Soviet bloc and its authoritarian and dehumanising form of industrial 'development', not only mentioning the Hungarian revolution of 1956, but also writing of the new Africa: 'The pretext of catching up must not be used to push man around, to tear him away from himself or his privacy, to break and kill him.'[87] This was nothing short of a socialist humanist third way, opposed to both Western style capitalism and Eastern statist communism.[88]

The penultimate chapter of *Wretched of the Earth* contains a burst of dialectical insight. Given his universalising humanist aims, Fanon asked whether nationalism was obsolete. Shouldn't the new African nations drop nationalism entirely in favour of universal brotherhood and sisterhood of peoples across the world? No, he argued, one cannot 'skip the national period', that of 'national consciousness'. Only through the particular, national consciousness can one get to the universal, humanism: 'The consciousness of self is not the closing of a door to communication. Philosophic thought teaches us, on the contrary, that it is its guarantee. National consciousness, which is not nationalism, is the only thing that will give us an international dimension.'[89]

Thus, the new nations of the emergent Third World could not skip over the stage of national self-consciousness, as the road towards universal human emancipation passed of necessity through the particular, provided that that national consciousness did not solidify into a separatist type of narrow nationalism.[90] Nor could the nations of Europe and North America skip over this either. They needed to recognise the fact that they had been complicit in systems of racist colonialism, not in order to wallow in guilt, but in order to make the kind of self-critique needed for a truly global human civilisation. And that global civilisation could be reached in full only by a revolutionary uprooting.

Fanon also famously advocated violence, and not only as a necessary tactic in struggles against intransigent, violently repressive colonial regimes like French-occupied Algeria. He also wrote of violence as personally liberating for oppressed peoples long dominated by a racist system that denied their very humanity. Whether or not this was influenced by Nietzsche, as some have maintained, its liberating force has been questioned by later commentators.[91] More problematically, Fanon's thought was for too long pigeon-holed – both by critics and supporters – as a philosophy celebrating revolutionary violence, in no small part because of the stress on this theme in Sartre's preface to *Wretched of the Earth*.

Fanon wrote at the dawn of the new Third World, fired with optimism but also deeply concerned about falling back into elitist, one-party rule, as in Nkrumah's Ghana, let alone more openly pro-imperialist regimes like Senghor's Senegal. At the time Fanon died in 1961, these dreams of a new humanism in Africa still seemed very concrete as an immediate and real possibility. To be sure, his socialist humanist vision of Africa's future did not come to pass, although there were for a brief period some interesting experiments, as in the *ujamaa* philosophy and politics of Julius Nyerere's Tanzania.[92]

I would argue that the failure of the revolutions of the 1950s and 1960s to develop new and positive forms of society – whether in Africa or in France in 1968 – came about not only due to imperialist or capitalist machinations, but also because of internal weaknesses. The latter included philosophical ones: for example, the leftist anti-imperialist tradition that had grown out of opposition to nuclear weapons and wars for empire remains intact today, but increasingly without much of a positive project. This leaves it open to the danger of opportunistically supporting various authoritarian and even reactionary forms of anti-imperialism, from Khomeini's Iran to Assad's Syria. There were some positive exceptions after the 1960s, as in revolutionary Nicaragua and Grenada during the early 1980s, but these were brutally crushed by US imperialism. In the case of Grenada, this was abetted by counter-revolution from within the revolution, as seen in the assassination of Maurice Bishop by the Stalinoid Bernard Coard, which paved the way for Reagan's 1983 invasion. By the 1980s, when Reagan–Thatcher–Pope John Paul II dominated the Western capitalist world, and perspectives as reactionary as Khomeini's radical Islamism came to the fore in the Middle East, this led to a situation aptly described by Raya Dunayevskaya in 1982: 'Without a new vision of revolutions, a new individual, a new universal, a new society, new human relations,' and 'without a philosophy of revolution, activism spends itself in mere anti-imperialism and anti-capitalism, without ever revealing what it is for.'[93]

By that time – the early 1980s – the vast majority of the global Left came to reject the possibility of a radical transformation of society in which workers would rule through the direct democracy of their councils, women would emancipate themselves and society from millennia of sexism, racial minorities like African Americans would conduct militant struggles that narrowed rather than widened the gap between them and the white workers, and Marxist philosophers would sketch out dialectical humanist visions to help transform the world. No, by the 1980s, and even more so after 1989, the Left got stuck between two very limited alternatives: (1) a sort of liberal left that supported democracy and civil society but no longer really challenged capital (Habermas et al.), and (2) a politics of difference that accepted uncritically even reactionary movements (Iranian Islamism, Farrakhanism) so long as they seemed to challenge imperialism and racism.

## RAYA DUNAYEVSKAYA: REVOLUTIONARY MARXIST HUMANISM

Raya Dunayevskaya's Marxist humanism had its roots in Marx and Hegel, but also appropriated critically many of the other strands of socialist humanism discussed above. An emigrant to the US from Russia, she came up through the US anti-Stalinist left, and then served as Leon Trotsky's Russian Secretary in 1937–8, during his Mexican exile. Without a university education and schooled in the radical movement, Dunayevskaya also had strong ties to the US black, labour and women's movements. Her theoretical career began not long after her break from the Left with Trotsky in 1939, when she opposed the Hitler–Stalin Pact as a Stalinist betrayal, whereas Trotsky defended it as a necessary tactic to preserve what he considered to be a Russian workers' state, albeit with bureaucratic deformations. By 1941, a year after Trotsky's assassination by a Stalinist agent, Dunayevskaya had elaborated a theory different from Trotsky's concerning the nature of the Soviet Union under Stalin, characterising it as a new type of class society, a state-capitalist totalitarianism. Among her earliest theoretical contributions was a debate in 1944–5 in the pages of the *American Economic Review*, a rarity for a Marxist, over Soviet state capitalism, in which she locked horns with the then Stalinist economists Paul Baran and Oscar Lange.

As Epstein notes in Chapter 1, she joined forces with the Afro-Caribbean philosopher and cultural theorist C. L. R. James in a dissident grouping within Trotskyism widely known as the Johnson–Forest Tendency (JFT) united around the James–Dunayevskaya theory of state capitalism. However, the JFT kept its distance from the specific language of humanism, which it viewed as fundamentally liberal and bourgeois. Within a few years of the breakup of the JFT in 1955, however, Dunayevskaya published *Marxism and Freedom* (1958), a book that placed humanism at the centre of Marx's thought, a type of vocabulary not found in the texts of the JFT, and in this sense, original to Dunayevskaya. In his preface to Dunayevskaya's book, Marcuse applauded her attempt 'to recapture the integral unity of Marxian theory at its very foundation: the humanistic philosophy'.[94] Dunayevskaya's translation of two of the key essays in Marx's 1844 *Economic and Philosophical Manuscripts*, 'Private Property and Communism' and 'Critique of the Hegelian Dialectic', was appended to the original 1958 edition.

In *Marxism and Freedom*, Dunayevskaya addressed humanism[95] in three contexts: the young Marx, the mature Marx of *Capital*, and the social movements of the period. In her chapter on the young Marx, Dunayevskaya quotes and then uses as a point of departure the core passages on humanism in the 1844 *Manuscripts* that had not been addressed by Marcuse in *Reason and Revolution*, the only previous substantial discussion of these texts in English. In so doing, she wove together in her trademark compressed form a number of issues, among them philosophical analysis of humanism in Marx, critique of the Soviet Union as an example of 'vulgar communism', and present-day humanism in the sense of the striving of human beings to be free of capitalistic alienation. Concerning the young Marx, she wrote:

> He drew the line so sharply between 'vulgar communism' and even 'positive communism', on the one hand, and his own philosophy of *humanism*, on the other hand, that it stands to this day as the dividing line between Marxism as the doctrine of liberation, and all who claim the name of 'Marxism', 'socialism', or 'communism' while they pursue an entirely different course, both in thought and in practice, from all that Marx stood for. 'Not until the transcendence of this mediation (abolition of private property) which is nevertheless a necessary presupposition does there arise positive Humanism beginning from itself', said Marx. In a word, another transcendence, *after* the abolition of private property is needed to achieve a truly new, *human* society which differs from private property not alone as an 'economic system', but as a different way of *life* altogether. It is as free individuals developing all their natural and acquired talents that we first leap from what Marx called the prehistory of humanity into its true history, the 'leap from necessity to freedom'.[96]

In this sense, Marx's humanism was itself the ground for a thoroughgoing critique of both statist communism in the East and formally democratic capitalism in the West.

A second humanist context was seen in the four chapters on *Capital* that formed the theoretical core of Dunayevskaya's book, with one of them entitled 'The Humanism and Dialectic of *Capital*, Volume I, 1867 to 1883'. She argued that the human being, the worker, remained at the centre of Marx's exposition and critique of capitalist value production:

> Marxism is wrongly considered to be 'a new critique of political economy.' ... By introducing the labourer into political economy, Marx transformed it from a science which deals with *things*, such as commodities, money, wages, profits, into one which analyzes *relations of men* at the point of production. ... It is characteristic of Marx, known the world over as the creator of the theory of surplus value, to

disclaim the honor because the theory was 'implicit' in the classical theory of labour value. What he did that was new, he said, was to make this explicit by showing what *type* of labour creates values and *hence* surplus values, and the *process* by which this is done.[97]

In keeping with this, Dunayevskaya devoted considerable attention to the understudied chapters of *Capital* on the working day and on machinery, in which the human condition – and oppositional force – of the working class came to the fore. These chapters were not 'sob story stuff' to convince the reader of the brutality of capitalist production, but at the core of Marx's analysis.[98]

Dunayevskaya highlighted not only the massive labour movement for a shorter working day, but also the struggle against machinery, towards which, she argued, uncritically pro-technology 'professional Marxists have too sophisticated an attitude'.[99] She also quoted a lesser-known passage from Marx's machinery chapter on this point: 'It would be possible to write quite a history of the inventions, made since 1830, for the sole purpose of supplying capital with weapons against the revolt of the working class.'[100] As she saw it, however, in *Capital* each new objective development of this sort not only created an objective transformation in capitalist production, but it also radically restructured the working classes, leading to new forms of consciousness and of revolt.

This type of consideration formed the foundation of a third humanist element of *Marxism and Freedom*, the discussion – in a chapter entitled 'Automation and the New Humanism' – of a new stage of capitalist production in the 1950s, automation, and the resultant movements of rank-and-file labour and African Americans of the 1950s. Marcuse took exception to this chapter in his preface, writing that he 'disagrees ... with the analysis of the contemporary position, structure and consciousness of the labouring classes'.[101] These differences would manifest themselves in Marcuse's *One-Dimensional Man* (1964), where he held that the new forms of production of automated capitalism, accompanied by the relatively high wages and benefits of the Fordist era, had not only transformed the consciousness of the working classes towards a more affirmative stance towards capitalism, but also that automation itself was laying the ground for a liberated future because its reduction in socially necessary labour time was creating the basis for a much shorter working day.

Contra Marcuse, Dunayevskaya held that when one considered the human condition of the worker, the new stage of automated production, far from liberatory, was resulting in both mass unemployment and a deepening alienation on the part of those who still had jobs. Moreover, automated production led to new types of revolt, like the thousands of 'wildcat' strikes that mushroomed from the rank and file, challenging not only capital but also a labour bureaucracy that since 1945 had become a player in the system. She also took up the mass creativity of the Montgomery Bus Boycott of 1955–6, a struggle by African Americans against racial segregation that persisted for a full year in the face of savage repression by the white power structure. In language that recalled Marx's writings on the Paris Commune, she concluded: 'Clearly, the greatest thing of all in this Montgomery, Alabama, spontaneous organisation was its own working existence.'[102]

Decrying a lack of creative development among Marxist theorists in response to the new forms of subjectivity, as in the wildcat strikes or Montgomery, Dunayevskaya suggested that the traditional relationship of theorist to ordinary people needed to change. She noted the deep thinking that had emerged from inside the working classes and the Civil Rights Movement during these new struggles: 'In truth, while the intellectual void today is so great that the movement from theory to practice has nearly come to a standstill, *the movement from practice to theory, and with it, a new unity of manual and mental labour in the worker, are in evidence everywhere.*'[103] Among other things, Dunayevskaya was referring to her conversations with striking coal miners, who had questioned not only wages and working conditions, but also the very nature of labour itself, especially the division between 'thinking and doing', which she connected to 'new Humanist impulses from ever deeper strata of the workers'.[104] The book concluded on a ringing humanist note: 'The totality of the crisis demands, and will create, a total solution. It can be nothing short of a new Humanism.'[105]

In the next decade and a half, Dunayevskaya modified her view that radical intellectuals had been entirely lacking in their response to the new forms of revolt of the post-war era. This can be seen in her *Philosophy and Revolution* (1973), which analysed critically, and drew into her own version of Marxist humanism insights from a number of radical humanist philosophical strains that had appeared since 1945, among them Sartrean existentialism, African socialist humanism and Eastern European Marxist humanism.

At first glance, it would seem that Dunayevskaya's engagement with Sartre was entirely critical, even polemical. For example, she entitled an early version of the Sartre chapter in *Philosophy and Revolution* 'Sartre's Search for a Method to Undermine Marxism' (1963). But a decade later, although the critique remained very sharp, there was also a measure of acknowledgement of Sartre's having helped to launch the turn by leftist intellectuals in the 1940s towards radical humanism: 'Immediately after World War II everyone from the theologians to Sartre took issue with Marx while at the same time "discovering" his Humanism.'[106] More importantly, Dunayevskaya critically appropriated Sartre in her elaboration of the most controversial philosophical argument of the book, the notion that Hegel's absolutes – rather than closed totalities that shut out all objectivity as Engels and the empiricists had maintained – needed to be reinterpreted for today as a new departure, as seen in the title of the book's first chapter, 'Absolute Negativity as New Beginning'. In developing this argument, she cited Sartre's critique of liberal relativism and tolerance in the face of Nazism from *What Is Literature?*, particularly his incorporation of a form of the absolute into his existential humanism: 'He said that what was original with Existentialists was that the War and the Occupation "made us rediscover the Absolute at the heart of relativity itself".'[107]

In the Sartre chapter of *Philosophy and Revolution*, subtitled somewhat less polemically as 'Outsider Looking In', Dunayevskaya acknowledges Sartre's search for a philosophy of revolution and his popularisation in the 1940s of the notion, previously restricted to Marxism, that philosophy must become revolutionary. Nonetheless, she took Sartre to task for merging together with Marx's own philosophy too many Stalinist ideological categories – among them a crude materialism and a deterministic theory of history – and then writing that Marxism therefore needed the additive of existentialism in order to address issues like individual subjectivity and choice, and to become a form of humanism. This problem could be seen in the major work in which Sartre declared himself a Marxist, *Critique of Dialectical Reason* (1960). That book was also burdened by elitist attitudes, seen most notably in Sartre's category of the 'practico-inert', a sort of fallback position of passivity and isolation towards which all human relationships tended: 'Sartre may have destroyed as many dogmatisms as he claims. But one unstated yet all-pervading dogmatism continues to be the underlying motif of all Sartre thinks, writes, and does. It is the dogmatism of the backwardness of the masses, now called "practico-inert" and including the individual as well as the masses.'[108]

Dunayevskaya also criticises Sartre's wavering towards Stalinism in the 1950s, as seen especially in his attacks on supporters of the Hungarian revolution of 1956. Here, Sartre's very desire to remain revolutionary, all the while imbued with the deep contradictions of his existentialist perspective, led him first towards the French Communist Party, which he uncritically defended during the 1950s, and later into an embrace of Maoism. Along the way, he also supported, sometimes with great courage, genuinely revolutionary movements, as in the Algerian Revolution against French colonialism, during which military reactionaries tried to assassinate him. In addition, Sartre lent his support to African revolutionaries like Patrice Lumumba and Frantz Fanon, writing a major, albeit flawed preface to the latter's *Wretched of the Earth* (1961). At the same time, however, he took too many uncritical positions towards various revolutions that had gone sour, especially in China.

To Dunayevskaya, the problem here lay not only in his overall existentialist framework, but also in a problem common to many revolutionary thinkers, 'the consequences of the abstract universal as methodology'.[109] The failure of the universal of freedom or humanism adequately to particularise itself meant that Sartre gyrated between individualist subjectivism, on the one hand, and capitulation to alienated forms of collectivity like Maoism, on the other. Concerning Sartre, Dunayevskaya concluded:

> The methodological enemy is the empty abstraction which has helped cover up soured revolutions and failed to disclose new roads to revolution in theory, not to mention in fact ... The philosophy of existence fails 'to merge' with Marxism because it has remained Subjectivity without a Subject, desire for revolution without the 'new forces, new passions' for revolution, and at present escapism into 'world revolution' at the very moment when what is required is the concretisation, the unity of philosophy and revolution on native ground, as the only ground for world revolution.[110]

As discussed below, this problem of an abstract universal was one that Dunayevskaya was also to find even among socialist humanists to whom she felt a greater affinity than Sartre.

In her writings on the African revolutions of the 1950s and 1960s, Dunayevskaya, who made a lengthy visit to West Africa in 1962, concentrated on humanist strains within African socialism, which were quite pervasive at the time. While her writings on Africa ranged widely,[111] I will concentrate again here on a chapter of *Philosophy and Revolution*, 'The African Revolutions and the World Economy', in which Dunayevskaya cited with enthusiasm anticolonialist leader Sékou Touré's call for African unity as a 'new humanism essentially founded on the universal solidarity and cooperation between people, without any racial and cultural antagonism and without narrow egoism and privilege'. It was Fanon, however, who stood out as the most significant theoretician of African socialist humanism: 'None looked at the African revolutions more concretely and comprehensively than did Frantz Fanon.'[112]

In keeping with her own theme of Hegel's absolute negativity as new beginning, Dunayevskaya cited as well Fanon's characterisation of the African struggle against colonialism as 'the untidy affirmation of an original idea propounded as an absolute.'[113] Dunayevskaya also incorporated Fanon's critique of European humanism as an abstract universal as the epigraph to the chapter, part of which read: 'Let us leave this Europe where they are never done talking of Man, yet murder men wherever they find them.'[114] As she noted, Fanon remained a dialectical humanist nonetheless, calling for a 'new humanism' based upon revolutionary solidarity for Africa and the world.

These early hopes of the late 1950s and early 1960s went largely unfulfilled, however, as the young African republics and liberation movements faced both the external dangers of neo-colonialism/Cold War politics, and deep internal contradictions between leaders and masses:

Despite the instant mass mobilisations and the search for new humanist beginnings that would unite philosophy and revolution, theory and practice, which was by no means limited to intellectuals but was a need most urgently felt by the masses themselves, we must soberly face the present bleak reality. For just as these revolutions reshaped the map of Africa in less than a decade, they just as rapidly reached the crossroads. Thus, though the revolutions emerged from deep indigenous roots, without capital of any sort, and by their own force and passion and reason achieved their political emancipation, independent of the 'East' as well as the 'West', after gaining power they did not remain quite so externally 'nonaligned'.[115]

Some, like Touré, sided with the East and gained Russian support. Others, like Senegal's Senghor, who had contributed an essay to Fromm's *Socialist Humanism*, sided with the West, including the former colonial power, France. Dunayevskaya chalks this up, again, to the dangers of an abstract universal: 'While President Senghor spoke most eloquently about African socialism, the country itself had undergone hardly any fundamental economic changes since gaining political independence. Senegal still follows France too closely, and not only in foreign policy.'[116]

Among the various strands of socialist humanism, with the possible exception of Fanon's version of African socialism, Dunayevskaya seemed to feel the greatest affinity for the Eastern European Marxist humanist philosophers, many of whom had appeared alongside her in Fromm's *Socialist Humanism* in 1965. During the period 1953–70, almost all of the uprisings and oppositional movements in Eastern Europe took place in the name of democratic or humanist socialism, as seen most notably in the Hungarian workers' councils during the 1956 revolution, or the 1968 Prague Spring that called itself an experiment in 'socialism with a human face'. The fact that this shifted by the 1980s, when the Solidarność movement in Poland came under the influence of right-wing Catholicism as represented by Pope John Paul II, should not obscure that previous period of socialist humanism. This is not to deny the importance of finally toppling the Stalinist regimes of Eastern Europe, which had espoused a fundamentally antihumanist ideology that was a caricature of Marxism.

In keeping with her state-capitalist theory, Dunayevskaya enthusiastically supported all of the Eastern European uprisings, calling, often vainly, upon the global Left to do so, just as it supported anticolonial and anticapitalist revolutions elsewhere. Already in *Marxism and Freedom*, she had viewed Hungary 1956 as a harbinger of the demise of the entire totalitarian system of Russia and Eastern Europe. But it was in *Philosophy and Revolution* that she discussed at greatest length the Marxist humanist philosophers of this region, while also taking up the Prague Spring, the greatest anti-Stalinist revolt of the period.

Among those whom Dunayevskaya saw as the most important thinkers of Marxist humanism was Kosík, who, as she saw it, 'had, in 1963 published an important philosophic work, *Dialectics of the Concrete*, which raised anew the question of the individual', and also spoken out, 'although in abstract philosophic terms, against the "dogmatic" Communist retrogressionism in life and thought'.[117] Soon after, in a

1974 critique of Adorno's *Negative Dialectics*, she contrasted the German 'ivory tower' philosopher with Kosík and Fanon, philosophers who had responded – and in her view profoundly so – to the new liberatory impulses within their respective societies.[118] In addition, the Eastern European Marxist humanists pointed to the problem of the individual within Marxist thought, while also rejecting Sartrean existentialism.

Dunayevskaya also singled out another Czechoslovak Marxist humanist, Ivan Svitak, for emphasising the need to overcome the division between mental and manual labour,[119] and the Yugoslav Mihailo Markovic, a founder of the *Praxis* journal that grouped a number of independent philosophers. Markovic defended a dialectical humanist perspective while also critiquing how the dialectic had been misused by the Stalinist ideologists. This touched upon a key issue, the question of why, even as Stalin transformed the Russian revolutionary regime into a state-capitalist one, he at the same time hewed publicly to a revolutionary line, rather than the reformism and open betrayal that Trotsky had predicted. As Dunayevskaya writes, 'Markovic calls attention to the fact that, "The use of dialectical phraseology created an illusion of continuity in method," where, in fact, it "has meant little more than a subsequent rationalisation of various past political conceptions and decisions. That is why Stalinism did not reject dialectic as a whole in the way it rejected negation of the negation."'[120] Thus, the Stalinists could justify their twists and turns – anti-fascist in 1936, pact with Hitler in 1939 and anti-fascist again in 1941 after Hitler attacked Russia – on the basis that revolutionary politics did not go on a straight line, but was dialectical. Later on, after Khrushchev revealed publicly some of Stalin's crimes, Soviet ideologues could then say that mistakes were 'of course' made but that progress is necessarily dialectical, i.e. full of contradictions.

At the same time, Markovic, Svitak and even Kosík spoke too often in abstract generalities, about humanity, freedom and the like, while failing to carry out specific Marxist analyses of their own societies, for example as to whether the population was divided by ethnicity, with some groups dominant and the others subordinate. A few years after Dunayevskaya's death, when the Balkan wars broke out in the 1990s, neither Markovic nor Kosík fully met the challenge. Markovic rapidly transformed into an apologist for the most virulent Serbian nationalism, drawing close to the genocidal Slobodan Milosevic, all the while continuing to mouth a universal language of humanism and universalism, and at the same time accusing the Bosnians and the Kosovars of ethno-religious separatism.

Kosík avoided that type of deep retrogression. However, when the Kosovo war started in 1999, he issued a denunciation of the US bombing that failed to mention the oppression of the people of Kosovo by the Serbian nationalist regime.

Dunayevskaya's Marxist humanism was deeply Hegelian, relying on her concept of Hegel's absolutes as new beginnings.[121] In this sense, she embraced what Marx referred to in *Capital* as the needed 'power of abstraction'.[122] At the same time, Dunayevskaya held to what Hegel called the concrete universal, whether in terms of the individual versus state power, or the specificities of race and gender, all the while attempting to avoid the twin dangers of empiricism and identity politics.

### CONCLUSION

This journey has taken us into some of the liberatory, creative aspects of the socialist humanist tradition. At the same time, we have found that some forms of socialist and Marxist humanism remained too often in the realm of the abstract universal. As we have seen, this was true of Fromm, and in a different way of Sartre as well. At a purely philosophical level, of course, Kosík's *Dialectics of the Concrete* avoided this problem, but the philosopher did not follow through adequately in terms of concretising his dialectics in a way that truly met the challenges of actuality. Only Fanon and Dunayevskaya succeeded in developing forms of socialist humanism that came down to earth and took up issues like race and colonialism in ways that both held on to universalising aspirations and acknowledged difference. Within the broad international discussion in the 1960s of socialist humanism, however, the strains upheld by Dunayevskaya, Fanon and Kosík were marginalised, relatively speaking, in the face of the towering influence of people like Fromm and Sartre. This left the Marxist humanists open to the type of attack the Foucaultians mounted after the 1960s, to the effect that they failed to address specific forms of resistance and were trapped in a generalised view of 'man'.

That process has now run its course as well. It is high time that critical philosophers and activists consider once again a socialist humanism that will give their opposition to global capitalism a type of content that points towards a new, liberated society in which women and men can exercise their self-determination in ways that are both social and individual. Much can be appropriated from the emancipatory universals of Sartre, Fromm and the Eastern European Marxist humanists, provided that we don't fall into the trap of the abstract universal once again. In this regard, we need to look especially closely at those forms of socialist humanism found in Dunayevskaya, Fanon and to a great extent Kosík – forms that allow for the universal to particularise itself. At the same time, we need critically to appropriate into a twenty-first-century Marxist humanism some of the insights from several decades of post-structuralist social critique, whether on language, prisons, the cultural legacies of imperialism, or gender and sexuality.

And yet we seem further off from this than one hundred years ago, when many workers and intellectuals dreamed openly of a socialist future, which they saw as a real possibility. Today, with the collapse of statist socialism in Russia (really state capitalism in my view[123]), we are faced with the received notion that there is no alternative to capitalism. The Foucaultian notion of resistance, with its circularity, operates in tandem with this. Thus, the problem facing us today is deeply philosophical. We are burdened not just by capitalism in general, or by thirty years of neoliberalism, but by ideological apparatuses on the Left as well.

Thus, while a critique of the limitations of much of the earlier radical humanism needs to be made, I think that once that operation is carried out, we would be left with some truly visionary perspectives that would help us to solidify and guide in a positive direction the revolutionary, anti-capitalist and democratic movements of today. It would be nothing short of a universalism that is more than merely strategic, rooted instead in the yearnings of human beings for an emancipatory future that would abolish the fetishisms of both capitalism and the state.

## NOTES

I would like to thank David Alderson, Barbara Epstein, Peter Hudis, Charles Reitz, and Robert Spencer for helpful comments.

1. Jean Paul Sartre, *What Is Literature? And Other Essays*, trans. Philip Mairet, Brooklyn: Haskell House, 1988 [1948], p. 177.
2. Ibid., p. 180.
3. Louis Dupré, 'Preface to the Morningside Edition', in Raya Dunayevskaya, *Philosophy and Revolution: From Hegel to Sartre and from Marx to Mao*, New York: Columbia University Press, 1979 [1973], p. xv.
4. Jean-Paul Sartre, *Being and Nothingness: A Phenomenological Essay on Ontology*, trans. Hazel E. Barnes, New York: Pocket Books, 1966 [1943], p. 561; *L'Etre et le Néant: Essai d'Ontologie phénoménologique*, Paris: Éditions Gallimard, 1970 [1943], p. 489. I have given references to both the

English and original French versions because English translator Hazel E. Barnes has garbled this passage. Instead I have used – in slightly modified form – the more precise rendering of Sartre's sentence provided by Richard Nice in his translation of Bourdieu's critique of Sartre (Pierre Bourdieu, *Outline of a Theory of Practice*, trans. Richard Nice, Cambridge: Cambridge University Press, 1977 [1972], p. 74). In the next block quote, I modify the Barnes translation myself.

5. Ibid., p 561 (English) and p. 489 (French).

6. Ibid., p. 562 (English) and p. 489 (French).

7. Bourdieu, *Outline of a Theory of Practice*, p. 75.

8. Ibid., p. 74.

9. Arnaud Tomes has argued that these kinds of critiques of Sartre by Bourdieu were not as new as they seemed, and that they bore striking similarities to Stalinist and other orthodox Marxist critiques in the 1940s of Sartre as a petty-bourgeois subjectivist: 'Pour une anthropologie conrète: Sartre Contre Bourdieu', *Les Temps Modernes*, No. 596 (1997), pp. 32–52.

10. Cited in Bourdieu, *Outline of a Theory of Practice*, p. 74.

11. Emile Durkheim, *The Rules of Sociological Method and Selected Texts on Sociology and Its Method*, trans. W. D. Halls, New York: Free Press, 1982 [1893], p. 62.

12. Recently, the American sociologist of culture Jeffrey Halley has argued that Bourdieu has ignored 'the ever developing and expanding part of the self as s/he accumulates new experiences. Dispositions are seen, in this optic [contra that of Bourdieu-KA], as less stable and more genetic, holding out the possibility for growth and education' ('Mondo Vino, un art comme les a(o)utres: Rationalisation et résistance dans les usages sociaux du vin', in Florent Gaudez (ed.), *Les Arts Moyens Aujord'hui*, vol. 1, Paris: Éditions L'Harmattan, 2008, p. 249).

13. Jean-Paul Sartre, *Search for a Method*, trans. Hazel. E. Barnes, New York: Knopf, 1963 [1957], p. 7.

14. Karl Marx, 'Alienated Labour', in Erich Fromm, *Marx's Concept of Man*, New York: Frederick Ungar, 1966 [1961], p. 101.

15. Karl Marx, *Capital*, vol. 1, trans. Ben Fowkes, New York: Vintage, 1976 [1867–75], pp. 283–4.

16. Ibid., p. 799. Here and elsewhere I have sometimes amended the existing Marx translations to render the German term 'Mensch' under its primary meaning of 'human being' rather than 'man' (the German 'Mann' refers specifically to the male human being). For the German original see Karl Marx, *Das Kapital*, in *Marx-Engels Werke*, vol. 23, Berlin: Dietz Verlag, 1962 [1867–75], p. 674.

17. Marx, *Capital*, p. 166.

18. Ibid., p. 173.

19. Louis Althusser, *Lenin and Philosophy and Other Essays*, trans. Ben Brewster, New York: Monthly Review Press, p. 181.

20. Ibid., p. 182.

21. Ibid., p. 181.

22. Raya Dunayevskaya, *Marxism and Freedom: From 1776 Until Today*, Amherst, NY: Humanity Books, 2000 [1958], p. 327.

23. Jacques d'Hondt emphasises this point in his critique of Althusser in *De Hegel á Marx*, Paris: Presses Universitaires de France, 1972.

24. Louis Althusser, *For Marx*, trans Ben Brewster, New York: Vintage, 1969 [1965], p. 116.

25. On this point, see Kevin Anderson, *Lenin, Hegel and Western Marxism*, Urbana: University of Illinois Press, 1995.

26. Ibid., p. 229.

27. Hondt, *De Hegel á Marx*, p. 225.

28. Ibid., p. 228.

29. Althusser, *For Marx*, p. 33.

30. Ibid., p. 230.

31. Marx, *Capital*, p. 165.

32. Althusser, *For Marx*, p. 230.

33. Althusser, *Lenin and Philosophy*, p. 90.

34. Ibid., p. 88.

35. Ibid., p. 93.

36. Ibid., pp. 93–4.

37. Michel Foucault, *The Order of Things: An Archaeology of the Human Sciences*, New York: Vintage, 1973 [1966], p. 262.

38. Cited in David Macey, *The Lives of Michel Foucault*, New York: Vintage, 1993, p. 175.

39. Foucault, *The Order of Things*, pp. 386–7.

40. Michel Foucault, *Discipline and Punish: The Birth of the Prison*, trans. Alan Sheridan, New York: Vintage, 1977 [1975], p. 141.

41. Cited in Lou Turner and John Alan, *Frantz Fanon, Soweto and American Black Thought*, Chicago: News & Letters, 1986, p. 40.

42. Fabienne Brion and Bernard E. Harcourt, 'The Louvain Lectures in Context', in Michel Foucault, *Wrong-Doing, Truth Telling: The Function of Avowal in Justice*, trans. Stephen W. Sawyer, Chicago: University of Chicago Press, 2014, pp. 277–8.

43. For the full text of the discussion, see Michel Foucault, 'Qu'est-ce qu'un auteur?', *Bulletin de la Societé Francaise de Philosophie*, Vol. 63, No. 3 (1969), pp. 73–104.

44. Ibid., pp. 97, 100, 104.

45. François Dosse, *History of Structuralism*, vol. 2, trans. Deborah Glassman, Minneapolis: University of Minnesota Press, 1997 [1992], p. 122.

46. Lucien Goldmann, 'The Dialectic Today' in Goldmann, *Cultural Creation*, trans. Bart Grahl, St. Louis: Telos Press, 1976 [1970], pp. 108–22.

47. Foucault, *Discipline and Punish*, p. 204.

48. Michel Foucault, *The History of Sexuality*, vol. 1: *An Introduction*, trans. Robert Hurley, New York: Vintage, 1978 [1976], pp. 95–5.

49. Herbert Marcuse, *Collected Papers of Herbert Marcuse*, vol. 5: *Philosophy, Psychoanalysis and Emancipation*, ed. Douglas Kellner and Clayton Pierce, New York: Routledge, 2011, p. 63.

50. John Holloway, *Change the World Without Taking Power*, London: Pluto, 2002, p. 40; see also Kevin Anderson, 'Resistance Versus Emancipation: Foucault, Marcuse, Marx, and the Present Moment', *Logos: A Journal of Modern Society & Culture*, Vol. 12, No. 1 (2013): <http://logosjournal.com/2013/anderson/>.

51. A detailed account of this episode, as well as a translation of Foucault's Iran writings and those of his contemporary critics, can be found in Janet Afary and Kevin Anderson, *Foucault and the Iranian Revolution: Gender and the Seductions of Islamism*, Chicago: University of Chicago Press, 2005. For other critiques of Foucault, see especially: Rosemarie Scullion, 'Michel Foucault the Orientalist: On Revolutionary Iran and the "Spirit of Iran"', *South Central Review*, Vol. 12, No. 2 (1995), pp. 16–40; and Ian Almond, *The New Orientalism: Postmodern Representations Of Islam from Foucault to Baudrillard*, London: I. B. Tauris, 2007. For a rare defence of Foucault's Iran writings, see Olivier Roy, 'Michel Foucault et l'Iran: Le Philosophe, le People, le Pouvoir et "l'énigme du soulèvment"', *Vacarme*, No. 29 (2004), pp. 34–8.

52. Michel Foucault, *History of Madness*, trans. Jonathan Murphy and Jean Khalfa, New York: Routledge, 2006 [1961], p. 491.

53. Ibid., p. 492.

54. Mary Wollstonecraft, *A Vindication of the Rights of Woman*, Amherst, NY: Prometheus Books, 1989 [1792], p. 122.

55. Edward Said, *Orientalism*, New York: Vintage Books, 1978, p. 204.

56. Aijaz Ahmad, *In Theory: Nations, Classes, Literatures*, London: Verso, 1992, pp. 178–9.

57. Michael Hardt and Antonio Negri, *Empire*, Cambridge, MA: Harvard University Press, 2000.

58. Recently, Peter Hudis has illuminated Marx's humanist concept of an alternative to capitalism in *Marx's Concept of the Alternative to Capitalism*, Leiden: Brill, 2012.

59. Jacques Derrida, *Spectres of Marx: The State of the Debt, the Work of Mourning and the New International*, trans. Peggy Kamuf, New York: Routledge, 1994, p. 3.

60. Goldmann, 'The Dialectic Today', pp. 112–13.

61. See, for instance, Kevin Anderson and Russell Rockwell (eds), *The Dunayevskaya–Marcuse–Fromm Correspondence, 1954–1978: Dialogues on Hegel, Marx and Critical Theory*, Lanham, MD: Lexington Books, 2012.

62. Erich Fromm, *The Sane Society*, New York: Holt, Rinehart and Winston, 1955, p. 205.

63. Fromm in Kevin Anderson, 'A Recently Discovered Article by Erich Fromm on Trotsky and the Russian Revolution', *Science & Society*, Vol. 66, No. 22, 2002, p. 271.

64. Erich Fromm, *Marx's Concept of Man*, New York: Frederick Ungar, 1966 [1961], pp. 4–5.

65. Ibid., p. 5.

66. Ibid., p. 1.

67. Ibid., p. 2.

68. Ibid., p. 5.

69. Ibid., pp. vii–viii.

70. Interestingly, Fromm rejected a contribution by Althusser, thus delaying by several years his entrance into the English-speaking world. See Louis Althusser, *The Humanist Controversy and Other Writings*, ed. François Matheron, trans. G. M. Goshgarian, London: Verso, 2003.

71. Erich Fromm, 'Introduction', *Socialist Humanism: An International Symposium*, New York: Doubleday, 1965, p. viii.

72. Ibid., p. viii.

73. Ibid., p. ix.

74. Fromm's letter appears in Dunayevskaya, *Women's Liberation and the Dialectics of Revolution*, New Jersey: Humanities Press, 1985, p. 242; Dunayevskaya's letters to Fromm from this period appear in Anderson and Rockwell, *Dunayevskaya–Marcuse–Fromm Correspondence*, pp. 208–10.

75. Karel Kosík, *Dialectics of the Concrete: A Study on Problems of Man and World*, trans. Karel Kovanda with James Schmidt, Boston: D. Reidel, 1976 [1963], p. 7.

76. Ibid., p. 8.

77. Ibid., p. 24.

78. Ibid., p. 30.

79. Ibid., p. 42.

80. Herbert Marcuse, *Reason and Revolution: Hegel and the Rise of Social Theory*, New York: Oxford University Press, 1941, pp. 251–9.

81. Kosík, *Dialectics of the Concrete*, p. 104.

82. Ibid., p. 105.

83. Ibid., p. 106.

84. Ibid., p. 134.

85. Frantz Fanon, *The Wretched of the Earth*, trans. Constance Farrington, New York: Grove Press, 1963 [1961], p. 313.

86. Ibid., p. 246.

87. Ibid., p. 314.

88. On Fanon's humanism, see Peter Hudis, *Frantz Fanon: Philosopher of the Barricades*, London: Pluto, 2015; also Lou Turner and John Alan, *Frantz Fanon, Soweto and American Black Thought*.

89. Fanon, *Wretched of the Earth*, p. 247.

90. Nigel Gibson separates Fanon as well from a form of politics more prominent today than in his own time, radical Islamism, in *Fanon: The Postcolonial Imagination*, Cambridge: Polity Press, 2003.

91. Marnia Lazreg, *Torture and the Twilight of Empire: From Algiers to Baghdad*, Princeton, NJ: Princeton University Press, 2007, pp. 217–19; see also Irene Gendzier, *Frantz Fanon: A Critical Study*, New York: Pantheon, 1973, pp. 200–9. Fanon's humanism was also ambivalent concerning the consciousness of the Western working classes: see *Wretched of the Earth*, p. 314.

92. Raya Dunayevskaya, *Philosophy and Revolution: From Hegel to Sartre and from Marx to Mao*, New York: Columbia University Press, 1989 [1973], pp. 243–4; see also Kevin Anderson, 'Tanzania's Ujamaa After Twenty Years', *Left Court*, Vol. 3, No. 1 (1985), pp. 30–44.

93. Raya Dunayevskaya, *Rosa Luxemburg, Women's Liberation and Marx's Philosophy of Revolution*, 2nd edition, Urbana: Illinois University Press, 1991 [1982], p. 194.

94. Herbert Marcuse, 'Preface' to Dunayevskaya, *Marxism and Freedom*, p. xxi. The intellectually rich dialogues between Marcuse and Dunayevskaya that form the backdrop to this preface can be found in Anderson and Rockwell, *Dunayevskaya–Marcuse–Fromm Correspondence*.

95. Here and below, I am concentrating on those parts of her work that explicitly address the themes of humanism in Marx or the 'new humanism' she saw in contemporary social movements and philosophies. This presents a difficulty, as Dunayevskaya referred to her entire body of work after her 1953 'Letters on Hegel's Absolutes' as a form of 'Marxist-Humanism', but as with the other thinkers considered in this chapter, I have concentrated on their engagement – for or against – with humanism. For more general assessments on my part of Dunayevskaya's work, particularly her critical appropriation of Hegel's concept of absolute negativity, see especially Peter Hudis's and my introduction to Raya Dunayevskaya, *The Power of Negativity: Selected Writings on the Dialectic in Hegel and Marx*, Lanham: Lexington, 2002, pp. xv–xlii.

96. Dunayevskaya, *Marxism and Freedom*, p. 58, emphasis in original.

97. Ibid., p. 106.

98. Ibid., p. 116.

99. Ibid., p. 116.

100. Ibid., p. 117.

101. Ibid., p. xxv.

102. Ibid., p. 281.

103. Ibid., p. 276, emphasis in the original.

104. Ibid., p. 285.

105. Ibid., p. 287.

106. Raya Dunayevskaya, *Philosophy and Revolution*, p. 79.

107. Ibid., p. 22.

108. Ibid., p. 200.

109. Ibid., p. 208.

110. Ibid., p. 210.

111. See, for example, her call for Western and African Marxist humanists to link up in 'Socialismes Africains et Problèmes Nègres par Une Militante de l'Humanisme Marxiste', *Présence Africaine: Revue Culturelle du Monde Noir*, No. 43 (1963), pp. 49–64.

112. Dunayevskaya, *Philosophy and Revolution*, p. 214.

113. Ibid., p. 215.

114. Ibid., p. 213.

115. Ibid., p. 217.

116. Ibid., p. 243.
117. Ibid., p. 219.
118. Raya Dunayevskaya, *Power of Negativity*, pp. 186–8.
119. Dunayevskaya, *Philosophy and Revolution*, p. 261.
120. Ibid., pp. 269–70.
121. See especially Dunayevskaya, *Philosophy and Revolution*, chapter 1.
122. Marx, *Capital*, p. 90.
123. See Kevin Anderson, 'Raya Dunayevskaya, 1910 to 1987, Marxist Economist and Philosopher', *Review of Radical Political Economics*, Vol. 20, No. 1 (1988), pp. 62–74.

# 3

# Postcolonialism is a Humanism

## Robert Spencer

> There is something in human history like retribution; and it is a rule of
> historical retribution that its instrument be forged not by the offended,
> but by the offender himself.
>
> Karl Marx, 'The Indian Revolt', 1857[1]

The aim of this chapter is to demonstrate the longevity and radicalness of
the tradition of Marxist humanism and in particular that tradition's value
when theorising the texts and contexts of the so-called 'postcolonial'
world. And yet humanism is one of those words that postcolonialists usually frown upon. For Martin Heidegger's influential 'Letter on
Humanism' of 1947, 'every humanism remains metaphysical',[2] which
pretty much sums up the view of it taken by the dominant strain of
cultural theory over the last thirty years or so, much of which is explicitly
indebted to Heidegger's 'destruction of metaphysics'. The definition
of 'Man' as a being with an essence, distinctive, rational and superior,
'dominates the destiny of Western history and of all history determined
by Europe'.[3] Postcolonial theory, in its programmatic entrenchment in
the British and American academy, has been premised from the outset
on a no less sweeping rejection of humanism's resources. Although they
might consider Heidegger, for a different reason, to be beyond the pale,
postcolonial theorists have long proceeded under the influence, as it
were, of the philosophical *anti*humanists Louis Althusser and especially
Michel Foucault. For instance, Bill Ashcroft, Gareth Griffiths and Helen
Tiffin, authors of three widely read and frequently reprinted guides and
introductions to the field, assert in their *Post-Colonial Studies: The Key
Concepts* that the 'assumption that there are irreducable [*sic*] features of
human life and experience that exist beyond the constitutive effects of
local cultural conditions ... is a crucial feature of imperial hegemony'.[4]
This allegation is repeated in the same authors' second edition of *The*

*Post-Colonial Studies Reader*, where it is accompanied by the odd claim that 'even the most apparently "essential" features of human life' are 'provisional and contingent'.[5] Really? All of them? This undiscriminating approach to humanism is shared by leading lights in the field like Gayatri Spivak, for whom '[t]here is an affinity between the imperialist subject and the subject of humanism'.[6] To reject one is presumably at the same time to reject the other. By thus tarring all humanisms with the same brush, many postcolonial theorists have slighted attempts by the first generation of anti-imperialist activists and movements to rescue the promise of universal human emancipation proclaimed (duplicitously) by capitalist imperialism from the exploitation and divisiveness that this system has meant in practice. A rich and critical humanist tradition, most of it produced by thinkers and activists explicitly opposed to imperialism, has therefore been kept hidden behind a straw man version that is branded 'essentialist' and 'Eurocentric'.

Nonetheless it is true that the unrepentant humanism of the field's founder, Edward Said, is not glossed over quite so embarrassedly these days. Said's repeated declarations that he was an unswerving humanist used to be met by his postcolonialist successors with a kind of uncomfortable silence. Now the situation is somewhat different. The war in Iraq and its calamitous aftermath no doubt alerted Said's heirs and interpreters to what Neil Lazarus has called 'the unremitting actuality and indeed the intensification of imperialist social relations in the times and spaces of the postcolonial world'.[7] As a result, those critics have perhaps been induced to look more favourably at Said's efforts to use humanism as a way of reproving imperialism and of imagining our way beyond it. The war in Iraq, in short, has made starkly visible a rampantly *in*human imperialist project that has obviously not, as our field's moniker suggests, been drawing to a close but has on the contrary been seeking to expand (or at least prolong) American hegemony, extend corporate power and hijack international institutions of governance. Said's humanism arraigns Iraq's assailants in the name of universal principles and a vision of social transformation. The second edition of Bill Ashcroft and Pal Ahluwalia's book on Said in the Routledge Critical Thinkers series contains a broadly sympathetic, albeit slightly grudging, section on Said's humanism,[8] as does R. Radhakrishnan's altogether more laudatory dictionary of Said's key concepts.[9]

It is well over a decade since Bruce Robbins marked 'a universalistic and humanistic impulse that has gradually emerged, within cultural studies generally and postcolonial studies in particular, but that was slow to be perceived as such because of the prevailing antihumanism.'[10] Notwithstanding this renewed interest in Said's humanism, I would maintain, however, that humanism's partial rehabilitation has not gone very far at all. It has not yet affected fundamentally the kind of work that we postcolonialists do. It is one thing to concede that when it comes to, say, the assault on Iraq it is legitimate to talk about rights and duties, about war crimes and crimes against humanity. That is part of our obligations and activities as citizens. It is quite another thing, however, to let such convictions guide or animate fully our professional lives as critics too. My point in this chapter is not that we should all carry a card with the word 'Humanist' emblazoned on it, nor that we should begin each argument with a paean of praise to the idea, nor even that we should bother to use the word more often. I suppose I am arguing that in addition to being a critical undertaking postcolonialism ought also to be a moral and a political one as well. This being the case, I want to say, at the risk of sounding facetious, that postcolonial studies should be exercised above all not by crimes against hybridity but by crimes against humanity and by the moral and political aspirations of those movements that seek to withstand such crimes and to overthrow the system that inflicts them. Ours is the effort to understand where colonialism comes from as well as how colonialism can be superseded; ours is the responsibility to make connections between local injustices and then trace these to the general and related injustices of state and class power; ours is also the obligation to give due emphasis to the achievement of texts of various kinds in dramatising those injustices and exploring alternatives. This is another way of saying that, although Said's humanism is not in such bad odour as hitherto, humanism has barely penetrated and informed the critical work that we do. Because humanism, at worst, conjures up images of men in pith helmets telling the world what to do, or else, at best, comes across as a quaint way of describing the convictions we employ when making political judgements, it has not been allowed to influence the priorities of a discipline that, alas, no longer sees itself, as its predecessors saw *them*selves, as part of a general movement for emancipation. It is now a trifling affair concerned with the 'liminal' spaces opened up by a global system that it either approves of or, more likely, that it despairs of being overturned.

Of course, it is not hard to find exclusionary and 'metaphysical' definitions of humanism that, far from being acclamations of universal rights and capacities, are in fact mere smokescreens for self-interest. Too many humanisms have excluded and denigrated certain groups whom they consider to be not (or at least not yet) fully human. This is especially true of the humanist rhetoric mouthed by the agents and spokespeople of colonial power. 'The Mediterranean is the human norm', according to the sententious narrator of A Passage to India, and through the Bosphorus and the Pillars of Hercules men 'approach the monstrous and extraordinary'.[11] So blatantly intolerable is this pompous and obnoxious way of thinking (remember it is, of course, not Forster himself speaking here) that Anthony Alessandrini observes that 'it is becoming increasingly difficult to find anyone within the field of postcolonial studies willing to defend humanism in its most traditional form'.[12] Impossible, in fact. What is more, it is of course quite right that this should be so. For the libertarian humanism that I am endeavouring to vindicate is as like the traditional version as a crab's like an apple. Let nobody labour under the illusion that I am foolish enough to endorse the sort of crass, self-seeking and ultimately racist humanism for which to be black, say, in Aimé Césaire's celebrated quip, is 'like being a second-class clerk': waiting for promotion, 'en attendant mieux et avec possibilité de monter plus haut'. What one wouldn't realise from the dismissal of humanism as a kind of unthinking belief in the superiority of white European men, is the sheer variety of humanisms that have come into being in response to such inadequate understandings of the term. In their Critical Humanisms, Martin Halliwell and Andy Mousley demonstrate the extraordinary durability and diversity of the humanist tradition.[13] One thinks, in addition to their examples, of the 'radical humanism' of the Holocaust survivor Jean Améry,[14] Karen Green's feminist humanism,[15] not to mention the variety of socialist humanisms enumerated by Barbara Epstein in this volume. Most of all, I believe our attention ought to be trained on the Marxist humanism of a tradition represented by Theodor Adorno, Ernst Bloch and Herbert Marcuse, and of Jean-Paul Sartre, to whose celebrated 1945 lecture 'Existentialism is a Humanism' this chapter's title is a respectful nod.

My claim here is that the rejection over these last decades of the idea that human subjects are possessed of intrinsic rights and capacities bears out one of Theodor Adorno's most cutting gibes: among its other functions, 'philosophy is capable of making people stupid'.[16] I therefore propose to describe what I believe are the deleterious consequences for postcolonial theory's development of its constitutive antihumanism and especially of

124 · FOR HUMANISM

its neglect of the liberating resources of a specifically Marxist humanism. I hope it is not unfair to observe that the dominant though persistently disputed and by now fairly beleaguered variety of postcolonial criticism shares several identifying marks, or let us say precepts and assumptions, that might with some justice be termed 'antihumanist'. I am referring less to such sophisticated as well as theoretically and politically distinct figures as Homi Bhabha and Gayatri Spivak, though I shall have a bit more to say in due course about the former, than to the myriad of other critics who draw on an idiom first promulgated by Bhabha and Spivak. I am not endeavouring to tick off, say, Bhabha for being a card-carrying antihumanist, not least because he has written in his preface to the new translation of Frantz Fanon's *The Wretched of the Earth* in a surprisingly sympathetic way about humanism.[17] Rather, in addition to showing that what Bhabha means by the term could scarcely be further from Fanon's extremely militant account of a 'new humanism', I want to identify a kind of disposition or outlook among most postcolonialists that is not so much stridently antihumanist, though God knows there is quite enough of that, as habitually or routinely and even automatically antihumanist. To be a postcolonialist, it seems, is to leave one's humanism at the door. To peruse the contents of any issue of the major journals in the field is more often than not to be confronted with theoretical disquisitions and analyses of texts that, whatever virtues of acuity and originality they possess and notwithstanding their informativeness, usually address their readers from a position that is tacitly antihumanist. They champion difference at the expense of equality, deal with narratives of cultural 'hybridity' without sufficient regard for the continuing exigencies of conflict and struggle, and choose to abide by the tenets and idiom of post-structuralism to the detriment of the revolutionary language and horizons of the previous generation of anticolonial militants. In so doing, my claim goes, many postcolonial critics have either forfeited or have else been completely oblivious of the very valuable resources of the language of humanism. They therefore leave unexplored the larger realities in which such texts and theories circulate, the world of imperialism, of capitalism (from which imperialism is inseparable) and of the counter-struggles of imperialism's victims.

The reasons for this aversion to humanism are complex, to put it mildly. They have to do with the discipline's snug consolidation within (as opposed to within *and against*) the Anglo-American university system as well as within those countries' radically neoliberal economic dispensations, dispensations which the world of higher education increasingly and quite willingly serves. Speaking only of the British system in which I work, it is a melancholy duty to have to report that any number of essential academic freedoms and responsibilities have been buried in the last few years beneath an avalanche of corporate waffle and management newspeak. Few of us will need reminding of the consequences of the annexation of British universities by the language and priorities of corporate power: of how large our class sizes have become, of the casualisation of the academic labour market, of funding crises and cost-cutting, of the extortionate price of tuition fees (the intention of which is not to save money but to turn students into indebted and thus pliant consumers), and of the distortion of scholarly research by measuring it against the risibly crude standard of 'economic contribution'. All of these developments deflect the inhabitants of these embattled institutions from the proper business of advanced education in the humanities, which is the cultivation of an aptitude for asking difficult questions about culture and society.[18] Postcolonial studies' materialist critics have long complained that the most prominent figures in the field, indeed the field itself, has been co-opted by its privileged position within this world of conformity and privilege.[19] And yet it would hardly be worth saying such things if universities were not at the same time also places in which it is still possible to foster the ability and the confidence to think knowledgeably, rigorously and above all critically about texts of all kinds and about the realities with which texts deal. My point is that the characteristic emphases of the postcolonial field cannot be understood without reference to its institutional, geographical and economic position. We need to be more self-conscious about that position and more willing to work both within and against it. Now more than ever there is a danger that if postcolonial studies does not present itself consciously as a discipline concerned centrally with questions of critique and liberation, then it will, at worst, end up as a kind of area office within an enfeebled humanities sector. At best, it will become a disgruntled subsidiary of the humanities, dissatisfied with the system of which it forms a part but whose favourite concepts are to that system like so many toy arrows.

To let fall the word 'revolutionary' where one might be accustomed to hearing terms like 'liminality' is already, therefore, to out oneself as a humanist. This is because the concern with systems and with systemic alternatives is usually seen as the preserve of an older anticolonial past rather than of the postcolonial present. By demonstrating the differences between Marxist humanism on the one hand and postcolonial *anti*humanism on the other, I hope at least to show that postcolonial theory as it is currently constituted does not possess anything like the system-challenging ambitions of humanism, which seeks to marry critical and theoretical work to the larger context of the struggle to replace the manifestly *in*human imperatives of imperialism and capitalism. This is a quintessentially theoretical question of course, by which I mean that it is a crucial question about the very purpose and context of the critical work that we undertake. We have, in my view, delayed for far too long a rigorous and open discussion of what I see as the very considerable disadvantages of the antihumanist theory that so many of us seem almost automatically to deploy. Imperialism and its transformation is the proper subject of our discipline; that being the case, we must return in a suitably critical and discriminating spirit to the humanist thinkers whose subject this was.

Neil Lazarus and Rashmi Varma have argued that postcolonial studies' 'constitutive anti-Marxism'[20] can be put down to its emergence as an academic enterprise in the late 1970s in a historical moment that saw a reassertion of imperial dominance in response to a broad crisis of profitability in global capitalism. The subsequent era witnessed the resurgence of American military power, the defeat and co-option of oppositional movements in the 'first' world, the final petrifaction and then dissolution of the nominally socialist 'second' world, and the 'rollback' of the social and economic achievements of large parts of the 'third'.[21] This is the period that witnessed the breaking and dissipation of what Ernest Mandel termed the 'long wave' of post-war growth.[22] It witnessed a concerted counter-revolution against the transformative goals of the preceding epoch. Lazarus's claim is that the principal motifs and preoccupations of postcolonial studies were affected by this moment of defeat. A sense of the system's resurgence as well as its permanence and ineluctability finds expression not, of course, in any overt championing of the counter-revolution, which many postcolonialists no doubt regret, but, as Lazarus and Varma argue, in the postcolonial field's reluctance to aver the 'grand narratives' of emancipation, revolution, socialism, internationalism and, they might have added, humanism.

Postcolonialists' radical energies are deflected instead into the privileging of 'a rhetoric of recognition over one of redistribution'.[23] This rhetoric values difference over universality, a difference that aspires to be respected by a social and economic system with which the previous generation of anticolonial thinkers and movements had sought unceremoniously to do away. The untranscendable horizon of world capitalism is thus the indispensable precept or *sine qua non* of postcolonial politics. This is the case whether the postcolonial ideology underlying theoretical disquisitions and critical readings is a reformist multiculturalism that craves the recognition of difference or the equally modest affirmation of a cultural 'hybridity' that is seen as being compatible with (and even, for some thinkers, engineered by) global capitalism. Sara Suleri is the best (or should I say worst) example of a postcolonial theorist for whom even the nebulous rhetoric of resistance is too radical. Her study of *The Rhetoric of English India* tells us that resistance 'precludes the concept of "exchange" by granting the idea of power a greater literalism than it deserved,'[24] power presumably being something that is less potent or objectionable than we usually imagine it to be and 'exchanging' with power something we might like to do instead of anything so doctrinaire as resisting power, still less overthrowing it. I contend that the rejection of humanism is part of this tacit abandonment by postcolonial studies of the goal of liberation, humanism having been an essential and ubiquitous part of the arsenal of anticolonial movements in the 1950s and 1960s. For the humanism that I am advocating threatens to overturn the system. It is a principle to set and protest against that system. It also provides a vision of a transformed global order.

My more specific point, therefore, is not that the antihumanists are always wrong or that their humanist antecedents were always right. What I am arguing is that the latter sought to understand capitalist imperialism, frequently in unexpectedly sophisticated and promising ways, as a dehumanising system. They therefore tried to think through the specific ways in which this system dehumanises its victims. They formulated, in addition, some pertinent ideas about alternative or emergent ways of living, ideas that deserve our attention though certainly not our uncritical approval. Naturally, these understandings and ideas must be scrutinised, assessed and updated. Yet I do not think I am overstating the point when I claim that unless theory is 'anti' rather than merely 'postcolonial', unless it concerns itself closely with what the thinkers in whom this chapter is interested present as a moral and political critique of imperialism in the name of a more humanly fitting alternative, then it might as well be 'pro-colonial'. Just as my own thoughts are offered here as matter for further debate, the theories formulated by the Marxist and anticolonial proponents of humanism whose work is discussed below will be treated in the same critical spirit. They provide, I hope to show, an authoritative and topical though far from infallible guide for reflecting on the larger questions of commitment and purpose that some of us have preferred to disregard. We have the wrong theory because we have chosen as our forebears the wrong theorists. Postcolonial studies ought to view and present itself not as what Alessandrini calls 'a particularly successful offshoot of postmodernism',[25] successful in terms of visibility, durability and institutional standing in the universities of the core countries of an unremittingly imperialist world system, but as part of a rich tradition descended from the Marxist thinkers and movements (as well as those influenced by Marxism) who struggled in the years after the war *against* that same system and *for* human liberation.

What do I – or rather *they* – mean by humanism? Two things. The first element of a distinctively postcolonial humanism would be the belief that humanity is, in a sense, not yet. One of the distinctive attributes of the human is, in other words, as Sartre argues, the capacity for self-creation, a capacity that is too often stymied by a social and economic system that coerces and controls the minds and bodies of human subjects. Human beings, with their diverse talents and inclinations, are not yet what they could be, and what they could be is nobody else's business but their own. Humanism means freedom and diversity. It does not mean, as humanism's reputation might lead us to believe, the positing of some prescriptive standard defined and enforced by the coloniser, the metropole or whoever. By definition, we do not know what freedom is, to paraphrase Adorno, only what freedom is not. Similarly, we do not yet know what the human is, but we can say with absolute certainty what *in*humanity looks like. A more humane order will strive not to instate some abstract or unilaterally conceived ideal of what it means to be human but only to rid itself of the most grievous wrongs: 'There is tenderness only in the coarsest demand: that no-one shall go hungry any more', in Adorno's moving formulation.[26] Put simply, a life of creative self-fashioning is not available to the man or woman whose stomach is empty. The first aspect of a putative postcolonial humanism is therefore meaningless without a second, further aspect. This second element of a postcolonial humanism is the assertion of those universal rights, to freedom from hunger for example or from exploitation, without which abstract avowals of freedom make no sense and are impracticable. A humanist postcolonial criticism will speak the language of rights and will be animated by the conviction that there *are* irreducible features of human life, not, of course, because it wants to ape the unsmiling and prescriptive humanisms of the past but, on the contrary, because it is convinced that only by eradicating the most devastating forms of inhumanity will the human, with all its variability and unpredictableness, come into its own.

## 'WESTERN' MARXISM'S ANTICOLONIAL CREDENTIALS

'Much of Western Marxism', according to Edward Said, at least 'in its aesthetic and cultural departments, is ... blinded to the matter of imperialism'. Even Frankfurt School critical theory, he goes on, 'is stunningly silent on racist theory, anti-imperialist resistance, oppositional practice in the empire'.[27] While it is true that the likes of Adorno, Bloch and Marcuse were hardly activists in the cause of anticolonial revolution, what Said says is demonstrably not true of another 'Western Marxist', Sartre, who was such an activist. And blindness to imperialism is scarcely something that one can lay at the door of those literally dozens of illustrious Marxists like Rosa Luxemburg, Andre Gunder Frank, Samir Amin, Paul Baran and of course Lenin and indeed Marx and Engels themselves, whom Said is careful to exclude from his stricture and who have plugged away in departments other than the aesthetic and the cultural but whose concerns were precisely those that Said lists. Indeed, Said is arguably not even right about the Frankfurt School. As we will soon see, Adorno et al. were not only surprisingly outspoken in their opposition to colonialism and neocolonialism, they also formulated pertinent insights into the nature of domination and its alternatives that positively beseech application to the world of colonial and anticolonial conflict. I am pointing here not to a fixed position but to a tradition developed by numerous thinkers who were not necessarily working together and who did not always agree with each other, a tradition nonetheless that shared a belief in the inextricable connection between social critique and the ideal of human liberation.

The classic 1965 volume on *Socialist Humanism* edited by Erich Fromm, allies the Marxist critique of capitalism to a humanist emphasis on the revolutionary transformation of an alienating and dehumanising society. The volume is introduced by Fromm as a meditation on the moral problem of how to create a more just and meaningful existence for human beings in a world in which the advanced state of the productive forces has for the first time made possible a universal freedom from fear and want.[28] To the practice of critique therefore, Marxist humanism adds a utopian stress on liberation. It is humanism that unites the leading lights of the British New Left such as Raymond Williams and E. P. Thompson, the Frankfurt School and the dissidents in the Soviet bloc whose voices began faintly to be heard after the partial thaw that followed Stalin's death and Khrushchev's speech to the twentieth party congress. It was in unmistakably humanist terms, albeit as we shall see tremendously nuanced and dialectical ones, that Marxists have criticised and envisioned alternatives to the established systems of social and economic power. They took aim at the sclerotic tyrannies of the Soviet zone and at a capitalism whose enormous productive power in these years took off at the cost of inequality and frustrated human potential in the apparently prosperous West as well as of the continuing super-exploitation of the colonial and then neocolonial world.

In his *Natural Law and Human Dignity*, for example, Ernst Bloch, striving after his defection from East Germany to make sense of the murderous wrong turns taken by Marxism, reasserted the principle of human rights, 'beyond all forms of contracts and contractors'.[29] Bloch sought to formulate a framework of rights and norms that any genuine socialism ought to realise. To this end he suggests that we rehabilitate the idea of natural law, that is, the moral basis of law and justice. There is hope and even a portent of utopia, Bloch contends, in a natural standard that exists independently of and can be used normatively to criticise existing laws, conditions and institutions. Revolutions are powered by the perennial human desire to, as he puts it in an appealing phrase, 'walk upright'. The quintessence of natural law is the postulate of human dignity: 'man, and not only his class (as Brecht said), is not happy when he finds a boot in his face'.[30] Bloch accepts that an essential part of human happiness is the possibility of self-flourishing or *eudaimonia*, which is a positive rather than a negative right but which cannot by definition be chosen for one by others. The aim is not human happiness as such, which is how *eudaimonia* is sometimes translated into English. Human flourishing describes a life made meaningful through, for example, devotion to others, intellectual, imaginative or creative achievement, or the full exercise of one's potentialities and abilities. Accordingly, natural law for Bloch 'is oriented above all towards the abolition of human *degradation*'.[31] Without such standards of what is right and just, exploitation cannot be reproved and a qualitatively different future society cannot even be foreseen, let alone brought into being. Bloch therefore devotes a great deal of his study to exposing the exclusions, illusions and aporias of bourgeois natural law. His aim is to demonstrate that a classless society is natural law's implicit goal. But human nature is not static for Bloch; it is not some standard to which individuals must aspire or be forced to conform.[32] Rather, since human beings are diverse, mutable, self-created creatures, the goal of any authentically radical politics is to bring about (by definition, voluntarily rather than forcibly) a world in which individuals dispose of the natural right to determine their own lives and in so doing unfold the various possibilities of their being.

This is also true of Herbert Marcuse, for whom politics, in a memorable phrase, is 'the day-to-day fight of men and women for a life as human beings'.[33] Socialism would be more humane because it would enable men and women to satisfy their individual and social needs without exploitation and with the minimum of toil and sacrifice. They would be free to realise their own talents and inclinations in a society that therefore conforms more closely to the kind of beings that humans are, i.e. possessed of an intrinsic capacity for creative self-realisation. Marcuse's *Eros and Civilization* is still one of the most original and compelling documents in the Marxist tradition of utopian speculation for this reason.[34] Its claim is that while all societies are repressive, requiring the subordination of gratification and desire to the discipline of work (the 'reality principle'), societies are not all repressive to the same degree. Marcuse argues that Freud was mistaken to assume that there is only one form of reality principle on the grounds, as Freud saw it, that there is only one form of society, a bourgeois society that compels a competition for scarce resources. Without exploitative social relations, however, and without the perceived need for incessant economic growth, in a world whose technological resources have made the need for exploitation, competition and breakneck growth entirely unnecessary, the 'surplus repression' exacted by capitalism might be done away with. Men and women will hardly be free from repression in such a society, but they will at least be liberated from capitalism's 'performance principle', which compels us to work for an apparatus which we do not control and which subordinates human need to the abstract and now entirely pointless goal of capital accumulation.

In the extraordinarily popular and radical series of texts that he penned in the United States in the three decades after the war, Marcuse bemoans an overdeveloped society's incessant and unnecessary augmentation of services and consumer goods. Those goods satisfy false or at least limited and destructive (because aggressive and acquisitive) needs at the expense of a life, which would only be possible in a qualitatively transformed society, lived in pursuit of peace, amity and beauty. In *An Essay on Liberation* Marcuse discusses a possible 'biological foundation for socialism', a phrase from which most postcolonial theorists would probably run a mile.[35] Yet Marcuse is not some naïve 'essentialist'. Nor is he claiming that there is some ideal of unchanging humanity to which we should be compelled to adhere. Rather, the emphasis in all of his work, from his critiques of the stultifying dictates of advanced capitalism to his equally damning appraisals of the repressive and bureaucratic form of Soviet socialism, is on the *liberation* of subjectivity.[36] Freedom would be a life no longer constrained by competitive performances and no longer impelled by the 'second nature' of consumption and aggression.[37] Moreover, the supersession of 'a system that makes hell of large areas of the globe'[38] could spell a more equitable distribution of resources and a reduction of the toil previously expended on the system's gratuitous and harmful expansion. Socialism would then be an arena of liberation in which equality and abundance meant the freedom of individuals to pursue creative activities more in keeping with their dynamic, many-sided natures. A just society would put behind it needlessly perpetuated repression, committing itself instead to 'the universal gratification of the basic human needs, and the freedom from guilt and fear'.[39] It would instate negative rights to freedom from affliction and want as well as the positive right to creative self-fulfilment, what Marcuse calls 'the free manifestation of potentialities'.[40] The aesthetic for Marcuse is therefore not just a realm of creative experience fenced off from the humdrum routines of everyday toil. It is also the promise and form of an existence in which individuals will be free to tap their own potential for creativity, imagination, sensuousness and play. To live humanly is to live freely: 'The goal of the revolution,' in Adorno's beautiful phrase, 'is the abolition of fear.'[41]

It is not just that, contrary to received wisdom, Frankfurt School Marxism grasped the colonial and neocolonial dimensions of advanced capitalism; as I have shown elsewhere in relation to Adorno's work,[42] the leading lights of the Frankfurt School were very precisely concerned with 'the fact that, in crazy contradiction to what is possible, human beings in large parts of the planet live in penury'.[43] Marcuse denounces as an 'obscenity'[44] the fact that the affluence of some societies is transforming the earth into an 'inferno ... concentrated in certain far away places: Vietnam, the Congo, South Africa, and in the ghettoes of the "affluent society": in Mississippi and Alabama, in Harlem".[45] Just as importantly however, the alternatives with which Adorno, Bloch and Marcuse contrast that society are inspired by a non-dogmatic humanism. They place the emphasis at all times on liberation and on the immanent critique of bourgeois civilisation's inability to realise its own ideals, even (we would say especially) 'in Asia and Africa' where, Adorno avers, 'the humanity of civilization is inhumane toward the people it shamelessly brands as uncivilized'.[46] The fact that the Frankfurt School did not get round to applying these ideas more methodically in colonial and anticolonial settings is no reason why we should not.

Perhaps no thinker has been more systematically and derisively dismissed by the antihumanists than Jean-Paul Sartre, but it was Sartre who in my view furnishes the most cogent account of how a libertarian humanism might be employed both to overturn colonialism and elaborate revolutionary alternatives. Indeed, it was Sartrean existentialism that structuralism and subsequently post-structuralism defined themselves against. But what remains truly fascinating about Sartre's work, not to mention profoundly useful and timely, is its insistence both on human subjectivity's mutability and on subjectivity's indispensability as a principle to be defended in the course of political action. Sartre is a humanist not because there is some 'essence' of humanity that needs to be exalted or restored. To the contrary, he is so because to be human means to win the freedom as well as the responsibility to fashion a personality that can never be anything other than precarious and contingent. Moreover, this claim about freedom is not separable from Sartre's well-known defence of anticolonial revolution. Famously, Sartre supported the Algerian war of liberation as well as Vietnamese resistance to American imperialism. The goal of anticolonial revolution is the establishment of a situation in which all people and all peoples are able to cultivate a meaningful and dignified (because free) existence. Humanism, for Sartre, did not exist; it had to be created.

One cannot justly say, therefore, that such a humanism is Eurocentric, because it emphatically does not require non-European peoples to measure up to an ideal of humanity already defined and sanctioned by Europeans. To the contrary, it avers that humankind has no essential identity or personality or rather, if the paradox can be tolerated, Sartre's humanism insists that humankind's essence is its freedom from essences and thus its consequent facility for self-creation. Sartre's humanism affirms the agency of the dispossessed, not that of the possessors. Why does this formulation of humanism represent a threat to postcolonial studies as it is currently constituted? The short answer is that it opens up a perspective on liberation. Where before postcolonial critics might have been content to deconstruct colonial power or to subject it to the gentle retorts of 'difference' and 'hybridity', a humanist postcolonialism will wish to excoriate colonial power for being systematically exploitative, humanly limiting and destructive. It will be confident about the humanist standard it uses to reach this judgement and about the humanist vision of which it avails itself when formulating and envisioning an alternative to colonial power. This is because, crucially, their emphasis on volition rather than prescription and on the dynamic rather than fixed nature of subjectivity mean that both the standard and the vision are no longer as vulnerable to accusations of Eurocentrism. Such a humanism will enable us to analyse postcolonial literary texts, for example, without being shy of discussing the overwhelming and exceptionable context of colonial and capitalist power that so many of them depict. I look forward to the day when humanism will also persuade us to stop overlooking those texts' capacities to articulate what is often an unmistakably humanist aspiration for a dispensation that is both more just and more free.

Human subjectivity is, of course, the principal focus of Sartre's early philosophy, most obviously in *Being and Nothingness*.[47] Subjectivity for Sartre is inextricably bound up with the objective world. The world is not dualistic, divided into reified subjects and reified objects. For one of the fundamental lessons taught by Sartre's great philosophical texts is that consciousness is always intentional; that is, consciousness is consciousness *of* something, which is a very different claim from saying that consciousness precedes the world, creates it and sustains it in being. Consciousness does not anticipate the world, though consciousness may endow the world with meaning. Similarly, the I or ego is actually a product of consciousness's involvement in the world. Sartre insists that reflective consciousness is actually capable of comprehending the self's mutability, an experience that results in a dizzying sense of anxiety or 'nausea'. There follows from this experience the possibility (or at least the willingness) either to embrace such radical contingency and in so doing to break consciously with one's falsely fixed self or, by convincing oneself that one's personality, identity and existence have already been determined once and for all from the outside, to give in to the self-deception of bad faith or *mauvaise foi* (of which racism, and especially anti-Semitism, is always the quintessential example in Sartre's writings). Sartre's thought therefore implores us to face the disconcerting truth that neither human history nor the individual human life is endowed with meaning or purpose by some transcendent creator. Everything is up in the air, for '[t]he essential thing', as Roquentin puts it in *La Nausée*, 'is contingency'.[48]

There is no possibility of avoiding the freedom to make and remake oneself since this freedom is as unavoidable a part of my sheer facticity or 'condition'[49] as my body or the world into which I am born. 'Existence precedes essence'[50] is the slogan coined in Sartre's 'Existentialism is a Humanism' lecture; the human being is a free as well as situated and embodied consciousness. Hence Sartre's provocative belief, at least in his early writings, that even in situations into which I am thrown such as war, I possess the freedom to shape my involvement, to thus make the war *my* war, a war for which I must therefore be held responsible: 'Man is nothing else but that which he makes of himself'.[51] It should be clear that there is nothing 'metaphysical' about this account of consciousness and subjectivity. Indeed, as Fredric Jameson explains, the human being is defined in *Being and Nothingness* precisely as *néant* or lack: 'the being of the individual is in reality a lack of being, an inability to be, to reach some ultimate and definitive stability and ontological plenitude'.[52] We need not be squeamish about endorsing Sartre's notion of authenticity, which is one of those words we have been trained to hold in contempt. The converse of *mauvaise foi*, Sartrean authenticity means the opposite of what we might think it means; authenticity is not some state of conformity with an existing identity or personality but rather a precarious condition of being that has been wrested freely and painstakingly from a condition of *in*authenticity. There are two types of humanism, according to Sartre's 1945 lecture: one inauthentic and one authentic. The first, which he rejects, is the 'absurd' and naïve 'theory which upholds man as the end-in-itself and as the supreme value'.[53] There is no humanity on which such a judgement could be passed: 'an existentialist will never take man as the end, since man is still to be determined'.[54] 'The cult of humanity', the hubristic belief that humanity is fixed as well as superior to nature and other animals, ends in fascism. The second type of humanism, which Sartre endorses, describes the human being's ability to go 'outside of himself' by choosing his own aims. We are 'forever present in a human universe',[55] not locked into our own subjectivity but capable of inventing and exceeding ourselves. Existentialism is a humanism because human beings are their own legislators. A world that enabled and encouraged those acts of conscious legislation would therefore represent humanity's full flowering: 'it is not by turning back upon himself, but always by seeking, beyond himself, an aim which is one of liberation or of some particular realisation, that man can realise himself as truly human'.[56]

So intense was Sartre's commitment in the 1950s and 1960s to libertarian Marxism and to the anticolonial movements in Algeria, Indochina and elsewhere, that his problematic insistence on the possibility of absolute freedom became tempered by a new stress on the political situations in which consciousness invariably finds itself and in which it is compelled to act. Yet no matter how moulded and hemmed in the individual may be, there is always an opportunity to understand and affect one's situation and in so doing assume responsibility for it. One of the significant advances made by Sartre's philosophy in this period is its increasing recognition that ethical behaviour (a system of ethics being something that Sartre promises at the end of *Being and Nothingness*[57] but which he never got round to writing) consists not just in one's own quest for authenticity but also in the self's ability, in Paige Arthur's words about Sartre, to 'see a freedom in the Other',[58] as well as to help remove the barriers that prevent the exercise of the Other's freedom. Besides, as Alexander Zevin has shown, in seeking to qualify Arthur's arguments, Sartre's work in the 1950s and 1960s was not so much ethical as forthrightly political.[59] In Sartre's work from this period we see a thinker acutely conscious of the overbearing global situation of decolonisation, Cold War and American and Soviet imperialism, but also of the opportunities this situation affords radical political movements to break with this comprehensive system of social and economic control and therefore of the philosopher's own responsibility to help such breaks to be effected. The human flourishing of the Other and not just of the self is the ethical and political goal of Sartre's philosophy, the true novelty and pertinence of which is its fervent and often courageous as well as unabashedly *humanist* conviction that this flourishing is the principal goal of intellectual and political action. This humanism could not resemble less the prescriptive humanisms that all postcolonialists rightly spurn; to the contrary, its sole value is the belief that thought and action should conduce to the promotion of freedom.

It might be worth observing at this point that some of the basic tenets of Sartre's early philosophy were subject to very searching criticism by Marcuse. Marcuse's specific objection is that Sartre's philosophy is unhistorical. Sartre's belief in the inviolability of human freedom is, in the Marxist sense, idealist. It mistakes a historically specific form of human existence for human existence per se.[60] But human beings are not yet free, Marcuse reminds us, for they have been reduced to objects in a thoroughly reified world: 'The anti-fascist who is tortured to death may retain his moral and intellectual freedom to "transcend" this situation: he is still tortured to death.'[61] Worse, behind existentialism's model of human self-determination is a capitalistic ideology of competitive self-assertion: Sartre 'presents the old ideology in the new cloak of radicalism and rebellion'.[62] Freedom for Marcuse is a goal, not yet a reality. Nonetheless, I would maintain that Marcuse's objections are to some extent satisfied by Sartre's acknowledgement in his later works of the objective and especially political and economic constraints that limit subjects' freedom. No doubt Simone de Beauvoir's exploration of the constraints placed on the freedom of women played a key part in that acknowledgement. Freedom, as Sartre increasingly recognised and as he theorised at length in the two massive volumes of the *Critique of Dialectical Reason*, is disfigured and held in check by both natural and humanly contrived (or 'practico-inert') constraints on the exercise of freedom. Such criticisms as those offered by Marcuse no doubt obliged Sartre in his later writings to emphasise the obstacles placed in the way of the realisation of freedom as well as to stress his conviction that freedom is a condition to be striven for, not a reality to be championed. And if nothing else, Marcuse's critique of existentialism as well as Adorno's in his *Negative Dialectics*[63] goes to prove that what I am endorsing here is a diverse tradition, not a homogeneous or unanimously espoused philosophy.

We come therefore to Sartre's exemplary anticolonialism. The reason why he should in my view be considered a model for us today is that Sartre's commitment to decolonisation is driven by his fidelity to the recognisably humanist principle of freedom. I am referring to Sartre's opposition to (and insights into) racism and anti-Semitism, the precocious internationalism of *Les Temps Modernes* (the journal he founded in 1945), his involvement in the pioneering pan-Africanist periodical *Présence Africaine*, his championing of *négritude*, his service on the Russell Tribunal on Vietnam, his backing for the Cuban revolution, his brave support for African and especially Algerian independence, and his later commitment to the struggles of regionalist movements and immigrant workers. My emphasis here is on the connection between Sartre's philosophical and his political espousal of freedom. Zevin too calls attention to what he describes as 'a kind of cross-pollination between

Sartre's philosophical ideas and his anti-colonialism.[64] Sartre's essay 'Colonialism is a System', for example, written at the height of the war in Algeria in 1956, demonstrates the impossibility of retaining Algeria as a colony while introducing reforms to ameliorate the impoverishment of its people. Impoverishment and even starvation were not the accidental results of maladministration or, as Camus saw it, of natural disasters.[65] Rather, Algeria had been colonised in the first place in order for the land to be stolen and its people exploited, an exploitation that continued and even intensified after World War II, and that could only be brought to an end by France's total withdrawal from the colony and by Algerians' wilful and determined attainment of their national freedom.

Freedom is the paramount value, the freedom of nations being a necessary although not sufficient precondition of the freedom of peoples. Hence Sartre's interest in the murder by Belgian special forces of Patrice Lumumba, the first prime minister of the former Belgian Congo.[66] For in that country and in most of the rest of Africa, colonialism had been succeeded by neocolonialism, in this case by a situation in which Western corporations continued to rule through a pliant and corrupt native bourgeoisie. Self-determination, Sartre concluded from his comprehensive study of Lumumba's ill-fated premiership, must be won not bestowed, and it must be total, that is, economic as well as political. Again, it ought to be clear therefore that humanism for Sartre is not a word that names a particular condition to which peoples ought to be forced to conform. In the hands of colonialism, humanism is nothing but hypocritical racism. France could reign over subject peoples because it ascribed to them no rights and no independent volition. Paratroopers could attach electrodes to their victims in the dungeons of Algiers because their supposedly superior civilisation claimed a right and even an obligation to control the destiny of a people they saw as only partly or incompletely human. 'One of the functions of racism is to compensate the latent universalism of bourgeois liberalism: since all human beings have the same rights, the Algerian will be made a subhuman', exploitable and torturable with impunity.[67] In the process, the coloniser also hardened and dehumanised himself. Confronted by Algerians' concerted seizure of their own destiny, Europeans

> must face that unexpected revelation, the strip-tease of our humanism. There you can see it, quite naked, and it's not a pretty sight. It was nothing but an ideology of lies, a perfect justification for pillage ...

[W]ith us there is nothing more consistent than a racist humanism since the European has only been able to become a man through creating slaves and monsters.[68]

Yet Sartre responds to the inhumanity of imperialism by waving the humanist banners that the army, the government and also the people of France had besmirched. The lesson Sartre teaches us is that unless it is guided by the category of humanity, which entails agency and responsibility and which identifies properties and rights, then the process of decolonisation will involve no substantive break with a colonial system that robs its victims of their freedoms, strips them of rights and stamps out their potentials.

Sartre's critique of the Vietnam War is therefore of crucial significance. The aim of the American state, according to Sartre, was to discourage other recalcitrant movements and nations from challenging either American violence or the worldwide system which that violence underpins. Contentiously, Sartre characterised the war as genocidal, such was the disparity between the peasant army of the Vietnamese and the immeasurably superior technological prowess of their American invaders. Confronted by determined guerrilla warfare, the US waged a war of extermination that paid no heed to the distinction between civilians and combatants. All moral compunctions were subordinated to the strategic desire to entrench and extend American hegemony:

It is guilty, by its own admission, of knowingly conducting this war of 'example' to make genocide a challenge and a threat to all peoples. When a peasant dies in his rice field, cut down by a machine-gun, we are all hit. Therefore, the Vietnamese are fighting for all men and the American forces are fighting all of us. Not just in theory or in the abstract. And not only because genocide is a crime universally condemned by the rights of man. But because, little by little, this genocidal blackmail is spreading to all humanity, adding to the blackmail of atomic war. This crime is perpetrated under our eyes every day, making accomplices out of those who do not denounce it.

In this context, the imperialist genocide can become more serious. For the group that the Americans are trying to destroy by means of the Vietnamese nation is the whole of humanity.[69]

Paige Arthur calls this passage 'overwrought'.[70] But I think it captures the most important and salutary aspect of Sartre's revolutionary humanism. The point is not that by treating the Vietnamese as expendable 'subhumans' US imperialism was preventing them from emulating some established ideal of humanity. Rather, by so doing US imperialism was appropriating their right to life and to freedom and therefore forestalling the advent of a more just and equal world. There is nothing 'eschatological' here, as Azzedine Haddour alleges,[71] since although Sartre is convinced that full freedom necessitates post-capitalist social and economic arrangements, he does not say that these arrangements are inevitable. Furthermore, he invariably takes care to describe those arrangements as democratic and to distinguish them from the 'prefabricated socialism'[72] of the Soviet bloc. Humanism for Sartre is by definition egalitarian, voluntary and universal.

## THE HUMANISM OF EDWARD SAID

No text has done more to establish the antihumanist ambience of postcolonial studies than Edward Said's *Orientalism*.[73] The discipline that Said's study effectively founded in the late 1970s and early 1980s continues to be distinguished, if that's the right word, by its aversion to the rhetoric and aspirations of humanism. Postcolonialists are, to say the least, suspicious of the belief that subjects have rights that can be denied or recognised as well as capacities and needs that can either be thwarted or nurtured, even natures that can be alienated or fulfilled. There is no little irony, then, in the fact that the author of an influential work that is usually read as *anti*humanist was himself a convinced, if never less than discriminating, defender of the humanist tradition, a commitment that Said reiterated time and again both before and after the publication of *Orientalism*. My aim in this section is to show that Said did not reject the resources of humanist critique, whatever this anomalous and sometimes contradictory work has led many of his successors to believe. Said's formative work on the complex connections between culture and empire and on the continuing grip that the culture and violence of empire exert even in a supposedly 'postcolonial' world, was in fact guided and enabled by an approach and by convictions to which no other name can be given than the one that he himself used: humanist. It is true that Said was suspicious of Marxism for what he perceived, in my view wrongly, to be Marxism's obliviousness to imperialism and anti-imperialism, and for what he saw, no doubt correctly, as Marxism's chequered political record. But I hope it will be recognised that Said's avowedly humanist oeuvre is compatible with and even belongs to the tradition I have been outlining so far. Assuredly, it does not belong to the antihumanist tradition to which it is usually assigned and to which, in a sense, *Orientalism* perhaps inadvertently assigned itself.

Orientalism is of course the name that Said gives to a dense system of prejudices and preconceptions about the Middle East, a discourse lasting from Aeschylus to E. M. Forster, and from Goethe to Gerald Ford. One gets the impression from *Orientalism* that it has not been the systematic colonial ventures of Western powers, let alone the inseparability of those ventures from the imperatives of capitalism, but instead some sort of inherited cultural ignorance or 'will to power', that brought the discourse of Orientalism into being. Readers of that book might even be forgiven for thinking not only that Orientalism is a process without a subject, but that it also lacks victims and opponents. It is not that Said is foolish enough to think that there were no victims or opponents, but rather that *Orientalism* is declaredly uninterested in them, concentrating as it does on the consistency and durability of the discourse not on its effects or even on the differences between the societies of the Middle East and what the crudely simplifying discourse of Orientalism says about them. Said has surprisingly little to say about these societies, except to acknowledge their existence and then focus instead on the discourse that obscures them. Yet without the kind of emphasis on organised opposition to colonial rule that 1993's *Culture and Imperialism*[74] would later seek to add to the thesis set out in *Orientalism*, the earlier book has the unfortunate effect of implying that European ideas about the Middle East were much more all-encompassing, more seamlessly operative and effectively unchallenged than in fact they were in a region that was rarely subjected to protracted or formal Western European domination and that never ceased to resent and typically prevail over such impositions.

*Orientalism* set the agenda for postcolonial studies with its portrayal of the sheer density and intransience of the discourses that underpin colonial power. In *Orientalism*, Said characterises the durable repertoire of 'Western' ideas about the Middle East not as an ideology but, in Foucaultian terms, as a discourse. Or rather, he does both and hedges his bets between Gramsci and Foucault, the concept of hegemony and that of discourse. Hegemony, of course, implies a set of ideas (essentially 'the idea of European identity as a superior one in comparison with all the non-European peoples and cultures'[75]) that are employed to justify a particular system of domination. Those ideas form a component part of what is ultimately a violent and oppressive system, albeit one that is susceptible to (indeed, that for these reasons urgently compels) both critique and transformation. Discourse, however, is a more neutral term that says nothing about domination and is largely silent about the origin and purpose of the phenomenon that it names. To characterise Orientalism as a hegemony is to trace it to the objectionable and dispensable institution of class power, while describing it as a discourse implies that it is somehow intrinsic to the 'episteme' of the West and therefore necessarily ineradicable.

This frequent resort in *Orientalism* to a Foucaultian methodology therefore obscures Said's fairly modest and more immediately political claim, derived from Gramsci and from the Marxist tradition from which the Italian Communist is inseparable, that orthodox representations of the Middle East are ideological and have played and continue to play a crucial as well as exceptionable and contestable part in maintaining European (and latterly American) control in the region. To characterise Orientalism as a discourse, as Said does almost in the same breath, is to make a much more ambitious and far-reaching claim about 'the enormously systematic discipline by which European culture was able to manage – and even produce – the Orient politically, sociologically, militarily, ideologically, scientifically, and imaginatively during the post-Enlightenment period'.[76] One assumes, of course, that Orientalism does not literally produce the Orient, out of thin air as it were, but that it serves to construct an image of a consistent and knowable entity that actually bears little comparison with what are in reality the infinitely more diverse and complex societies of the Near and Middle East. But formulations like the one above go against every one of the emphases contained in the concept of hegemony: i.e. that power is pervasive but mutable and that its effects are comprehensive yet always limited and contested. A discourse, however, is so 'enormously systematic' that it is difficult, if not impossible, to get outside of and to censure.

So intensive and all-embracing is discursive power in Said's account, so insinuatingly efficient and so detached from the invidious business of physical coercion, that it runs the risk of ignoring the potential (and even the manifest fact) of organised political opposition to power. Of course, Foucault famously insists that power invariably engenders its opposite: 'Where there is power, there is resistance and yet this resistance is never in a position of exteriority in relation to power.'[77] Resistance takes place, Foucault concedes, but it does so at power's behest. This being the case, it hardly merits the term. For this kind of resistance is surely a poor substitute for revolution. If the latter indicates irreconcilable antagonism then the former denotes a kind of dependent or symbiotic relationship with power. As Moishe Postone argues, the rhetoric of resistance often goes hand in hand with an inability to identify the system supposedly being resisted or even really to countenance that system's transformation:

> The notion of resistance ... says little about the nature of that which is being resisted or of the politics of the resistance involved – that is, the character of determinate forms of critique, opposition, rebellion, and 'revolution.' The notion of resistance frequently expresses a deeply dualistic worldview that tends to reify both the system of domination and the idea of agency. It is rarely based on a reflexive analysis of possibilities for fundamental change that are both generated and suppressed by a dynamic heteronomous order.[78]

The idea of resistance extols agency but offers no judgements about the type of agency that should be undertaken by the oppressed. Moreover, it says nothing about strategy and goals. Nor does it name the system that is being resisted or even envisage openly that system's deposal and replacement, restricting itself instead to the reactive and defensive manoeuvres implied by the word in both English and French. Thus Bill Ashcroft's account of postcolonial resistance defines it as the 'subtle' and 'unspoken' 'form[s] of defence' by which 'an invader is "kept out"'. This kind of resistance is not organised or concerted or even conscious, and is not dedicated to anything as dogmatic as prevailing over or even opposing the thing it resists. 'Can one even resist without obviously "opposing"? The answer to this is obviously "yes!"'[79] That sort of answer is inseparable from a perception of helplessness, as Postone has argued; it connotes survival and defiance but not transformation. Indeed, Postone attributes what he calls 'the current impasse of the Left'[80] to the abandonment of an older anticapitalist idiom and the advent of a far less rigorous worldview that fails to identify the target of resistance and that fails to interrogate the often reactionary politics and frequently terroristic strategies of many self-styled 'resistance' movements. Indeed, by blurring distinctions between very different forms of political action, the undiscriminating acclamation of resistance leads to some crass political misjudgements.

We postcolonialists are not, surely, in favour of all reactions to dominant forms of power, but only of those responses that possess the moral and political resources necessary to supplant those forms. Postone reminds us that militant Islamism, for example, may be a form of resistance but it is hardly revolutionary. It has less to do with any genuine confrontation with dictatorship and with the precipitate economic decline in many predominantly Muslim countries than with anti-Semitism, misogyny and a totalitarian vision of a 'purified' society, none of which were top of the Left's traditional wish list. What Postone does not add, perhaps because he does not trace the popularity of the notion of resistance to the esteem in which Foucault's work is still held, is that Foucault himself made the very same misjudgement, as Kevin Anderson discusses in this collection, when his articles in the Italian newspaper *Corriere della Sera* trumpeted the Islamic forces that hijacked the Iranian revolution.[81]

In the end, the notion of resistance does nothing but cement in place the system it purports to oppose, which ironically is what Foucault believes to be the fate of the idea and practice of humanism: 'The man described for us, whom we are invited to free, is already in himself the effect of a subjection much more profound than himself.'[82] In Foucault's view, subjectivity is both the effect of power and the means by which power is articulated and enforced. To be a subject is already to be subjected, and therefore to inscribe humanist slogans on one's banners is unwittingly to confirm and endorse that subjection. Indeed, in a celebrated and lyrical passage, Foucault bids farewell not just to the idea of a unified and all-determining human subject (which the mostly Marxist thinkers against whom Foucault defined his own thinking had already rejected) but to human subjectivity itself:

> If the [arrangements of knowledge since the sixteenth century] were to disappear as they appeared, if some event of which we can at the moment do no more than sense the possibility – without knowing either what its form will be or what it promises – were to cause them to crumble, as the ground of Classical thought did, at the end of the eighteenth century, then one can certainly wager that man would be erased, like a face drawn in sand at the edge of the sea.[83]

This aversion to the prospect of a transformed and emancipated subjectivity has a deleterious effect on Foucault's work. Foucault leaves himself bereft of any vision of subjective freedom to set against the subject's domination by power. As Peter Dews has argued in relation to Foucault, 'a theory of power with radical intent requires an account of that which power dominates or represses, since without such an account relations of power must cease to appear objectionable'.[84] Candidates for this role in Foucault's work include, in *Madness and Civilization*, the expression of impulse and spontaneity, popular justice in the *ultra-gauchiste Discipline and Punish* of 1975 and the body and its pleasures in the later *History of Sexuality*. 'What is Enlightenment?', one of Foucault's last texts, even calls for a more nuanced approach to humanism and the Enlightenment, this last perhaps, Janet Afary and Kevin Anderson speculate,[85] as a result of having his fingers burnt by the tragic outcome of the revolution in Iran and the furore surrounding his support for its Islamist turn.

It is perhaps his awareness of these shortcomings in Foucault's work that led Said, in several texts written after *Orientalism*, to offer a lengthy appraisal of what he saw as the limitations of Foucault's characterisation of power. 'Criticism Between Culture and System' concedes that Foucault had done very constructive work in exposing the interestedness and violence frequently hidden beneath the discourses of rationality and scientific objectivity. Yet Foucault had neither illuminated the sources of power nor laid enough emphasis in his work on power's limitations and weak points. Indeed, Foucault had actually obscured power's origins in ruling classes and dominant interests. His work portrayed power instead, misleadingly, as 'a spider's web without the spider'[86] and, Said might have added, without any flies either. Why power is exercised and by whom are questions rarely if ever broached by Foucault. Moreover, contests between classes, societies and ideologies are largely absent from Foucault's work, which 'takes a curiously passive and sterile view not so much of the uses of power, but of how and why power is gained, used, and held onto'.[87]

> In understandably wishing to avoid the crude notion that power is unmediated domination, Foucault more or less eliminates the central dialectic of opposed forces that still underlies modern society, despite the apparently perfected methods of 'technocratic' control and seemingly nonideological efficiency that seem to govern everything. What one misses in Foucault is something resembling Gramsci's analyses of hegemony, historical blocks, ensembles of relationship done from the perspective of an engaged political worker for whom

the fascinated description of exercised power is never a substitute for trying to change power relationships within society.[88]

Said soon recognised that Foucault's portrayal of power as inexorable had induced him to ignore the possibility and desirability – quite apart from the manifest *actuality* – of political struggle against the effects of discursive power and against the social and economic order on which discursive power rests.

No matter how it may be made to appear in texts or how it looks from privileged cultural perspectives, power rarely manifests itself in history in ways that are unproblematic and unopposed, let alone non-corporeal: 'history', Said reminds us, 'is not a homogeneous French-speaking territory but a complex interaction between uneven economies, societies, and ideologies'.[89] To pretend otherwise is to characterise power as ineluctable and, just as unhelpfully, to portray power as a kind of performance addressed not to the body but, as Foucault puts it, to the soul. Yet to speak of power becoming a discourse is, to borrow a phrase from Susan Sontag, a breathtaking provincialism.[90] Foucault's scholarly work, which is barely far-reaching enough to be called Eurocentric, never addresses situations in which direct physical violence (as opposed to disembodied techniques of control) is still the principal means by which power is inflicted, most of which are outside the region with which his work is immediately concerned and many of which have been controlled historically by the nations whose histories interest him above all others. This soft-pedalling of power's inseparability from violence is especially problematic when it comes to giving an account of how power operates in the colonial and postcolonial worlds. The reason for Said's more or less total renunciation of Foucault's work and therefore also the reason why I think postcolonial scholarship should likewise ditch Foucault's characteristic emphases and look instead to other, more enabling antecedents, is that we cannot come close to an accurate theorisation of colonial power without acknowledging its inseparability from violence and its fallibility as well as its resulting vulnerability to moral critique and political transformation. Foucault's work's most grievous flaws, for Said, are its inadvertent parochialism and its tendency to depict power as all-penetrating and inexorable. Resulting from this was Foucault's inability to even countenance revolutionary historical change.[91] The point is that the critic, if he or she is to merit that title, has an obligation not just to describe power but also to explain its existence, trace its origins, criticise its effects and beseech its dissolution.

I have gone to some trouble to demonstrate and explain the reasons for Said's renunciation of the antihumanist dimensions of Foucault's work. This was so I can now go on to show in precise terms how and why Said subsequently sought to present the processes of colonial power and of revolutionary opposition to colonial power from an unmistakably, indeed avowedly, humanist perspective. It is worth pausing to note, however, that the discipline his early work inspired has not followed him down that path. 'Power' for Foucault is ubiquitous and perdurable; it is attended by 'resistance', which is similarly everywhere and everlasting. Foucault makes no moral judgements about power or about resistance. Content with describing this *pas de deux*, his philosophy contains no perspective on liberation. In Said's work, by contrast, precisely because that work is inspired by humanist convictions, 'power' is characterised quite differently, as a historical (rather than a metaphysical) phenomenon, as a system to which a name can be given, that can be subjected to critique and that has been placed on borrowed time by political projects that aim not just to resist but actively to transform and replace power.

Nobody needs me to tell them that *Orientalism*'s influence in postcolonial studies, a discipline it effectively founded and whose characteristic methodological and political emphases it therefore helped to shape, has been immense. Yet that book decidedly exaggerates the durability, scope and intensity of the colonial discourse it maps out, it obscures colonialism's origin and purpose, and it postpones until later work any attention to those *anti*colonial projects whose aspirations were so far-reaching and, at least in their early years, so staggeringly successful that it would be simply churlish to dismiss them as mere acts of 'resistance'. 'Colonial discourse', a concept whose adoption is in many ways postcolonial theory's original sin, has been portrayed as an expansive, subjectless and ineluctable phenomenon insinuated through discreet rituals and performances. Even when texts are declared to 'hybridise' colonial discourse, or else subject it to the rejoinders of 'difference', there is rarely any sense that colonial discourse might fundamentally be undermined, let alone overthrown – the Sisyphean labour of 'subverting' colonial discourse being what keeps us in work. Postcolonial critics have commonly been suspicious of categories like class. Little wonder, because capitalism is not a word frequently heard from their lips. Indeed, the discipline has been prone to muffle ongoing forms of imperial domination with the comforting rhetoric of globalisation and hybridity. Postcolonialists are indignant about 'Eurocentrism' (which is an idea) but rarely exercised by ongoing forms of imperialism (which is also a particularly brutal practice), in addition to being curiously silent about capitalism (which has been as willing as ever to bare its teeth since the 1970s and without reference to which the phenomenon of imperialism becomes literally incomprehensible). As far back as Aijaz Ahmad's *In Theory* (1992), postcolonial theory's left wing has arraigned the discipline for its most prominent critics' frankly idealist belief that it was not capitalist imperialism that structured and explained the world but more cultural or 'discursive' constructions like Eurocentrism, racism or nationalism:

> An obvious consequence of repudiating Marxism was that one now sought to make sense of the world of colonies and empires much less in terms of classes, much more in terms of nations and countries and races, and thought of imperialism itself not as a hierarchically structured system of global capitalism but as a *relation*, of governance and occupation, between richer and poorer countries, West and non-West. And whether one said so or not, one inevitably believed that ideas – 'culture' was the collective term in most mystifications, or 'discourse', but it mainly meant books and films – and not the material conditions of life which include the instance of culture itself, determine the fate of people and nations.[92]

Eurocentrism, racism and nationalism, along with patriarchy for that matter, precisely because they were seen as mostly cultural phenomena, could be opposed by defending difference or invoking hybridity, laudable endeavours of course but also incomplete or at least insufficient. The consequences of what Arif Dirlik has called this 'shift in attention to questions of cultural identity in postcolonial discourse'[93] are at once theoretical and practical; theoretical because the phenomenon of capitalist imperialism thereby escapes our conceptual nets, practical because energies are then devoted to 'hybridising' the West or defending difference from it, undertakings for which the category of capitalism, let alone the practice of *anti*capitalism, is simply nugatory. This is the 'postcolonial unconscious' as Lazarus defines it. Postcolonial theorists look for 'resistance' in 'mimicry', 'migrancy', 'hybridity', 'ambivalence', 'subalternity', 'liminality' or the 'multitude', all of which are terms that have in common an assumption that struggle takes place not against the system of capitalist imperialism (though it is rarely called that) but within that system and even at its behest.

Happily, Said's later work set about qualifying and even repudiating many of the key claims made in what would prove to be a quite anomalous early book in the context of a sizeable oeuvre that remained militantly humanist in both its methodology and its political convictions. Insofar as it has hitched its wagon to post-structuralist philosophies like that of Foucault, postcolonial theory has, by contrast, been dragged too far from the political and intellectual commitments of its founding thinker and, in what amounts to the same thing, from the original convictions and aspirations of anticolonialism. *Orientalism*'s readers were led astray by the unnecessary and incongruous references to Foucault, who if Lazarus is to be believed was perhaps name-checked in that book for tactical reasons in order to ease the book's reception by 'leftist' scholars for whom Foucault was *de rigueur* at the time of *Orientalism*'s publication. Said's humanism, however, presents the 'discourse' of Orientalism very differently. The whole of the rest of Said's work, from his early work on the philosophy of 'beginnings' through his advocacy of the rights and aspirations of his Palestinian compatriots to his later writings on music and aesthetic style, is premised on an unmistakably and avowedly, not to mention gleefully and sometimes provocatively unrepentant, *humanist* stress on the limits to discursive power. Said was no Marxist of course, or at least he professed himself, understandably enough, extremely ambivalent about Marxism's political record.[94] But Said's desire to attend not just to the cobweb but to the spider, to the fly and to the web's frailty certainly makes his work in my view compatible with Marxism. His later work is adamant in particular that the limits to discursive power are set and exemplified by the ideas of human solidarity and human freedom which were articulated most powerfully by the first generation of anticolonial movements, whose achievements Said celebrated, whose defeat he mourned and whose transformative aspirations he longed to reignite.

Said, in short, traced his own approach not to Foucault, whose name continued to be ubiquitous in postcolonial scholars' work long after he had ceased dropping it, but to the premises and principles of humanist intellectual practice articulated by half-forgotten American literary critics like R. P. Blackmur, Richard Poirier and Lionel Trilling, and especially by German comparative philologists like Erich Auerbach and Leo Spitzer.[95] In one of his last books, *Humanism and Democratic Criticism*, Said outlines what he sees as the two chief precepts of humanist practice. The first is the deceptively straightforward proposition that that which has been humanly made (and which is subject neither to the laws unearthed by the natural sciences nor to the unchanging verities pondered by metaphysicians) is uniquely susceptible to analysis and change. Societies, dogmas, texts and the very mores and ideas of the self are variable products of human work. Because they were conceived and made they can be reconceived and remade. Knowledge, however, is not uncontroversial or easily gained. Glossing Vico, Said remarks upon the mind's fallibility, its passionate rather than dispassionate nature and its unavoidable entanglement with interests and situations. Knowledge of what is humanly constructed is always incomplete and provisional, a thing to be negotiated, interrogated and improved. Hence humanism entails a taste for self-renewal and a restless impatience with the mind's dogmas: 'humanism is critique'.[96] Indeed, this is the special vocation of the humanities in general, which provoke critical scrutiny of humanly produced institutions and ideas. What makes humans human, in other words, is their distinctive capacity for critical self-knowledge or, in the philologist Leo Spitzer's memorable phrase, 'the power bestowed on the human mind of investigating the human mind'.[97] The distinctive (though not necessarily superior) human capacity, the thing that allows us in Sartre's words 'to establish the human kingdom as a pattern of values in distinction from the material world',[98] is consciousness or, if you like, the consciousness of consciousness. Self-criticism, then, is the first precept of Said's humanism. The second is the kind of cosmopolitan moral intelligence that can result from self-criticism. Humanists' interrogation of partial and limited perspectives can engender a newly ecumenical respect for humanity in its entirety. If self-criticism is one of the twin poles of humanistic endeavour therefore, then the second is the potential of self-criticism to broaden one's sympathies as well as one's sense of moral and finally political obligation. Said is a defender of humanism in the sense of what the humanities do (which is to examine humanly made phenomena like texts, ideas and institutions) as well as humanism in the sense of human rights (that is, the belief in the dignity, equality and value of all human life contained in Seneca's great dictum: 'nothing human is alien to me').

Having established the twin principles of humanistic endeavour, *Humanism and Democratic Criticism* goes on to elucidate the special attributes required of the American humanist in the wake of 9/11 and the United States' belligerent response. For a start, democratic humanism contrasts with the provincial version of this creed espoused by the enthusiasts for 'humanitarian intervention'. Nor does it have anything to do with any unselfconscious defence of one's own culture against interlopers, not just because America – as Said is at pains to stress – is a society made up of immigrants and therefore in conception if not always in fact a multifarious and hospitable place, but more importantly because it is of the very nature of humanistic activity to upset, interrogate and reformulate ostensible certainties. They cannot long survive the knowledge of self and world to which humanistic scrutiny gives rise. Critical consciousness or, put differently, a biting distrust of received wisdom is the humanist's customary mode. A form of incessant questioning, humanism necessitates a militant critique of jingoistic ideologies and a practical refusal to tolerate distant suffering:

> Principally it means situating critique at the heart of humanism, critique as a form of democratic freedom and as a continuous practice of questioning and of accumulating knowledge that is open to, rather than in denial of, the constituent historical realities of the post-Cold War world, its early colonial formation, and the frighteningly global reach of the last remaining superpower of today.[99]

Without criticism, as W. J. T. Mitchell has argued, glossing Said, humanism tends to be a sterile and complacent reverence for the cultural superiority of the West; without humanism, however, criticism is nothing but empty quibbling.[100]

Saree Makdisi has argued that Said's inclusive humanism was inseparable from his vision of a 'one state solution' in Israel/Palestine. Peace there will be the outcome not of the various ideologies of ethnic, racial or religious distinctness and separation but of an acceptance, which is clearly far easier to say than to do, that 'the other' is human and has rights. For the Israelis, whose superior political and military clout and whose blame for expelling, occupying and tyrannising the Palestinians over the decades places on them a greater responsibility to bring such a reconciliation about, peace means resolving to treat the Palestinians not as bothersome nuisances that obstruct and frustrate Israel's exclusive entitlement to the land and its resources but as partners in pursuit of a just settlement. For the Palestinians, it means abandoning the millenarian fantasies of religious sects and the futile dream of overpowering their adversaries by force of arms, while talking to persuadable Israelis, campaigning in the West for pressure to be placed on governments that indulge Israel's unconscionable occupation and repudiating the failed and unimaginative policies of their own undemocratic, short-termist leadership. In Makdisi's words, 'the idea of Palestine is a struggle for the articulation of a new sense of what it means to be human'.[101] In Said's:

> The real strength of the Palestinian is just this insistence on the human being *as a detail* – the detail likely to be swept away in order for a grandiose project to be realized. The Palestinian therefore stands on a small plot of land stubbornly called Palestine, or an idea of peace based neither on a project for transforming people into nonpeople nor on a geopolitical fantasy about the balance of power, but on a vision of the future accommodating both of the peoples with authentic claims to Palestine, not just the Jews [...] In the end, it is finally the humblest and the most basic instrument that will bring peace, and certainly that instrument is not a fighter plane or a rifle butt. This instrument is self-conscious rational struggle conducted in the interests of human community.[102]

Humanism = critical thinking + the ideal of solidarity.

## CONCLUSION

The likes of Sartre and Fanon were faced with an ideology – Western humanism and the discourse of rights – that excluded most of the world's population. 'What was required, therefore,' as Robert Young argues in his preface to the Routledge collection of Sartre's essays on colonialism and neocolonialism, 'was either to do away with the concept of humanism altogether, or, more positively, to articulate a new anti-racist humanism, which would be inclusive rather than exclusive, and which would be the product of those who formed the majority of its new totality.'[103] Why hasn't this second approach found a more receptive audience among postcolonialists? Paige Arthur notes the suspicion in France in the 1970s of Sartre's Marxism. She mentions the *nouveaux philosophes'* crude equation of communism with totalitarianism and their equally simplistic attribution of dictatorship in the *tiers monde* to the original objectives of anticolonial nationalism. The system had stood firm against the revolutionary swell of May 1968 and against the feeble barbs of that event's Maoist progeny. The likes of Bernard-Henri Lévy made a good living out of retro certainties about the Cold War and *la mission civilisatrice*. No doubt this anti-Marxist reaction was part of a wider intellectual hostility to the *grands récits* of enlightenment and emancipation, which as we have seen is also part of the intellectual climate of postcolonial theory, a discipline that was brought into being at this time. Yet while such objectives might have seemed passé to a disenchanted Western intelligentsia, they retain their force for thinkers and movements in (or concerned with) other parts of the world. There the goal of universal emancipation has lost none of its urgency in the overbearing context of neocolonial retrenchment. As Patrick Williams observes, 'too many critics have been unable to get beyond the simple equating of humanism with the unsatisfactory Enlightenment version', thereby 'ignoring and jettisoning' all that the likes of Césaire, Fanon and Sartre hoped for.[104]

Still, I think we can be quite optimistic about the future of the discipline. For even one of the authors I criticised earlier for conflating the idea of a 'common humanity' with imperialism, Helen Tiffin, accepts in a recent book on postcolonial studies and the environment (co-written with Graham Huggan) that humanism might not have attracted quite so many adherents over the years had it represented nothing more than a bellicose assertion of the sovereignty of white men over the rest of the world. Tiffin and Huggan manage to affirm the longevity of a tradition, which this chapter has tried to commend and explain, as well as indicate the nature of future theoretical and critical work, when they acclaim a 'postcolonial humanism' for which 'the historically necessary decolonisation of the "human" leads not to a *post-* but a *pan-*humanism that opens up more generous understandings of the human defined in terms of cross-cultural solidarity and achievement rather than those more likely to seek shelter in comforting notions of cultural particularity and the privileges of birth'.[105]

Only now, prompted perhaps by the resurgent imperialism of the 'war on terror' and by the perennial inequalities made worse by the unabated (if not accelerating) project of neoliberalism, is postcolonial theory beginning to attend, in its theoretical as well as its critical work, to the specifically *human* dimensions of oppression and liberation. Iraq's assailants, openly scornful of international law and conspicuously motivated by corporate voracity, have unwittingly done us the service of discrediting the postcolonial field's constitutive assumption that we come *after* colonialism and not in colonialism's turbulent midst. By all means let us agree to keep the term 'postcolonial', provided we construe it not as a descriptive category, the temporal or historical prefix of which can mislead us into thinking that the work of decolonisation has been completed or at least that the world's persistent imbalances are just a legacy of extinct structures, but rather as a goal or aspiration, one to which the connotations of transformation and liberation are attached.

I have been calling for a return to the libertarian dimension of Marxism. The responsibility for the low esteem in which even libertarian strains of Marxism are held cannot all be laid at the door of the anti-Marxists. Since Marxism, in the shape of the slow death of the Soviet bloc under Brezhnev and his successors, of the gigantic catastrophes and convulsions of China under Mao, of the deformed and deflected revolutions of the 'Third World' and of the depressing sclerosis of the labour movement in Western Europe, had shown itself incapable of real introspection and reform, *post*-Marxism came along to bury it. Only a humanist Marxism can resist this fate. Stalinism was the result of the Bolsheviks' failure to replace, or even to resist the temptation to intensify, the authoritarian methods of the state they had inherited. The Left has failed to surmount this legacy, and no doubt will continue to do so, unless and until it finds a way of repudiating the methods of coercion and manipulation that characterise the system from which it seeks to break free. That the quest for libertarian values with which to guide this process has been undertaken most promisingly by a diverse tradition from *within* Marxism (rather than by theoretical and political traditions taken up *against* Marxism) is the main claim for which I have been trying to provide evidence.

One looks in vain in the works of the thinkers I have been examining for any assertions that subjectivity is static, unitary, centred or entirely self-determining. Rather, human subjectivity is conceived there as dynamic and developing in history. 'We may not know what absolute good is or the absolute norm,' as Adorno argues, 'we may not even know what man is or the human or humanity – but what the inhuman is we know very well indeed.'[106] Humanity constitutes a principle of opposition and an agent of transformation. A postcolonial humanism would therefore be a humanism based not just on humanist conceptions of the value and equality of human life but also on a rigorous critical approach towards all those complacent and unselfconscious humanisms that have bedevilled the world since the concept's revival in the eighteenth and nineteenth centuries: the racist humanism of the Comte de Gobineau, the colonial humanisms of the European powers, and what Chomsky has called the 'new military humanism'[107] of the twenty-first century. What I have been objecting to is the mistaken assumption that one local, self-serving definition of humanity should be taken to be true of all humankind. In Said's terms, this is political humanism shorn of its intellectual complement, an ambitious universalism bereft of self-knowledge.

Though they might dislike the term 'postcolonial', the many materialist critics who are working within that field as well as against some of its primary emphases, have sought to sharpen postcolonialism's critical and political edges by keeping alive the memory of an anticolonial tradition that is, as Benita Parry has put it, 'grounded in a Marxist humanism'. That tradition has 'inveighed against the abuse of humanism and universalism when these ideas were mendaciously invoked to disguise capitalist exploitation and colonial malpractices'. But it did not, crucially, 'disown their ethical potential or abandon their liberatory usages, a stance shared by theorists in colonized worlds who aspired to realize the *unfulfilled* enlightenment notions of reason, justice, and egalitarianism'.[108] Humanism may have been put to use by imperialism but that does not make all humanisms imperialist.

A commonly heard criticism of human rights discourse is that it is, to use Samuel Moyn's term, depoliticising.[109] That discourse implies and sometimes explicitly asserts that it is the responsibility of the powers that abuse those rights to desist and treat their victims differently. No perspective on transforming or replacing those authorities is contained in the discourse. Rights discourse, Jodi Dean adds, shrinks 'the scope of political claims to those of victims needing recognition and redress'.[110] To speak at all one must demonstrate one's weakness and vulnerability, thus conferring the responsibility for redress to established powers that inflicted the injury in the first place. The systematic nature of the problem and the comprehensive character of the solution are therefore concealed. The plight of the Palestinians, for example, is often referred to as a 'humanitarian crisis', as though they were the helpless victims of a flood whose fate is to be managed by outside powers, dealt with and occasionally relieved. Minority discourse must instead be seen as a step taken towards a substantive ideal of equality not a desperate form of special pleading that leaves the system itself intact. Respect for human rights, especially the radical social and economic rights contained in the Universal Declaration (rights to work, a decent pension, a minimum wage, an education, free healthcare and so on), cannot be achieved without also addressing the massive inequalities that structure the world: 'There can be no true installation of human rights without the end of exploitation, no true end of exploitation without the installation of human rights', in Bloch's invaluable dictum.[111]

The more postcolonialism recognises the importance of this formulation the more I believe it will start to grasp the pertinence and cogency of its Marxist antecedents, or, in other and simpler though possibly more contentious words, the more Marxist it will become. I am therefore repeating the call issued by the editors of an important volume on the state of the discipline for postcolonial studies to envision transformative and even utopian alternatives to this situation: '[W]hat visions of a postcolonial world can we as humanists offer that will interrogate, perhaps even interrupt, the forms of globalization now dictated by politicians, military strategists, captains of finance and industry, fundamentalist preachers and theologians, terrorists of the body and the spirit, in short, by the masters of our contemporary universe?'[112]

Postcolonialists ought to recognise the sheer magnitude and durability of a world system that has succeeded in halting and frequently reversing many of the achievements of anticolonial movements since independence. They also need to name that system and beseech its transformation. Ultimately, postcolonial criticism is a discipline guided by moral and political investments.

The task I have set myself is to show that this libertarian humanism or, as Edward Said calls it, democratic humanism has nothing whatever in common with the Eurocentric, exclusionary and teleological version that postcolonialists have understandably repudiated. Postcolonialism is a humanism because humanism gives us a rhetoric with which to reprove the system of imperialism and both a guide and motive for combating it. Humanism gives us a vocabulary with which to denounce the failings of a form of social and economic organisation that sacrifices human potential, human need and even human life to abstract goals of profit and utility. Humanism also enables us to distinguish reactionary and even fascist anti-imperialisms from progressive anti-imperialisms. We need to be clearer about our adversary – which is capital and its indispensable partner-in-crime imperialism, both of which are occluded by abstract references to 'the West' and 'Empire' – as well as much more confident and unambiguous about our goals. Decolonisation is the wilful and insistent seizure of the status of humanity, of a subjective freedom that is even today under mortal threat both from local despots and from the intercessions of those states that march into their former colonies under the duplicitously raised banner of universal human rights. Ideas about humanity and rights have been used as a justification for exploitation and control right down to the present vogue for 'humanitarian intervention'. But those ideas could hardly exercise such appeal and fascination, could not in fact aspire to be hegemonic, if they did not also contain a promise of liberation. As ever, humanist principles are more honoured in the breach than the observance. In fact they have been misused to such an extent that they sometimes no longer mean what they should mean or what they might have meant had numerous groups not been discouraged for centuries from participating in the process of their definition. Nevertheless, humanism remains the only feasible basis of protest and transformation. 'If only I knew a better term than humanity', as Max Horkheimer once lamented: 'that poor, provincial slogan of a half-educated European. But I don't.'[113] That's because there isn't one.

## NOTES

1. Karl Marx, 'The Indian Revolt (1857)', in Robert J. Antonio (ed.), *Marx and Modernity*, Oxford: Blackwell, 2003, pp. 190–3.
2. Martin Heidegger, 'Letter on Humanism', in *Basic Writings*, ed. David Farrell Krell, London: Routledge, 1993, p. 226.
3. Ibid., p. 232.
4. Bill Ashcroft, Gareth Griffiths and Helen Tiffin, *Post-Colonial Studies: The Key Concepts*, London: Routledge, 2000, p. 235.
5. Bill Ashcroft, Gareth Griffiths and Helen Tiffin, *The Post-Colonial Studies Reader*, 2nd edition, London: Routledge , 2006, p. 71.
6. Gayatri Chakravorty Spivak, *In Other Worlds: Essays in Cultural Politics*, London: Routledge, 1988, p. 202.
7. Neil Lazarus, 'Postcolonial Studies after the Invasion of Iraq', *New Formations*, 59 (2006), pp. 10–22, p. 16.
8. Bill Ashcroft and Pal Ahluwalia, *Edward Said*, 2nd edition, London: Routledge, 2008, pp. 142–8.
9. R. Radhakrishnan, *A Said Dictionary*, Oxford: Wiley-Blackwell, 2012, pp. 42–7.
10. Bruce Robbins, 'Race, Gender, Class, Postcolonialism: Toward a New Humanistic Paradigm?', in Henry Schwarz and Sangeeta Ray (eds), *A Companion to Postcolonial Studies*, Oxford: Blackwell, 2000, p. 567.

11. E. M. Forster, *A Passage to India*, London: Edward Arnold, 1987 [1924], pp. 270–1.

12. Anthony C. Alessandrini, 'The Humanism Effect: Fanon, Foucault, and Ethics without Subjects', *Foucault Studies*, 7 (2009), pp. 64–80, p. 78.

13. Martin Halliwell and Andy Mousley, *Critical Humanisms: Humanist/ Anti-Humanist Dialogues*, Edinburgh: Edinburgh University Press, 2003.

14. Jean Améry, *Radical Humanism: Selected Essays*, ed. and trans. by Sidney Rosenfeld and Stella P. Rosenfeld, Bloomington: Indiana University Press, 1984.

15. Karen Green, *The Woman of Reason: Feminism, Humanism and Political Thought*, London: Continuum, 1995.

16. Theodor W. Adorno, *Lectures on Negative Dialectics: Fragments of a Lecture Course, 1965/66*, ed. Rolf Tiedemann, trans. Rodney Livingstone, Cambridge: Polity, 2008, p. 19.

17. Homi K. Bhabha, 'Foreword: Framing Fanon', Frantz Fanon, *The Wretched of the Earth*, trans. Richard Philcox, New York: Grove Press, 2004 [1961], pp. vii–xli.

18. Among the many incisive critiques of these developments are Priyamvada Gopal, 'How Universities Die', *South Atlantic Quarterly*, Vol. 111, No. 2 (2012), pp. 383–91; Stefan Collini, *What Are Universities For?* Harmondsworth: Penguin, 2012; and Chris Lorenz, 'If You're So Smart, Why Are You under Surveillance? Universities, Neoliberalism, and New Public Management', *Critical Inquiry*, 38 (2012), pp. 599–629.

19. See Aijaz Ahmad, 'The Politics of Literary Postcoloniality', *Race and Class*, Vol. 36, No. 3 (1995), pp. 1–20.

20. Neil Lazarus and Rashmi Varma, 'Marxism and Postcolonial Studies', Jacques Bidet and Stathis Kouvelakis (eds), *Critical Companion to Contemporary Marxism*, Leiden: Brill, 2008, p. 309.

21. Neil Lazarus, *The Postcolonial Unconscious*, Cambridge: Cambridge University Press, 2011, p. 9.

22. Ernest Mandel, *Long Waves of Capitalist Development*, Cambridge: Cambridge University Press, 1980.

23. Lazarus and Varma, p. 312.

24. Sara Suleri, *The Rhetoric of English India*, Chicago: University of Chicago Press, 1992, p. 2.

25. Anthony C. Alessandrini, 'Humanism in Question: Fanon and Said', in Henry Schwarz and Sangeeta Ray (eds), *A Companion to Postcolonial Studies*, Oxford: Blackwell, 2000, p. 448.

26. Theodor Adorno, *Minima Moralia: Reflections from Damaged Life*, trans. E. F. N. Jephcott, London: New Left Books, 1974, p. 156.

27. Edward W. Said, *Culture and Imperialism*, London: Vintage, 1994, p. 336.

28. Erich Fromm (ed.), *Socialist Humanism: An International Symposium*, New York: Doubleday, 1965, pp. ix–iv.

29. Ernst Bloch, *Natural Law and Human Dignity*, trans. by Dennis J. Schmidt, Cambridge, MA: MIT Press, 1987 [1961], p. xxix.

30. Ibid., p. 203.

31. Ibid., p. 205.
32. Ibid., p. 192.
33. Herbert Marcuse, *An Essay on Liberation*, Harmondsworth: Penguin, 1972 [1969], p. 88.
34. Herbert Marcuse, *Eros and Civilization: A Philosophical Inquiry into Freud*, London: Abacus, 1969 [1955].
35. Marcuse, *An Essay on Liberation*, p. 17.
36. See Douglas Kellner on how, rather than abandoning subjectivity, Marcuse envisages subjectivity's progressive transformation. Douglas Kellner, 'Marcuse and the Quest for Radical Subjectivity', in John Abromeit and W. Mark Cobb (eds), *Herbert Marcuse: A Critical Reader*, London: Routledge, 2004, pp. 81–99.
37. Marcuse, *An Essay on Liberation*, pp. 20–1.
38. Ibid., p. 23.
39. Marcuse, *Eros and Civilization*, p. 115.
40. Ibid., p. 137.
41. Theodor Adorno, 'Letter to Walter Benjamin', in Theodor Adorno et al., *Aesthetics and Politics*, London: Verso, 1977, pp. 120–6, p. 125.
42. Robert Spencer, 'Thoughts from Abroad: Theodor Adorno as Postcolonial Theorist', *Culture, Theory, Critique*, Vol. 51, No. 3 (2010), pp. 207–21.
43. Theodor W. Adorno, *Can One Live after Auschwitz? A Philosophical Reader*, Stanford, CA: Stanford University Press, 2003, p. 121.
44. Marcuse, *An Essay on Liberation*, p. 17.
45. Marcuse, 'Political Preface 1966', *Eros and Civilization*, p. 12.
46. Theodor W. Adorno, *Negative Dialectics*, trans. E. B. Ashton, London: Routledge, 1996 [1966], p. 285.
47. Jean-Paul Sartre, *Being and Nothingness: An Essay on Phenomenological Ontology*, trans. Hazel E. Barnes, London: Routledge, 1958 [1943].
48. Jean-Paul Sartre, *Nausea*, trans. Robert Baldick, Harmondsworth: Penguin, 2000 [1938], p. 188.
49. Jean-Paul Sartre, *Existentialism is a Humanism*, trans. Philip Mairet, London: Methuen, 1948, p. 46.
50. Ibid., pp. 26–8.
51. Ibid., p. 28.
52. Fredric Jameson, *Marxism and Form: Twentieth-Century Dialectical Theories of Literature*, Princeton, NJ: Princeton University Press, 1971, p. 268.
53. Sartre, *Existentialism is a Humanism*, p. 54.
54. Ibid., p. 55.
55. Ibid., p. 55.
56. Ibid., p. 56.
57. Sartre, *Being and Nothingness*, p. 628.
58. Paige Arthur, *Unfinished Projects: Decolonization and the Philosophy of Jean-Paul Sartre*, London: Verso, 2010, p. 69.
59. Alexander Zevin, 'Critique of Neo-Colonial Reason', *New Left Review*, 70 (2011), p. 148.

60. Herbert Marcuse, 'Existentialism: Remarks on Jean-Paul Sartre's *L'Être et le Néant*', *Philosophy and Phenomenological Research*, Vol. 8, No. 3 (1948), p. 311.

61. Ibid., p. 331.

62. Ibid., p. 335. This essay appeared in an edited version in Marcuse's 1972 *Studies in Critical Philosophy*. The postscript praises Sartre's efforts to reconcile his politics and his philosophy in the years after the first publication of Marcuse's essay in 1948.

63. Adorno, *Negative Dialectics*, pp. 49–51.

64. Zevin, 'Critique of Neo-Colonial Reason', p. 143.

65. See Azzedine Haddour on Camus' and Sartre's very different approaches to the 'crise en Algérie'. Azzedine Haddour, 'The Camus–Sartre Debate and the Colonial Question in Algeria', in Charles Forsdick (ed.), *Francophone Postcolonial Studies: A Critical Introduction*, London: Arnold, 2003, pp. 66–76.

66. Jean-Paul Sartre, *Colonialism and Neocolonialism*, trans. Azzedine Haddour, Steve Brewer and Terry McWilliams, London: Routledge, 2001, pp. 175–223.

67. Jean-Paul Sartre, *Critique of Dialectical Reason*, vol 1, trans. Alan Sheridan-Smith, London: Verso, 1991 [1960], p. 51.

68. Jean-Paul Sartre, 'Preface' to Fanon, *The Wretched of the Earth*, trans. Constance Farrington, Harmondsworth: Penguin, 1990, p. 21.

69. Jean-Paul Sartre, 'On Genocide', in Peter Limqueco and Peter Weiss (eds), *Prevent the Crime of Silence: Reports from the Sessions of the International War Crimes Tribunal*, London: Allen Lane, 1971, pp. 364–5.

70. Arthur, *Unfinished Projects*, p. 162.

71. Azzedine Haddour, 'Introduction: Remembering Sartre', in Jean-Paul Sartre, *Colonialism and Neocolonialism*, trans. Azzedine Haddour, Steve Brewer and Terry McWilliams, London: Routledge, 2001, p. 13.

72. Jean-Paul Sartre, *Between Existentialism and Marxism*, trans. John Matthews, London: Verso, 2008, p. 92.

73. Edward W. Said, *Orientalism*, Harmondsworth: Penguin, 1985 [1978].

74. Edward W. Said, *Culture and Imperialism*, London: Vintage, 1993.

75. Said, *Orientalism*, p. 7.

76. Ibid., p. 3.

77. Michel Foucault, *The Will to Knowledge, The History of Sexuality*, vol. 1, trans. Robert Hurley, Harmondsworth: Penguin, 1990 [1975], p. 95.

78. Moishe Postone, 'History and Helplessness: Mass Mobilization and Contemporary Forms of Anticapitalism', *Public Culture*, Vol. 18, No. 1 (2006), p. 108.

79. Bill Ashcroft, *Post-Colonial Transformation*, London: Routledge, 2001, p. 20.

80. Postone, 'History and Helplessness', p. 102.

81. See also Kevin Anderson, and Janet Afary, *Foucault and the Iranian Revolution: Gender and the Seductions of Islamism*, Chicago: University of Chicago Press, 2005.

82. Michel Foucault, *Discipline and Punish: The Birth of the Prison*, trans. Alan Sheridan, Harmondsworth: Penguin, 1991, p. 30.

83. Michel Foucault, *The Order of Things: An Archaeology of the Human Sciences*, London: Tavistock, 1970, p. 387.

84. Peter Dews, *Logics of Disintegration: Post-structuralist Thought and the Claims of Critical Theory*, London: Verso, 1987, p. 145.

85. Afary and Anderson, *Foucault and the Iranian Revolution*, p. 137.

86. Edward W. Said, 'Criticism Between Culture and System', *The World, the Text, and the Critic*, Cambridge, MA: Harvard University Press, 1983, p. 221.

87. Ibid., p. 221.

88. Ibid., pp. 221–2.

89. Ibid., p. 222.

90. Sontag's original formulation, aimed at Baudrillard's bluster about the first Gulf War, says that '[t]o speak of reality becoming a spectacle is a breathtaking provincialism.' Susan Sontag, *Regarding the Pain of Others*, London: Hamish Hamilton, 2003, p. 98.

91. Said, 'Criticism Between Culture and System', p. 188.

92. Aijaz Ahmad, *In Theory: Classes, Nations, Literatures*, London: Verso, 1992, p. 41.

93. Arif Dirlik, 'Rethinking Colonialism: Globalization, Postcolonialism, and the Nation', *Interventions*, Vol. 4, No. 3 (2002), p. 432.

94. Edward W. Said, *Power, Politics and Culture: Interviews*, ed. Gauri Viswanathan, London: Bloomsbury, 2004, pp. 158–61.

95. The subsequent discussion of Said is based on my reflections on Said's *Humanism and Democratic Criticism* and *From Oslo to Iraq and the Roadmap* in 'Edward Said and the War in Iraq', *New Formations*, No. 59 (2006), pp. 52–62. See Edward W. Said, *Humanism and Democratic Criticism*, New York: Columbia University Press, 2004; and Edward W. Said, *From Oslo to Iraq and the Roadmap*, London: Bloomsbury, 2004.

96. Said, *Humanism and Democratic Criticism*, p. 22.

97. Quoted in Ibid., p. 26.

98. Sartre, *Existentialism is a Humanism*, p. 45.

99. Said, *Humanism and Democratic Criticism*, p. 47.

100. W. J. T. Mitchell, 'Secular Divination: Edward Said's Humanism', *Critical Inquiry*, Vol. 31, No. 2 (2005), p. 463.

101. Saree Makdisi, 'Said, Palestine and the Humanism of Liberation', *Critical Inquiry*, Vol. 31, No. 2 (2005), p. 443.

102. Edward W. Said, *The Question of Palestine*, New York: Vintage, 1992 [1979], pp. 234–5.

103. Robert J. C. Young, 'Sartre: The "African Philosopher"', in Sartre, *Colonialism and Neocolonialism*, p. xvii.

104. Patrick Williams, '"Faire peau neuve": Césaire, Fanon, Memmi, Sartre and Senghor', in Charles Frosdick and David Maurphy (eds), *Francophone Postcolonial Studies*, London: Arnold, 2003, pp. 181–91.

105. Graham Huggan and Helen Tiffin, *Postcolonial Ecocriticism: Literature, Animals, Environment*, London: Routledge, 2010, p. 208.
106. Theodor W. Adorno, *Problems of Moral Philosophy*, ed. Thomas Schröder, trans. Rodney Livingstone, Stanford University Press, 2002, p. 175.
107. Noam Chomsky, *The New Military Humanism: Lessons from Kosovo*, London: Pluto, 1999.
108. Benita Parry, 'Liberation Theory: Variations on Themes of Marxism and Modernity', in Crystal Bartolovich and Neil Lazarus (eds), *Marxism, Modernity and Postcolonial Studies*, Cambridge: Cambridge University Press, 2002, p. 134.
109. Samuel Moyn, *The Last Utopia: Human Rights in History*, Cambridge, MA: Harvard University Press, 2010.
110. Jodi Dean, *Democracy and Other Neoliberal Fantasies: Communicative Capitalism and Left Politics*, Durham, NC: Duke University Press, 2009, p. 5.
111. Bloch, *Natural Law*, p. xxix.
112. Ania Loomba, Suvir Kaul, Matti Bunzl, Antoinette Burton and Jed Esty, 'Beyond What? An Introduction', in Loomba et al. (eds), *Postcolonial Studies and Beyond*, Durham, NC: Duke University Press, 2009, p. 13.
113. Max Horkheimer, *Dawn and Decline*, London: Seabury Press, 1978, p. 153.

# 4
# Queer Theory, Solidarity and Bodies Political

## David Alderson

As Barbara Epstein comments in Chapter 1, one of the things that distinguishes socialist humanism is a conviction that human beings possess a nature that is characterised by 'specific needs, abilities, and limits to those abilities'. It is this that renders such humanism apparently conservative in the view of its opponents, since to speak of specificity and limitation is also to invoke norms that define the human. Queer theory, by contrast, places a premium on antinormativity.[1] The predication of norms, it tends to argue, is rather the means by which the human is produced, thereby constraining us to or excluding us from conformity to that category. On this view, normativity is conservatism.

The account of human nature I would defend, though, is a dynamic one. Norman Geras dispels the myth, promoted by Althusser especially, that Marx rejected the concept of human nature, and argues instead that he was right to embrace it.[2] Human nature, as Geras explains it, consists in the relation between the needs we all have and the distinctively creative human capacities we possess to satisfy them in different ways. He therefore suggests that human nature is responsible for the immense diversity of societies and culture – the very thing that antihumanists frequently cite as grounds for repudiating the concept. As Geras argues, human nature is necessarily therefore an abstraction, but it is a valid abstraction.[3] It follows that there can be no final 'realisation' of that nature in any possible society, but society can and must be held accountable to it, since it is both the basis and the means by which we can achieve whatever satisfaction is or may become available to us.

The implication of endorsing this position is that I do not view humanism as the binary opposite that antihumanism appears to require as its naïve and unsophisticated opponent, but rather as restoring the dialectical emphasis that strong versions of social or discursive construction attempt obsessively to expel, as if doing so were necessarily to perform some progressive political function. It is because we possess the physical and intellectual capacities we do that we construct, and are not merely constructed by, our societies. As Sartre put it, writing of individual subjects, 'we are not lumps of clay, and what is important is not what people make of us but what we ourselves make of what they have made of us'.[4] Even if the focus on an exceptional figure such as Genet led Sartre to overemphasise existential freedom, the point is valid even if it is abstract.

The rather more complex matter to grasp is that in constructing our societies, they may become alien to us, forces set against us that will not permit us the rest, security or satisfaction we require. Our limits, as much as the apparent ones of the material world, may go unacknowledged under a capitalist modernity in which 'all that is solid melts into air'.[5] Even our pleasures – and especially our erotic needs – may be exploited mercilessly to this end as both stimulus to production and justification for that process. In Herbert Marcuse's sense, such needs are false, not because they are not 'real', but because they bind us to the system rather than directing us towards the transformation of it; for him, true and false are teleological terms, not mere factual descriptions of what is or is not the case.[6] For this reason, they are critical terms that may encourage agency, even if the preponderance of false needs led Marcuse to despair of one-dimensional man.

All of this draws our attention to questions of form and formation; that is, to the dynamism of and limits imposed by both corporeal and social forms, as well as the relations between the two. These relations are material, as I have just been emphasising, but they are also grasped symbolically in ways that are consequential. We speak, for instance, of the body politic or the social body, but actual bodies are also often read as evincing the qualities of an 'ideal' general condition – of health and vigour, of discipline and conformity, of appropriately gendered spheres, of racial integrity or, negatively, of degeneracy. Modes of embodiment are imbued with values associated with the 'proper' functioning of society, even as the inclusive recognition of bodies diversifies. According to the work ethic of our austere times in Britain, for instance, it is apparently important for their dignity that disabled people should work rather than become 'dependent' on benefits, and to make the point a great many of them are humiliated by punitive state assessments of their capacities.

Queer theory's way of thinking about subjective formation is as subjectification by power. Ethically and politically progressive action is generally associated with unpicking this process through modes of desubjectification that can never be complete. As Judith Butler argues in *Bodies That Matter*, 'the subject is constituted through the force of exclusion and abjection, one which produces a constitutive outside to the subject, an abjected outside, which is after all, "inside" the subject as its own founding repudiation'.[7] Butler therefore tends to regard humanism itself as formative in its positive definitions of the human because it consequently abjects those who do not qualify; the ethico-political project she is committed to focuses on the expansion of representation so that the abject may be 'recognised' and achieve 'legibility'. That process must entail the breakdown of those borders that construct inside and outside, a spatial deconstruction that is also temporal, since it concerns subjective development.

A good deal of this chapter focuses on Butler's work, but it is not about Butler; it rather engages with her as an exemplary voice within the queer theory with which I am concerned in the sense both of representing that theory and doing so powerfully, precisely because her voice is distinctive and important. I acknowledge solidarity with a great deal of the insightful commentary she has produced on political matters – on freedom of speech, for instance, or the politics of Israel/Palestine – but I nonetheless find her consistent commitment to antihumanism problematic and even puzzling, since it leads her into unnecessary inconsistencies and carries political implications. This chapter therefore begins with some reflections on her arguments about the ethical and political, and goes on to establish an important context for the priorities that have been central to her thinking, governed as they were by the redefinition of the Left that took place during and after the 1960s. This includes what have come to be known – regrettably, but too often accurately – as 'identity politics'. I then consider the autonomisation of gender as a category, both generally and within queer theory and activism, as one mutation of those identity politics to which Butler has significantly contributed through her engagement with this formative term. In a final section, I turn more explicitly to the questions of political economy and its 'queering' in order to propose a different set of political priorities to which those concerned with the erotic in its broadest definition might contribute. My aim is to assert the need for a more purposeful and coherent politics than is possible within antihumanist terms.

## POLITICS, ETHICS, HEGEMONY

'It seems to me,' Butler has suggested recently, 'that queer has to be part of a broadening struggle.'[8] The sentiment resounds through much queer theory, especially in more recent times. Though I am sympathetic to it insofar as it expresses the hope for an inclusive programme of the Left, I am less attached than many to the category of queer itself, because it is theoretically prescriptive in ways this chapter obviously seeks to resist: any affiliation with it appears to demand of us a commitment to what has come to be known as post-structuralist theory, whether of a primarily Deleuzian, Derridean, Foucaultian or Lacanian inflection. It might even be argued that queer has above all become an institutionalised training in such theory, prescribing certain habits of thought that dispose one to arrive at conclusions regarded as 'radical' in its terms, though it has also been disseminated beyond the academy in consequential ways I touch on here in section three. In part because of my own detachment from post-structuralism, it occurs to me to respond to Butler's comment with the unfashionably teleological question: struggle for what?

This, of course, is where the trouble starts, since to ask such a question suggests that there may be an ultimate goal, or set of goals, to that struggle. Queer theorists have mostly resisted such conclusions, since goals are normative and therefore suggest exclusion and an 'author-itarian' disposition on the part of those who would set them. If one were to point out that to be without goals would imply being without a guide as to which projects might legitimately form a part of the weave of that apparently singular struggle Butler invokes, queers and other post-structuralists are likely to ask: who gets to decide what is legitimate, and who will be *de*legitimated in the process? Above all, queer addresses exclusion; it is, in this sense, a reactive project.

Does the fact of struggle, then – of apparently being ranged against power – demand recognition in itself? Are all formations good simply in virtue of being 'new'? Surely this position is to be romantically on the side of protest or against the state, and that danger is especially potent in neoliberal times that have promoted economic deregulation and equated freedom of the individual with the freedom of markets. David Harvey, for instance, contrasts the 'embedded liberalism' of Fordist/Keynesian societies and the disembedded, 'globalised' and deregulated ones that have been actively forged under neoliberal governance.[9] In my view, one aspect of plausible struggle, at least in the immediate term, should be for the defence of existing, as well as the further extension of, democratically accountable state responsibilities and the reigning in of the market; for *more* constraint, in short.

Of the various institutions that come in for critique by Butler, however, it is mostly the state that is targeted. In a work such as *Excitable Speech*, for instance, with its powerful critique of appeals for the regulation of hate speech, she tends to regard the state as necessarily conservative by contrast with a civil society that is contestatory and pluralistic. Surrendering responsibility to the state, she argues, is always dangerous, because the state will use its enhanced power for its own purposes. Censorship, moreover, is a form of productive power: it actively fashions subjects through the determination of what is speakable.[10] As others have argued, Butler presents a contradictory view of the state in this book, but tends to regard its power as undifferentiated;[11] she also has a tendency to romanticise civil society in which the performative resignification of terms may take place without acknowledging the constitution of that rather vaguely defined sphere. Ellen Meiksins Wood has argued that, as a concept, civil society lumps together an assortment of different institutions simply by virtue of their detachment from the state; it is a sphere whose distinctive combination of public and private is specific to capitalism, and the power relations that constitute it tend to be overlooked.[12] This preference for civil society over state helps explain why, in my view, Butler privileges ethics over politics, and even defines politics as a kind of ethics in ways I shall return to.

Butler places such faith in civil society because it is there that 'radical democracy', in her conceptualisation of it, might flourish. That term was originally coined by Ernesto Laclau and Chantal Mouffe in their inaugurating work of post-Marxist thought, *Hegemony and Socialist Strategy* (1985), but it is one that circulates more generally on the post-structuralist Left. It is both an idealised abstraction and yet also the source of disagreement among various commentators about how it should be theorised in ways I do not have the space to consider here.[13] For the sake of efficiency, I refer to Moya Lloyd's helpfully succinct formulation of Butler's way of understanding it:

> Like other poststructuralist radical democrats, Butler stresses the disruptive rather than rational nature of democratic activity; assumes power relations are intrinsic to society, including democratic society; and views radical democracy not as an alternative to liberal democracy

but as a process of 'incessant contestation' over, and thence radical-
ization of, 'the key terms of liberalism' – equality, freedom, justice,
humanity – so as to make them 'more inclusive, more dynamic
and more concrete' [...] Radical democracy is thus a constitutively
open-ended rather than teleological process, sustained by its very
unrealisability.[14]

The reason that radical democracy must be conceived as open-ended
is because of a principled conviction that a social order and the norms
on which it is based must entail certain formal, discursive and therefore
social exclusions that will occasion various new demands for recognition.
Butler's broader agenda is geared to forms of social justice, then, but it is
not directed at determinate social transformation, since determinacy is
the very thing that gives rise to desirable struggle as she sees it.

The state is the object of critique by Butler, then, because of its
formalising power, not least through its necessarily limited and limiting,
but thereby also productive, recognition of who counts as a citizen and
in what respects; radical democracy, by contrast, holds out deformalising
potential. Butler's language of freedom is one couched in terms of 'ability'
– liveability, speakability, even grievability for those defined by the state
as unworthy of our concern. Something of her attitude in this respect is
conveyed in the celebrated debate she published with Ernesto Laclau and
Slavoj Žižek in 2000. Here she argues that the universal constitutively
excludes certain people by rendering them 'unspeakable and unspoken
for'. This 'unspeakability' – the allusion to abjection is clearly intended
– is determined by both the functioning of a given language and also
the hierarchies among languages that render them incommensurable. By
contrast with the way that the universal currently functions, she proposes
in place of linguistically or discursively determined exclusions a process
of translation that 'belongs to no single site, but is the movement between
languages, and has its final destination in this movement itself'. The
effects of this process, she anticipates, 'will not only relieve the state of
its privileged status as the primary medium through which the universal
is articulated, but re-establish as the conditions of articulation itself the
human trace that formalism has left behind, the left that is Left'.[15]

It is worth exploring this argument in greater detail, perhaps by trying
to envisage what she hopes to convey by it. One explicit influence on
her thinking about such translation is Homi Bhabha.[16] Though Butler
does not specify which aspects of his work are important for her, his

elaboration of a Third Space is surely one thing she has in mind, though it overlaps with other theoretical terms he elaborates. Bhabha claims that that space is the product of a complex hybridity, that 'it is the "inter" – the cutting edge of translation and negotiation, the *in*-between space – that carries the burden of the meaning of culture [...] by exploring this Third Space, we may elude the politics of polarity and emerge as the other of our selves'.[17] The suggestion, like those about radical democracy, is once again abstract. For an attempt to give the notion some concretion, I find it instructively necessary to resort to fiction in the form of Salman Rushdie's novel, *The Satanic Verses*, on which Bhabha's thinking was an explicit influence. Rushdie once said that the novel 'celebrates hybridity, impurity, intermingling, the transformation that comes of new and unexpected combinations of human beings, cultures, ideas, politics, movies, songs'.[18] It famously begins with the explosion of a plane, *Bostan*, the dispersal of its diverse passengers and contents, and the fantastical mutation of Gibreel Farishta and Saladin Chamcha into angelic and devilish figures respectively on their descent. The symbolism of all of this resides in the potentiality of airspace, even in spite of certain attempts to constrain it:

> [it is] that soft, imperceptible field which had been made possible by the [twentieth] century and which, thereafter, made the century possible, becoming one of its defining locations, the place of movement and of war, the planet-shrinker and power-vacuum, most insecure and transitory of zones, illusory, discontinuous, metamorphic – because when you throw everything up in the air anything becomes possible.[19]

In this, there is that wholly characteristic sense of hybridic possibility through consequences that outstrip intentions, and of specific material developments giving birth to indeterminacies that are troubling and therefore provoke attempts at regulation ('planet-shrinker and power-vacuum'). In Butler, Bhabha and Rushdie, instability is idealised; it appears to be inherently progressive. Consequently, the new is fetishised.

One thing Rushdie's novel does not highlight, however, is that the greatest boost to the expansion of air travel in the later twentieth century was an epoch-defining act of disembedding, the neoliberal abolition of currency controls pioneered by Margaret Thatcher; it was her first act on coming to power in 1979, placing pressure on other states to follow suit.[20] The idealisation of movement and flux in these writers as corrosive of the domination of a power identified with the nation-state is therefore all too easily viewed as a positive spin placed on neoliberal globalisation, but it masks the dependence of such movement on the actions of states. In Rushdie's novel, it is resistance of various sorts to translation and hybridity that is stigmatised. Thatcher's Britain is certainly a focus of Rushdie's attack, but mostly for its intolerant nationalism, whereas, as Stuart Hall once argued, such conservatism formed only one part of a contradictory 'authoritarian populism' that also embraced 'a revived neoliberalism – self-interest, competitive individualism, anti-statism'.[21] Rushdie's own trajectory, after being targeted by one form of fundamentalist resistance to the flux he idealised, was to embrace the US as an authentic upholder of democracy and freedom.[22] This is often considered a betrayal of his earlier leftist affiliations, but it is just as easily regarded as a logical trajectory. It is not one that either Butler or Bhabha have followed, of course.

If Butler's politics are substantially directed *at* the state, then, that is not as a result of any conviction about the desirability of the Left *taking power*, since her definition of 'the left that is Left' is *anti*-formalist. Unsurprisingly, therefore, her 'political' interventions are directed at eroding the normative restrictions placed on recognition. Hence the importance she attaches to the processes of signification that render certain subjects legible or illegible. In her wonderfully suggestive essay on 'Violence, Mourning, Politics', she presents the disposition towards recognition as an ethical one facilitated by the infantile vulnerability that precedes the hardening process of our subjectification, thereby rendering the individual potentially open to the Other in spite of that subsequent development. It is through an involuntary ec-stasy – the Heideggerian condition of being beside, or outside, oneself – rather than through any process of reasoning that this may occur. The recognition facilitated by our common, original vulnerability is ethical because it represents the resignification of those norms through which that vulnerability is recognised. Butler steadfastly resists any description of this mode of thinking as humanist, in part no doubt because it relies not on an assertion of autonomy (which she acknowledges to be politically important) but the opposite, a weakening of our individualisation.[23] Nonetheless, she leaves unclear by what process we might give ourselves over to our undoing; Lauren Berlant presumably has this in mind in criticising her work for its ethical intentionalism.[24]

Some of the further reasons for Butler's resistance to humanism are also touched on in her essay, which seeks to challenge the restrictions on grievability determined by the (US) nation-state: 'To what extent,' she asks, 'have Arab peoples, predominantly practitioners of Islam, fallen outside the "human" as it has been naturalised in its "Western" mold by the contemporary workings of humanism?' The very terms of this question are symptomatic of a more general theoretical tendency to reify humanism *as* Western,[25] and to see the power of an imperialist US as governed by the necessary development of that tradition. But who would think of George W. Bush and Donald Rumsfeld – the figures in office when Butler wrote those words – as primarily *humanists*? Not them, I reckon.

Butler's question raises others about the relations between the categories of human, Arab and Muslim. For all but the actually racist, there is surely no problem in recognising Arabs and Muslims as human, though dehumanising propaganda – some of it promoted by Islamists – is sadly too prevalent. But Arab and Muslim are distinct and, in both cases, heterogeneous and even conflicted terms, and to recognise both as human implies not merely a challenge to a narrow grasp of that category insofar as this is a feature of certain Western perceptions, but simultaneously to any narrowly nationalistic, sectarian or religious conceptualisation of solidarity that the claim to an Arabic or Muslim – or Christian or Jewish or atheistic or Western or Japanese or Australian, and so on – identity may entail. It moreover implies a critique of Islamic or other religious or traditional codes that seek to constrain the human potential for freedom – liveability, if you prefer – within narrowly moralistic limits. That critique is implicit in the practical solidarity those of us on the Left express with forces we recognise as progressive in societies that are Arabic and/or – substantially, predominantly or by repressively theocratic decree – Muslim. Furthermore, it seems to me relatively straightforward to distinguish between those whose vision of human rights is consistent, if necessarily pragmatic, and those who invoke feminism or LGBT rights, for instance, for the purposes of furthering racist or imperialist agendas, as is the case with what Jasbir Puar labels 'homonationalism'.[26]

Butler's essay leaves many questions unanswered, among them that of the relation between subjective ethical and institutional political recognition. I may very well empathise with Palestinians in their truly appalling, and seemingly relentless, plight, but how might that translate into effective action? Any answer to that would clearly require some understanding of the powerful forces of resistance to such action, and therefore of how we might impact on state and supra-state institutions in spite of them. What form might *political* recognition entail?

But the further question that preoccupies me here is that of why certain people may be disposed to find outrageous the repressive tolerance that gives equal weight at best to Israeli and Palestinian perspectives in spite of the massive imbalance of forces between them and the genocidal campaign against the latter that this facilitates? Why are some of us better informed and more inclined to feel solidarity? After all, it would be a naïve humanism indeed that treated empathy as spontaneous. The answers clearly have to do with our positive socialisation as a result of our involvement in dissident milieus of one sort or another, through which we acquire the virtuous habit and disposition to be critical and to question the official line on who our enemies are – and, indeed, who 'we' are. The theoretical collapse of socialisation into subjectification by power is a grievous error, and it is the reason why Raymond Williams, for one, argued for the recognition of residual and emergent, as well as dominant, social formations and values.[27] Another important category in this respect that I shall come to later is subculture.

In a sense – and this constitutes a partial rejoinder to Berlant's criticism – Butler acknowledges this, since she highlights the potential of those whose suffering and grief, as a result of AIDS for instance,[28] has itself gone unrecognised to recognise the vulnerability of others. Her account is not merely voluntaristic, then. In this way, she is implicitly addressing the potential of constituencies who may be regarded as nonconformist, queer, dissident, perhaps explicitly on the Left. I want to leave aside for the moment the question of whether it is indeed necessary to have experienced such marginalised suffering to be capable of empathy, however, in order to focus instead on these constituencies and their demands for recognition, since they ultimately condition the position from which Butler speaks. Frequently, indeed, she has spoken in their defence; they are the subjects and objects of radical democratic action.

Butler's way of understanding radical democracy as a resignification of liberalism's key terms appears to accept as a given the structural determinations of them. It therefore aspires to a radicalisation, rather than displacement, of liberalism, and it seems plausible to understand that process as conditioned by the intensified individualism, incoherence and rapidity of change characteristic of what some call post-Fordist capitalism (though I prefer to speak of a combination of neoliberalism and flexible accumulation). Something, indeed, of this sort has already been suggested by Žižek in his critique of the political projects of both Butler and Laclau:

> it is contemporary global capitalism with its dynamics of 'deterritorial-isation', which has created the conditions for the demise of 'essentialist' politics and the proliferation of new multiple subjectivities [...] my point is *not* that the economy (the logic of Capital) is a kind of 'essentialist anchor' that somehow 'limits' hegemonic struggle – on the contrary, it is its *positive condition*; it creates the very background against which 'generalized hegemony' [or radical democracy] can thrive.[29]

This observation – which I have been anticipating and endorse – serves to highlight the shift in meaning of the key terms of the debate that proposals for radical democracy have effected. Hegemony, Gramsci argued, is achieved by persuading the majority that class domination in fact represents the universal interest. In Laclau and Mouffe's account, by contrast, hegemony is aspired to by an abstract Left that has abandoned its illusions of the necessary primacy of class to socialist struggle, but seeks nonetheless to 'articulate' the social movements spontaneously generated by the social.[30] To persist in this view grievously fails to acknowledge the realities as argued for by David Harvey of neoliberal-ism as a project couched in terms of liberty of the subject, but designed to restore the power of an elite, even if that project has also resulted in the reconfiguration of that elite. The emphasis in Laclau and Mouffe's work, and in other accounts of radical democracy, obscure the social *intention* at work in the abstractly designated 'social'.[31]

The neoliberal project has been remarkably successful, though it has been advanced not merely through persuasion and the formation of subjective dispositions, but also through violence and coercion. The implication of Žižek's argument is that proliferating demands for recognition are not generated by the static, conservative form of politics and society, but rather by the dynamism of the market.[32] Moreover, it is precisely the operations of the market that capitalist states – but also supra-state institutions such as the European Union, the Interna-tional Monetary Fund and the World Bank – function to secure. These institutions are not merely conservative; indeed, it is a mistake to regard them as predominantly so. The plausibility of this claim resides in the fact that the market they disembed is not a moral force: its progressive, detraditionalising, denaturalising properties have often been observed and approved by those on the Left, including Marx, and for good reason (and this is the quandary we struggle with).

Plenty of queer theory serves to confirm Žižek's point about deterritorialisation, though often in terms that differ from the Deleuzian ones he deploys. Kevin Floyd, drawing on Lukács, argues that the reification of desire that took place over the late nineteenth and twentieth centuries nonetheless led to the emergence of lesbian and gay liberation movements that have been progressive, creating new demands for liberty.[33] Judith Halberstam suggests that the kind of 'inverted' female masculinity that is explored in Radclyffe Hall's novel, *The Well of Loneliness*, attests to 'a fantasy of transformation and an economic model of desire based on exchange value [...] For Stephen [Wonham, Hall's protagonist], this transformation occurs through the act of dressing'.[34] And transgender theory of the sort that can be traced back through the work of Susan Stryker and Sandy Stone to Donna Haraway's inspirational 'myth' of the post-human cyborg as hybrid of the human and broadly speaking technological – and whom she claims will be 'a creature in a postgender world' – must acknowledge that such beings are 'the illegitimate offspring of militarism and patriarchal capitalism, not to mention state socialism'.[35] The subversive potential of such cyborgs, as well as the other identities highlighted here, resides in the illegitimacy attributed to them in their potential to contest the authoritarian forms that gave birth to them. But, as Wendy Brown has commented in direct response to Haraway, 'liberal, capitalist, disciplinary discourses [...] are installed in the very structure of *desire* fuelling identity-based claims: the psyche of the bastard child is hardly independent of its family of origin'.[36]

The recognition performed by radical democracy is therefore exercised in a dynamic context of identity production to which the arguments of Floyd, Halberstam, Haraway and others attest. While post-structuralists, queers and radical democrats claim to be anti-teleological for reasons I began this section by outlining, they nonetheless appear to be confident that things can go on indefinitely in the way they have under neoliberalism and flexible accumulation, rather than be subject to the kinds of systemic contradiction that have generated economic shocks with increasing frequency in recent years. Such shocks hold the potential to intensify still further in the future,[37] with considerable potential to generate modes of 'resistance' incompatible with liberal democratic conceptions of desirable change, however radicalised. There are those who would harness certain political energies generated by such crises – Nigel Farage, Marine le Pen and Donald Trump to name a few – but to sinister ends. This danger has long been present; in his critique of cosmopolitanism as it is dominantly configured and practiced, Timothy Brennan nonetheless warned twenty years ago of:

> a populist and right-wing [US] nationalism [that] has arisen from below, attacking the partnership of big business and government for being indifferent to the interests of the American people, and demanding that the United States be separate and apart and superior by privileging the concerns of the white 'mainstream' in what is seen as a return to an inward-directed patriotism poised against foreigners.[38]

The most urgent task of the Left, it seems to me, is to establish an agenda that is able to offer a coherent alternative to such powerful and spreading versions of anti-globalisation (to the extent that the agendas I have alluded to may be adequately defined as such; mostly they are contradictory on this point). How the constituencies to whom these agendas appeal have formed is my next concern.

## IDENTITY POLITICS

Accounts of radical democracy are theoretically indebted to the post-structuralist prioritisation of difference, but that term is meaningless as an abstraction; it might relate to anything. The more specific priorities it attends to were determined by the ferment of the 1960s: the innovations, trajectories and aftermath of the New Left and counterculture. The thinking of Laclau emerged out of affiliations with the Argentinian socialist and subsequently the Eurocommunist Left, whereas Butler's affiliations were less formal, and therefore more characteristic of the diffuse radicalism of the US context.[39] I turn here to the latter because of the enormous influence it has had on political imaginaries globally, not least through the theory that is generated out of the prestigious academic institutions that are ironically one symptom of the US dominance that theory frequently critiques.[40]

The New Left first emerged in the West, though its influence rapidly spread; it was an amorphous phenomenon. Alan Sinfield, speaking primarily of the British context, has described it as a subculture: it was middle class and therefore substantially differentiated economically and culturally from the working class that frequently preoccupied it. Indeed, it tended to be judgemental of working class tastes for their commercialism. For Sinfield, a subculture – which he does not regard as necessarily defined by youth, musical taste or class, but by marginalisation or dissidence – holds positive potential, since it may be the basis for political identifications that do not inevitably emerge out of class, gender or racial identities.[41] Nonetheless, the fact of being a subculture must surely represent a limitation for a movement that aspires in its rhetoric at least to change the world; it suggests we may rather be talking to ourselves. The rarefied nature of New Left theorising (including this chapter) would seem to confirm that. The New Left has, after all, largely centred on higher education, with few organic connections to working class people of whatever race, gender or sexuality. Of course, many students who pass through the academy pick up ideas that may continue to influence them over their lives – and there is in this loose sense a form of dissemination with which I shall be concerned shortly – but students are a diverse body destined for various social positions; mostly they seek to 'better' themselves.

It is important to acknowledge four influences on the New Left in its highly influential US form as these have contributed to the emergence of identity politics. The first, as highlighted by Fredric Jameson, is the anticolonial movements of the post-war world whose language of liberation, self-determination and autonomy was taken up by the Left more generally and deployed in various contexts.[42] Anti-colonialism thereby established a language through which those other movements understood their own struggles, and the appropriateness of it in each case was largely taken for granted. This consequently assisted in generating certain illusions about the commonality of the projects being pursued across the world. Solidarity often proved awkward between movements for national autonomy being pursued in the Third World and those demanding subjective autonomy in the overdeveloped West. Gay socialists visiting Cuba in the early 1970s, for instance, returned disenchanted by official 'homophobia', prompting some to commit themselves more resolutely to their own, i.e. identitarian, struggles.[43]

The second is the prototypical and rightly central status of the black civil rights movement initially from the mid-1950s, and then in the more autonomous form of Black Power from the mid-1960s. It is difficult to overestimate the importance of this struggle to the US Left's political imaginary, establishing race not only as a priority, but also as a further model and touchstone for other struggles and political dynamics. In 1972, in reaching for an analogy for the general liberation homosexuals proposed, Dennis Altman drew what appeared to him an obvious analogy: 'It is the fate of the Negro, James Baldwin once wrote, to carry the burden of both white and black Americans. It may well be the fate of the homosexual to liberate both gays and straights.'[44] Such analogies proliferated and have persisted: Judith Roof notes the comparison made by one lesbian feminist in the early 1970s between the butch lesbian and the Uncle Tom figure;[45] when expressing outrage at the claim of the radical feminist, Janice Raymond, that 'all transsexuals rape women's bodies', Sandy Stone wonders 'what if she had said, e.g., "all blacks rape women's bodies"?'[46] Such loose analogies can be misleading, however. Raymond's comment, for instance, did not draw on a deep-seated and popular 'fear', such as that held by whites in relation to black men's sexuality; the comment is rather self-evidently obnoxious and ridiculous, a theorisation from the margins of political discourse. Of course, that is not to say that transsexuals have not suffered from distinctive modes of stigmatisation and violence, but rather that a specific claim to political legitimacy is being made through the analogy.

The third influence is more complex, and had to do with the displacement and disparagement of the Old Left by something that was very confidently New, but that also made a virtue of its inchoateness. The spirit of this newness permeated a variety of causes as apparent confirmation again that something larger, even systemic, was being challenged, even as the lack of specificity about what that system was tended also to be regarded as a virtue. Language was again important, but as an indicator of a certain structure of feeling that came to privilege feeling and intuition themselves. This was an *experiential* politics related to the formation of the New Left among the young and mostly privileged. Maurice Isserman and Michael Kazin, for instance, contrast the Communist, Socialist and Trotskyist movements of the 1930s who prided themselves on analytical, conceptual and oratorical sophistication and 'a kind of emotional and moral plain-speaking [...] among S.D.S. [Students for a Democratic Society] leaders. Authenticity, usually described as "commitment", was the political and personal value New Leftists were most eager to display, a quality that could best be established by the willingness to "put your body on the line".[47] If the Old Left was austerely theoretical, even dogmatic, and focused explicitly on a narrowly socialist politics, the New Left privileged a different set of terms of quite deliberately uncertain valence, but more in keeping with US political idioms: 'radicalism' supplanted substantive commitments, because 'socialism' was considered unpronounceable in political discourse,[48] and 'democracy' was to be radicalised by becoming *participatory*.

There was much that was specific in the founding document of the SDS, the *Port Huron Statement*, but its principal legacy was a conflation of means and ends, if not a direct identification of them: participatory democracy was to be the principle of organisation of SDS, as well its ultimate objective, though on a more general scale. *Port Huron* spoke positively of the value of community and consensus, but dissensus was often enough the practice of students precisely through different SDS branches' suspicion of the centre and its right to take decisions. Timothy Brennan is right to lament the absence of what he calls an organisational imaginary in the post-1970s, culturalist Left,[49] but in truth these anarchistic – and often anarchic – tendencies were anticipated during the more uncompromising 1960s. Paradoxically, it was the exploitation of such anti-hierarchical sentiment that led to the Progressive Labour Party taking control of SDS, the resulting split with Weatherman, and the disintegration of the whole organisation in 1969.[50]

This diffuse spirit of radicalism conditioned the 'personalism' of 1960s activism that has been widely remarked on as definitive of it, and was evident in a new *sensitivity* that became consequential in the conduct of politics. It was not merely in feminism that the personal was believed to be political. One consequence of the new sensitivity, however, was the heightened potential it entailed for causing and taking offence. This became a particular feature of the assertion of identity politics as a means of highlighting the exclusion or marginalisation of this or that constituency, or of subgroups and even individuals within those constituencies, on the basis that a particular experience, way of life or sensibility was being overlooked or denigrated. To be guilty of the latter was to be culpable of exclusion and authoritarianism, and it is out of this that the demand to respect difference ultimately emerges in both its positive corrective to perspectives that fail to examine their own grounding in privilege, but also its negatively debilitating tendency to generate sectarianism and pander to individualism. The difficulty resides in how one may distinguish one from the other; who might be the arbiter?

The fourth influence resides in the negative ground for the emergence of identity politics. As Wendy Brown argues, it is the US middle class that 'precisely embodies the ideal to which nonclass identities refer for proof of their exclusion or injury'. For this reason, and because the white, masculine, middle class ideal serves to naturalise capitalism through its familial and prosperous dimensions, she proposes that identity politics may function both to obscure the critique of capitalism and sustain 'the invisibility and inarticulateness of class'.[51]

That is a compelling argument, but it perhaps elides another negation that is more awkward for the Left to acknowledge; after all, it is easy to bash a rarely very well-defined 'middle class'. What this masks, however, is the presumption – and often the actuality – that took hold during the 1960s that the working class white male was assimilated and conservative, patriotic, pro-war, straight, racist and newly integrated into the work and consumption regimes of Fordist capitalism. Herbert Marcuse, writing in his most influential, if least typical, book, *One-Dimensional Man* (1964), noted the 'assimilation of blue-collar and white-collar population, of leadership types in business and labour, of leisure activities and aspirations in different social classes'.[52] Whereas the European Left evinced a persistent attachment to socialist, and even Marxist, traditions, these were largely absent in the US, especially after the McCarthyite persecutions of the 1950s. Indeed, Theodore Roszak coined the term 'counterculture' quite specifically to highlight this difference, and to celebrate the *superiority* of the US Left through its rejection of socialism and appreciation that the working class had always proved itself to be reactionary. Hope resided instead in an educated youth that was critical, somewhat detached from the system by its location in the university, and consequently had time on its hands.[53] Such a constituency stood no chance, of course, of overthrowing a system that mostly remained vaguely defined. Still, the presumption that there was indeed a coherent entity that must be opposed facilitated the view that in challenging it at one point you were striking at something bigger, and were therefore in solidarity, if not necessarily agreement, with other self-styled radicals.

There is nonetheless a connection between the classes Brown and I focus on. In 1972, Dennis Altman endorsed the claim that Black Pride, the New Left, the counterculture and its different components, including gay liberation, were united in challenging what was essentially WASP (white Anglo-Saxon Protestant) hegemony. Pointedly, however, he noted that 'while the blacks at least put their challenge to whites from outside the family, the young challenged from within – the most rebellious among the young tended to be upper middle class and either W.A.S.P.S.

or Jews – and hence the hostilities and insecurities they brought forth.[54] This sense that young radicals were challenging authority as it was mediated through the family, the most intimate instrument of social-isation, was another crucial feature of the period, determining the particular significance ascribed to sexual liberation, especially of the queer sort. The family was regarded as a kind of micro-state, headed by the (potentially) authoritarian father.

The body featured prominently in all of this. It was the very sign of exclusion in the case of people of colour. But it was also the self-conscious means of differentiation pursued by those who cultivated what Marcuse described in *An Essay on Liberation* (1969) as 'the new sensibility': the rejection of the self-discipline symbolised by the white working and middle class male. This was an aesthetic protest, and culture therefore took on a new significance, as Roszak's term highlights, through its potential to prefigure a different reality principle. 'Reality,' Marcuse wrote, 'has to be discovered and projected. The senses must learn not to see things anymore in the medium of that law and order which has formed them.'[55] Countercultural rebelliousness, he argued, constituted 'the subverting forces in transition'.[56] This was a humanist argument predicated on the possibility of a transformed human nature that could no longer tolerate 'the aggressiveness, brutality, and ugliness of the established way of life'[57] because that nature's historically constituted needs would be transformed away from those determined by what Marcuse termed the performance principle (in other words, mass production through alienation and exploitation, as well as the consumerism that sustained it).

The New Left, however, never realised the potential Marcuse saw in it, in part because much of it never shared his sense of what was taking place. In the event, counter-revolution triumphed, with the result that Marcuse shifted his view, and argued in the transformed conditions of the 1970s for a renewed (self-)discipline, realism and purpose. 'Do one's thing, yes', he argued, 'but the time has come to learn that not *any* thing will do, but only those things which testify (no matter how silently) to the intelligence and sensibility of men and women who can do *more* than their own thing, living *and working* for a society without exploitation'[58] (the emphasis on work here is Marcuse's own). The New Left had by now isolated itself through its radicalism, he argued, both because socialist theory was alien to the majority and because a free society was incon-ceivable by it. 'Liberation thus appears a threat: it becomes taboo.'[59]

The New Left subculture remained centred institutionally on the universities, but the dominant strain of theory that chimed with the pessimism of the 1970s was increasingly antihumanist structuralism and post-structuralism. Symbolically, perhaps, Foucault sought to displace the influence of the 'Freudo-Marxism' of Marcuse in *History of Sexuality, Volume 1*, published in French in 1976 and translated into English in 1978; he was largely successful. In this process, the New Left emphasis on the subject was preserved, but negatively reconfigured as necessarily subjectification *by* ideology or power/discourse. Moreover, the particular US context determined the politicised reception of 'French theory' there, as François Cusset summarises: 'if Derrida or Foucault deconstructed the concept of *objectivity*, the Americans would draw on those theories not for a reflection on the figural power of language or on discursive constructions, but for a more concrete political conclusion: *objectivity* is synonymous with "subjectivity of the white male."'[60] Through this elision of theory and politics, another appeared to follow: that challenges to WASP, and more broadly Western, hegemony entailed acceptance of the theoretical critique of objectivity as such.

A great deal of ink has been spilt in retrospect on the relations between counterculture and the market, but there was always a self-consciousness in more sophisticated quarters that 'youth' was a market reification.[61] The question was whether its political aspirations were necessarily limited by its enabling conditions. Inevitably, with the decline of the Left in the 1970s, the spirit of nonconformity and the desires unleashed during the 1960s were addressed by an increasingly 'flexible' market. In 1982, Dennis Altman anticipated all the more recent concerns about lesbian and gay assimilation, or homonormativity, in *The Homosexualisation of America*.[62] The tone of this volume is markedly different from his earlier focus on liberation, and was largely appreciative of the extent to which queers had become visible as urban trendsetters and had thereby established more relaxed sexual attitudes as the cosmopolitan norm.

But countercultural tendencies persist – the 1960s remain a potent 'myth' with different valences for Left and Right – and some would argue that my use of the term queer in relation to assimilation fails to recognise its persistent dissident potential. That may be so, but I would also caution against self-congratulation on this point. The counterculture may be understood as part of the tradition of the Bohemian whose history is traced by Elizabeth Wilson. This rootless figure emerged out of a precise context, the turbulent urban environment of early nineteenth-century

France, among those who found themselves socially out of place – or deterritorialised, if you prefer. He (mostly) was a member of 'an oppositional fraction of the bourgeois class [...] which preserved cultural values and was therefore a "civilising fraction",[63] even as he consorted with the socially disreputable. That romantic combination of dissidence and spiritual superiority has persisted in various reconfigurations of this persistent Bohemian myth. Subcultures indebted to it, consciously or otherwise, may of course encourage the kind of re-education of the senses Marcuse admired among 1960s youth, but insofar as they remain cultural protests cut off from plausible movements for general social transformation, they fall prey to the charge advanced by Bourdieu of 'contesting one culture in the name of another [and] in so doing they fulfill the traditional role of a cultural avant-garde which, by its very existence, helps to keep the cultural game functioning'.[64]

To the extent that the category of the white working class is not itself a reification conjured into being by this cultural game, its emergence from the 1960s on the side of reaction was hardly triumphant. Barbara Ehrenreich has charted the pervasive demonisation of the working class as authoritarian at this time, not least in film,[65] and Susan Faludi has detailed the impact of these cultural attitudes, along with defeat in Vietnam, the 'feminisation' of the labour force, the commodification of gender and the effects of deindustrialisation and neoliberalism on post-war ideals of manhood, precipitating a much-discussed 'crisis of masculinity'.[66] Similar processes have been at work elsewhere in the West, and perhaps especially in post-imperial Britain – to which I turn in the final section – reinforcing the sense of a connection between geopolitical decline, economic reconfiguration and the erosion of masculine purposefulness. The political attention to gender generated out of feminism, to which I turn in the next section, has been pioneered in this shifting context, substantially in response to it – facilitated, indeed, by it.

Nonetheless, to speak of the 'new social movements' that emerged out of the 1960s as forms of identity politics is one that strikes me as deeply problematic. As we have already seen in Altman's comments on the project of lesbian and gay liberation, the hope was to effect a more general transformation in human sexuality, and other struggles shared those universalist objectives. In this respect, they were no more inherently identitarian than the focus on class in prevailing trade union forms that seek merely to represent the sectional interests of labour. The difference is that, whereas in the more ambitiously socialist argument class solidarity represents a plausible agency for change because of its structural and majoritarian power, responsibility for achieving the universal aspirations of the social movements of the 1960s devolved on marginal and minoritarian groups (even women may be regarded as a minority in the Deleuzian sense of being relatively disempowered, rather than numerically inferior). If universalist aspirations have given way to the politics of difference, queer radicalism nonetheless remains faithful to the desire of the 1960s to resist assimilation to what continues to be corporeally figured through the white (working class, presumptively straight and generally reactionary) male. I want now to turn to one dimension of that radicalism.

## THE AUTONOMISATION OF GENDER

Sex and gender were theorised as distinct terms within what has come to be known as the 'second-wave' feminism that emerged from the 1960s.[67] Sex is the given of anatomical distinction, male and female, while gender is the set of dichotomised attributes, masculine and feminine, mapped on to it. The feminist claim is that this dichotomy is conventional, instilled in individuals and policed, though presented as if it were natural. The result of this intensive process of socialisation is that it is often experienced as such. Indeed, men and women have both invested in and derived pleasure from their gendered status. Crucially, the *purpose* of this feminist account of the sex/gender distinction was not to elaborate modes of identity, but to draw attention to and challenge the ideological means through which women are subordinated in relation to men.

The most frequently cited account of this distinction was developed by Gayle Rubin, who argued that sex/gender systems were predicated on the traffic in women highlighted in the anthropology of Lévi-Strauss and theorised under conditions of modernity by Freudian and Lacanian psychoanalysis. According to this way of thinking, gender is 'a product of the social relations of sexuality. Kinship systems rest upon marriage. They therefore transform males and females into "men" and "women", each complete half which can only find wholeness when united with the other.'[68] Thus, Rubin established (hetero)sexuality, rather than, say, divisions of labour, as fundamental to the transformation of sex into gender; feminism therefore required 'a revolution in kinship'. Crucially, this might be facilitated in modernity by kinship's redundancy as the principle of social organisation; it is a powerful hangover from the past.[69] Effectively, though without saying so explicitly, Rubin was drawing attention to capitalism's progressive dynamics in respect of gender, and highlighting therefore the greater potential for transformation in societies in which relations based on kinship had been most powerfully eroded.

All of this will be familiar to many, and yet it would appear to bear repetition, since in everyday usage gender has come to be used synonymously with sex, and often by those who are aware of and grasp perfectly well this theoretical distinction. We commonly speak, for instance, of achieving a 'gender balance' on academic conference panels, not in order to refer to the equal representation of temperaments, but to parity between men and women. When official forms ask for your gender, they do not mean to inquire how robust you feel. An older discourse of 'sex discrimination' now sounds archaic, but why? In other words, much of the time – and these days practically always – we do not merely fail to observe the conventional feminist distinction, but habitually contradict it. Moreover, it is always gender that substitutes for sex, never sex for gender, even though on the basis of the feminist claim just outlined it would make far more sense to suggest that clothes or activities, for instance, are sexed – implying that they are reserved or designated for men or women – than it does to claim that my gender is male or female. Strictly speaking, the latter is a bit like describing the colour of one's clothing as trousers.

Indeed, the current situation is even more confused than this, since the precision of the sex/gender distinction – whatever its merits – has given way to a situation in which the expansive category of gender is used quite permissively even within supposedly critical discourse to refer not merely to sex, but almost on a whim to ideology or normativity, identity (positively or negatively understood), performance (in Judith Butler's sense) and essence (as in the claim often made that surgery for transsexuals facilitates conformity to a primary gender). Often it is unclear what a given reference to gender means or implies. I am not sure whether this incoherent ubiquity is cause or effect of the autonomisation of gender I describe here; possibly it is both. By 'autonomisation' I mean the tendency towards the term's separation from and displacement of the category of 'sex'.

What can be said, however, is that factors other than a slippage in common usage have been at work in the privileging of the term. Joan

W. Scott, for instance, suggests that 'gender' displaced 'women' in the titles of historiographical scholarship during the 1980s as a means of rendering that work more scholarly and 'disinterested'. 'Gender,' she writes, 'seems to fit within the scientific terminology of social science and thus dissociates itself from the (supposedly strident) politics of feminism.'[70] This claim that the shift in terms emerged in part out of institutional pressures towards respectability is interesting, because the substitution is often perceived instead as a mode of radicalisation associated with the emergence of anti-essentialist third-wave feminism and its focus on culture and representation, as distinct from the material conditions and experiences of actual women and their struggles. Indeed, during the 1990s in particular the designation 'Women's Studies' came frequently to be modified or displaced by 'Gender Studies', generating significant controversy.[71] This tendency was also symptomatic of the broader, antihumanist theoretical shift to viewing persons as instruments of discourse.

Other pressures contributed to the analytical focus on gender, including a burgeoning interest in masculinity, at first through the emergence of 'men's liberation'. Initially conceived as a mode of self-scrutiny intended to complement feminist praxis,[72] the focus on masculinity paralleled that of gender studies more generally, becoming more scholarly and emphasising the diversity of masculinity historically and across cultures, thereby differentiating between masculinit*ies*. Masculinity also came to be understood, not merely as involved in regulating the 'proper' spheres of men and women, but as bound up with class and racial formations. Thus, for instance, manliness was a nineteenth-century imperial ideal in Britain that resulted in the stigmatisation of the colonised as feminine, and the idle, aristocratic elite as effeminate; according to Herbert Sussman, for instance, manliness was a virtuous condition predicated on a rapacious masculinity that required subjective control.[73] Sussman draws on Klaus Theweleit's extraordinarily ambitious Deleuzian and evolutionary-anthropological account of masculinity and its apparently teleological consummation in proto-Nazi and Nazi forms. The argument views masculinity as a mode of aggressively defensive psychic and political territorialisation.[74] Masculinity–repression–authority–fascism; the linkages are characteristically countercultural, especially for the German Theweleit, *and* post-structuralist.

A different strand in the study of gender emerged through the celebration of dissident modes associated especially with subcultures.

The gay male masculinity that characterised gay liberation in the 1970s has often been regarded as ironic, for instance, though both Alan Sinfield and David Halperin have more recently challenged that view.[75] For Sinfield, gay liberation represented a shift towards differentiation according to sexuality away from a prior differentiation on the basis of gender, under which queers were viewed and viewed themselves as effeminate. It is an insight prompted by transgender activism and theory. Camp, indeed, has been variously dissected and celebrated ever since Susan Sontag's 'Notes on "Camp"' (1964), and others have focused on the history of the category of effeminacy. An analogous move to the emphasis on camp has been made through the recovery of butch/femme lesbian traditions against the radical or lesbian feminist insistence that gender identification represented a mode of false consciousness, since gender was/is what feminists have wanted to do away with.[76]

Largely through its connection with dissident sexuality, therefore, gender came to be recognised not merely as the sphere through which power secured conformity, but as facilitating a positive mode of transgression. Note, however, the instructive tension here between an emphasis on gender dissidence as critical through its denaturalising possibility, with the potential perhaps to contribute towards a dissolution of the ideological dimension of sex/gender systems, and another that stresses its subjective value as identity within subcultural traditions. Such identities may paradoxically acquire virtue precisely because they are transgressive; they have often been associated with Bohemianism.

Diverse experiences, analyses and purposes have governed escalating tensions in this field. As trans commentators often observe, the feminist desire to see gender disappear has traditionally been wedded to an idealisation of androgyny that threatens their identities.[77] Perhaps, however, the real problem with the category of androgyny is that it does not remove us from the spectrum of gender, but rather envisages a general convergence on some ambiguous centre ground. But if the problem with talk of androgyny is therefore that it appears prescriptive, and in my view tends to encode certain class-based norms, this need not mean that the only plausible alternative must entail retention of the category of gender, at least through the appropriation and resignification of its polarising tendencies. There is no reason other than convention for regarding short hair, a forceful personality and expertise on a motorbike as masculine in whatever combination with sex. The question, which I do not mean to pursue here, might then become: what subjective investment is being made through the insistence on that identification?

Judith Butler's highly influential arguments in *Gender Trouble* therefore emerged out of and consolidated more general trends towards the reification and ubiquity of gender as a (pluralistic) thing to be scrutinised across the historical and cultural differences that shaped it. At the time, however, her arguments appeared counter-intuitive to many of us who were so steeped in the sex/gender distinction. Butler views gender as an instance of power in the Foucaultian sense of being a productive, subjectifying force. Up to this point, the argument is consistent with the critical discussion of masculinity and femininity as not merely ideological, but formative. However, she goes further by taking the deconstructive step of arguing that the belief in sexual difference may be regarded as an *effect* of discursive gender. 'Whether sex or gender is fixed or free,' she writes, 'is a function of discourse which [...] seeks to set certain limits to analysis or to safeguard certain tenets of humanism as presuppositional to any analysis of gender.'[78] The syntax as much as the argument of this sentence, then, highlights that an emphasis on gender facilitates the freedom to *think* without constraints (and it is worth noting that the book itself originally appeared in a series called 'Thinking Gender'). The body, where it is *not* understood as an effect of gender, figures as the (humanist) limit on thought.

*Gender Trouble* is a complex, at times bewildering book, not least because it seems to me to perform the colonisation of sex by gender it effectively argues for. Its most influential aspect has been its emphasis on gender as *per*formative – that is, as constituted through imitative acts for which there is neither an original nor any 'internal' necessity. But, once again, Butler goes further than this in adopting and adapting Nietzsche's disputation of the ultimately grammatical assumption that there is a doer behind the deed; gender takes place, as it were, regardless of the intention of the individual. This is crucial to Butler's argument, and she has repeatedly insisted on it. Since gender functions through imitation or repetition, the gender order cannot help but *fail* to reproduce itself according to its own ideal terms. If that is an accurate summary of the case, however, it seems to me best regarded not as an account of agency at all, but rather a complex theory of social evolution: the doer – gender *itself*, the object of our meditations – has not disappeared, but has been rendered impersonal.

If all of this sounds rather bleak – at least to a humanist – it should be stressed that there is a utopian dimension to Butler's case, since she imagines as the outcome of this process a desirable plurality: 'the loss of gender norms,' she writes, 'would have the effect of proliferating gender configurations, destabilising substantive identity, and depriving the naturalising narratives of compulsory heterosexuality of their central protagonists: "man" and "woman".'[79] Except for the argument that it may be necessary to rid ourselves of the terms man and woman because they are inherently prescriptive, the rest of this is wholly consistent with Rubin's argument in 'The Traffic in Women'.

Anyone who has taught *Gender Trouble* will testify to the difficulty one has in getting the point about agency across to those who wish to put Butler's theory to use to inform self-consciously subversive gender activism. Annamarie Jagose has recently commented that 'even more than twenty years later, the idea that the political could survive being detached from a notion of the agential subject is not at all a critical truism in most queer contexts'.[80] There are, nonetheless, highly ambiguous sections of the text that endorse the message some activists have taken from it. When Butler argues, for instance, that 'the critical task is [...] to locate strategies of subversive repetition enabled by [social construction], to affirm the local possibilities of intervention through participating in precisely those practices of repetition that constitute identity and, therefore, present the immanent possibility of contesting them', a great deal depends on what is meant by such verbs as 'to locate' and 'to affirm'.

Are we not back in the realm of intention and purpose that Butler seems so committed to eliminating? Thus, when she rejects 'the unnecessary binarism of free will and determinism',[81] she is not herself cutting the Gordian knot everyone else struggles to untie, but rather appears tacitly to be endorsing a dialectical possibility: that our options for agency are socially determined precisely *by* the inconsistency and outright contradiction of the social (under which category I would subsume, without privileging, discourse and signification). We are compelled in such circumstances to think and act, to make difficult choices, sacrifices or compromises; we may be pleased with, regret or be permanently unsure of the wisdom of the decisions we take.

But perhaps the key part of the sentence I have just quoted is 'the critical task'. If so, Butler is again privileging analysis and thought, the work of the theorist who recognises the true diversity of individual performances as well as the general situation of which they form a part. That reading is certainly rendered plausible by Butler's hope for a new politics that 'would surely emerge from the ruins of the old' (by which she means the presumption of the Left that given agents have interests): 'Cultural configurations of sex and gender might [...] proliferate or, rather, *their present proliferation might then become articulable within the discourses that establish intelligible life*, confounding the very binarism of sex, and exposing its unnaturalness' (my emphasis).[82] Such statements help to justify Žižek's claim that Butler's thought comes close to confirming 'the empiricist opposition between the infinite wealth of reality and the abstract poverty of the categories by which we try to grasp reality'.[83] But that only partially captures what is going on here. What we have, rather, is a striking combination of empiricism with the idealism I have been highlighting so far. Through this combination something approaching the infinite wealth of reality may appear to us by becoming known, recognised or perhaps even discursively *produced* as such. This idealist empiricism – *presuming* a complexity that nonetheless awaits its symbolisation – is not particular to Butler's thought, but is rather characteristic of a range of post-structuralist work that seeks to disclose the 'difference' that subverts identity, but has a habit rather of multiplying it. Moreover, it does so in the kind of productive, 'deterritorialising' conditions to which Žižek has drawn attention, and therefore as their complement.

I have pursued a particular critique of Butler's arguments here; others have made different kinds of objections that also relate to the kind of rigour Butler is intent on pursuing. Among these, Toril Moi suggests that the argument about sex being a construction of gender is theoreticist – in other words, that it is a response to a problem generated by the terms of theory itself – and argues that it is simply unnecessary for feminists to argue in this way; the only important thing is to deny biological determinism, the view that sex determines gender. Moreover, she suggests that the belief that it is necessary to regard sex as a construct of gender perhaps betrays a suspicion that if we *could* prove the existence of sexual difference this would open the door to biological determinism.[84] Whether or not this is true of Butler, it is so for those genderqueer activists who celebrate her work as formative for them, and who believe that the categories of man and woman can *only* be understood normatively, and therefore negatively, as binaries that cannot account for them personally.

While Moi regards the sex/gender distinction as useful for the specific feminist task of highlighting the ways in which women are constrained by limiting, essentialist ways of representing them, she regards it as unhelpful for thinking about subjectivity, and instead seeks to clarify the arguments of Simone de Beauvoir in *The Second Sex* (1949) by detaching them from their pervasive interpretation through the sex/gender distinction. Instead, she re-establishes the book's philosophical relations with Sartre, Merleau-Ponty and Fanon. All these thinkers reject the scientific, objectifying view of the body as an inert biological fact. It is rather the dynamic *situation* through which an individual realises her projects in the more general situation of the world. For Beauvoir, the nature/culture dualism – and by extension the sex/gender one – could only be considered a problematic dichotomy for thinking about subjectivity because it suggests that it is possible to distinguish securely between the two, whereas the living body is dynamic: 'For Beauvoir,' writes Moi, 'a woman defines herself through the way she lives her embodied situation in the world, or in other words, through the way in which she makes something of what the world makes of her. The process of making and being made is open-ended: it only ends with death.'[85]

This restores a focus on intention as a part of agency, but of course the project of making and being made will depend on one's consciousness of what that process might entail and the context in which one finds oneself. In Moi and Beauvoir, the body is conceived positively as the reason for, possibility of and limit to agency, but the individual is far from wholly autonomous. In this account, 'sex' is not the limitation placed on an analytics of gender, but rather the agential principle that may be limited by, or challenge, the conventional norms of gender.

I have suggested that the background to *Gender Trouble* was the increasing prominence of gender in theoretical and cultural debate, but the book also needs to be understood in relation to its effects. If feminism once sought ultimately to bring about the disappearance of gender as a regulatory framework, Butler reinforced an opposing tendency, because her claim was that we could not escape from it; we could only exert pressure through immanentist modes of subversion. If gender may be considered formative of the category of sex, it becomes the privileged term, acquiring greater substance. Indeed, gender matters, in the sense that it confers value on subjects and is therefore formative in materialising the body.[86] Gender is everywhere; it has legs.

Something of this is evident in a brief, insightful essay by Eve Kosofsky Sedgwick, 'Gosh, Boy George, You Must Be Awfully Secure in Your Masculinity'. Sedgwick argues that masculinity often has nothing to do with men, because it is performed by women; that masculinity and femininity may be orthogonal, rather than oppositional (which is to say that some people might be both masculine *and* feminine, 'just plain more gender-y',[87] than others); that gender distinctions can function as 'threshold effects' through which one passes over from one into the other; and that self-recognition mediates between our corporeal essence and the potential free play of gender (the argument restores the sex/gender distinction). In other words, she amply demonstrates that our assumptions about gender are incoherent; or, rather, she does so on the basis of an understanding of gender in terms of its stylistic, commodified forms as these contribute to the sense of proprietorial identity, to gender as 'presentation'. Masculinity is not understood here as a structure of power between men and women, because under her first proposition Sedgwick wants us to 'resist [...] the presupposition that what women have to do with masculinity is mainly to be treated less or more oppressively by the men to whom masculinity more directly pertains.'[88] Having demonstrated gender's incoherence, however, Sedgwick does not argue for its dissolution; the point is further to insist on its complex, and often pleasurable, ubiquity.

This is typical of a tendency to detach discussion of gender from what feminists considered its primary purpose. It may be that Sedgwick and others are tacitly focusing on specific contexts (subcultural, academic, privileged?) in which such subordination is less evident. Judith Halberstam, for instance, has made a case for regarding female masculinity as an autonomous tradition independent of the masculinity performed by men. She struggles, however, to be consistent or to frame a satisfactory feminism that can accommodate her case. Engaging with an argument made by Susan Cahn that women's participation in sport is limited by the presumption that the skills required for it are masculine, and the conclusion Cahn reaches that these skills should be redefined as 'human', Halberstam rather peremptorily asserts that 'the only way to extend such attributes to women [...] is not simply to make them "human" but to allow them to extend to women as masculinity'.[89] The emphasis on extension here appears to undercut Halberstam's more general case about autonomy, but it seems in any case oddly prescriptive to suggest that women should have to identify with masculinity in order to participate fully in sport. Why? An emphasis that appears transgressive in a subcultural context turns out to be specifically reactionary in its more general application. This raises the difficulty of how we understand transgression in relation to projects of social transformation. Does it not thrive on the persistence of dominant definitions that are presumed to remain intact?

Deborah Cameron argues that the very prefix in the word 'transgender' testifies to the persistence of the assumption that there is an 'appropriate' relation, however conceived, between sex and gender. She asks why it is necessary to speak of *trans*gendered identities at all rather than simply gendered ones, and concludes that this represents a failure for feminism.[90] Her argument is important, and testifies to the way in which an emphasis on transgression may serve to limit the potential for more general transformation,[91] but more needs to be said both about this particular term and others that have evolved out of transgender politics, especially through its articulation with queer theory.

According to various sources, it was Leslie Feinberg's *Transgender Warriors* that popularised, even if it did not initiate, the category as a capacious term to describe those who 'traverse, bridge, or blur the boundary of the *gender expression* they were assigned at birth', including but in no way presuming those who choose to take hormones or have surgery.[92] Feinberg's way of putting this itself blurs, or even collapses, various distinctions: most obviously, between sex and gender as the thing that is 'assigned' at birth, and between assignment and expression (elsewhere in the book, these are at variance). Moreover, hir – Feinberg's preferred pronoun, along with ze – own account draws attention to the complexity of identity formation, and is self-conscious of the difficulties attending what might superficially be read as an ahistorical way of reading the past as teleologically unfolding towards a contemporary trans liberation.

Nonetheless, Feinberg's political formation took place in the context I discussed in the previous section and it differentiates hir thinking and activism from subsequent kinds. Ze accounts for hir subjective development as someone who, physically and in terms of conduct, never conformed to feminine norms, and was consequently viewed with suspicion, hostility and derision. The search for work in the economically depressed 1970s ze recounts as a key experience, accentuating hir stigmatisation. 'The more I tried to wear clothing or styles considered appropriate for women,' ze writes, 'the more people believed I was a man trying to pass as a woman.' Consequently, ze sought to pass as a man and took up work as a builder; ze also took hormones to grow a beard in order to facilitate the ease with which ze could do this. On moving to New York, Feinberg became increasingly involved in politics and joined the Workers World Party (WWP), which supported hir development of a trans politics.

In *Transgender Warriors*, Feinberg explores the history of transgender modes of embodiment, and takes hir cue from Engels' *The Origin of the Family, Private Property and the State* (1884) in attributing the taboo on them to the historical emergence of private property and the patriarchal need to secure it within the male line. Proscription on gender ambiguities, ze argues, were a consequence of the subordination of women in class society. Thus for Feinberg transgender identity and politics were inseparable from an awareness of larger political economic frameworks. Hir arguments do seek to establish a loose continuity of transgender embodiment, identity and experience across different cultural articulations of it, as well as trans suppression through the spread of systems based on private property and the family and especially through Western imperialism. Significantly, however, Feinberg did not presume that identity automatically translated into progressive politics: embracing the latter had to be a conscious decision. Hir identification as 'an anti-racist white, working class, secular Jewish, transgender, lesbian, female, revolutionary communist'[93] seems designed to emphasise complexity over singularity and exclusion; to some these labels may seem to embrace contradiction.

Whatever the plausibility of Feinberg's historical account of transgender – and I am not the one and do not have the space to establish it – its appeal lies in what it seeks to achieve through its unfashionable 'metanarrative'.[94] In the context of the US, at least, Feinberg's account serves to identify WASP hegemony under capitalism, with *its* accompanying sex/gender system, as the persistent political problem, the binding force of a particular conservatism that ideologically overrides divergent class interests. It is this hegemony that determines what counts as 'difference' in the US, as Feinberg's identifications and their qualifications illustrate; crucially, for instance, ze finds it necessary to specify that ze is '*anti-racist* white, working class'.

As the editors of the *Transgender Reader* highlight, however, Feinberg's 'particular theory of history has not attracted widespread support in transgender communities, [but] hir work has gained a devoted and grateful following for the powerful way it calls upon transgender people to recover their historical legacy, and to harness that knowledge to the current struggle for a more just society'.[95] In other words, its systemic critique has been neglected in favour of identitarian emphases, including those that seek to recover past traditions. Critical attention, indeed, has mostly focused on the subjective, substantially autobiographical experience distilled in hir novel, *Stone Butch Blues*.[96] Thus, the reception of Feinberg's writing has contributed to a distortion of its distinctive political purposes. This may have something to do with hir party-political affiliations and their tendency to reinforce pervasive perceptions of Marxism as inevitably authoritarian: the WWP is Stalinist in orientation, as evident from its persistent support for the 'self-determination' of the North Korean regime.

There is an obvious overlap between the categories of transgender, as defined by Feinberg, and genderqueer. In some ways, both categories seek to trouble binary distinctions, which is how they understand the categories of man and woman. In other respects, however, they have inaugurated and consolidated binarisms of their own. If there are those who identify as non-binary, for instance, this is surely by contrast with those who are presumed to be binary on the basis of their 'gender presentation', but who have never opted for – and may even indignantly reject – any such description of them. After all, it goes against feminist thinking virtually in its entirety to think of men and women in binaristic terms. In this context, Rubin's observation forty years ago that 'far from being an expression of natural differences, exclusive gender identity is the suppression of natural similarities' between men and women[97] takes on a striking new significance. A similar point has to be made in relation to the term 'cisgender', which manifestly consolidates the normative relation between sex and gender, presuming that this can only be disrupted by those who are/identify as 'trans'.

The trajectory in any case is clear: the more general sensitivity to difference, combined with the autonomisation of gender, has encouraged trends towards interpreting the 1960s emphasis on 'the personal as political' as the wholesale subsumption of the latter by the former. The norms governing 'safe space' arrangements offered by the group, Genderqueer Chicago, for instance, evince a paranoid sensitivity to privacy:

- Consent for touching: ask before you touch someone else.
- One Diva, One Mic: respect folks by not interrupting.
- Don't assume: we respect each other by trying not to assume anything about anyone's identity, gender or otherwise.

- Las Vegas Rule: what is said in GqC meetings, cannot be repeated outside of the space.
- Oops/Ouch: if someone says something you find hurtful, you can say 'ouch.' They then say 'oops' and we all work it out, either during or after the meeting.
- Respect everyone's name/pronoun preference inside and outside the space. Check in with folks about names/pronouns so you don't accidentally out them.
- Own it: To keep things in perspective, try and speak from your own experiences using 'I' phrases.[98]

Drawing on arguments by Wendy Brown I have already outlined, Jack Halberstam rightly draws attention to the ways in which this kind of development in trans cultures both reflects and consolidates neoliberal pressure to pass off individualised suffering as social activism.[99] But the problem is also bound up with theory. In claiming that gender is about (non-intentional) doing rather than being, Butler confers on the desirable pluralisation of gender the status of agency itself.

One way to reconnect with purpose may be through the critique of paranoia.

### QUEERING THE ECONOMY?

In her essay, 'Paranoid Reading and Reparative Reading', Eve Kosofsky Sedgwick speaks of the effect on her of a particular insight in relation to AIDS activism articulated by Cindy Patton. It is the effect itself that matters here, since this 'opened a space for moving from the rather fixated question' about whether something is true to that of '*how* [...] is knowledge performative, and how best does one move among its causes and effects'.[100] Note here what will by now be the familiar spatial metaphor in this idealist prioritisation of movement over fixity. Thinking once again becomes a mode of liberation, as thought itself is rendered performative, which is to say as participating in the received wisdoms through which the world is discursively constructed. On this basis, Sedgwick proceeds to challenge what she regards as the paranoia of Left modes of analysis and the way they pessimistically render the world predictable because rigorously determined by power; nothing can surprise those of us in the know. Though Sedgwick clearly frames her argument by reference to the idea of performativity Butler has done so much to promote, she nonetheless illustrates this paranoia in part by reference to *Gender Trouble*. Drawing on a distinction found in Sylvan Tomkins's work on affect, she contrasts strong theory, which seeks to account for everything according to established principles, and weak theory, which is more open to unforeseen possibilities and seems for this reason preferable.

From an avowedly orthodox Marxist position, Donald Morton is suspicious of this argument. It is, he suggests, Sedgwick's 'response to class struggle: reparative reading is aimed at the blurring of social antagonisms and at the affective "healing" of economic wounds'.[101] From the perspective argued for by Sedgwick, such a response may only to be expected – which serves to illustrate just how difficult it is to escape from 'paranoia'. As I read the essay, however, Sedgwick does not really propose that we can or should simply abandon strong theory, and by contrast with Morton I am struck by her attentiveness to the historical conditions in which she articulates her case, which after all has targets other than Marxism in its sights. She points out that the 'paranoid' Foucaultian interrogation of 'secular, universalist liberal humanism' has been pursued most rigorously in the 'xenophobic Reagan–Bush–Clinton America where "liberal" is, if anything, a taboo category; and where "secular humanism" is routinely treated as a marginal religious sect'.[102] What might we say of the fate of humanism of any sort in the future in relation to Trump's project to restore American greatness?

I shall return in my conclusion to what I consider the potential value of Sedgwick's essay. First, I want to reflect on its influence in the sphere of political economy as developed by J. K. Gibson-Graham (two people who write under this pen name). Their work claims to be both feminist and queer, though it is not conspicuously concerned with questions of sexuality or gender, but rather asserts these affiliations on the basis of shared philosophical and methodological principles. Gibson-Graham's aim, initially outlined in *The End of Capitalism (As We Knew It)* (1996), is to generate detotalising accounts of transactions and relations that might broadly be described as economic in order to dissipate our sense of 'the Economy' as something overwhelming, global and, because of its sheer scope, unalterable – something, that is, that might be thought of as capitalist. They effectively collapse – or, if one prefers, deconstruct – ontology and epistemology. Their subsequent work, *A Postcapitalist Politics* (2006), continues this critique of the 'hegemonic discourse' of an essentialist, determining Economy. 'We have imagined,' they write, 'that a language of economic diversity might provide webs of meaning and intimations of possibility that could distinguish and invigorate a new economic politics.'[103] One striking effect of their particular resignification of the category of hegemony, however, is the unification of the political spectrum of apologists and critics of capital. Those of us who believe that it is neoliberalism that is truly hegemonic and in need of opposition are identified with those who impose it, but it is we who are in need of feminist and queer correction, not the Right.[104]

In proceeding discursively to (de)construct the world in conformity with these purposes, Gibson-Graham therefore again combine the elements of idealism and empiricism we have seen somewhat differently aligned in Butler through their recognition of a world of economic diversity. Their initial critical focus, before going on to consider the potential for practically implementing their project, is on the subjectification of the Left. They note in passing, but avoid engagement with, the substantive points raised by those who are sceptical about their work, and instead diagnose those critics' paranoia, in the sense Sedgwick speaks of, and Left melancholy, a Benjaminian term invoked by Wendy Brown to refer to 'a certain narcissism with regard to one's past political attachments and identity that exceeds any contemporary investment in political mobilisation, alliance, or transformation'.[105] Brown particularly highlights the ultimate conservatism of this pessimism's tendency to emphasise the disabling effects of identity politics and post-structuralism.[106]

Gibson-Graham choose to illustrate the differences in sensibility between themselves and the traditional Left by reference to two British films from the 1990s instructively concerned with deindustrialisation, *Brassed Off* (Herman, 1996) and *The Full Monty* (Cattaneo, 1997). The first focuses on the divergent fortunes of a coal mine destined for closure as part of the programme announced by John Major's Tory government in 1992, and the competitively successful, though existentially imperilled, brass band that has been the cultural accompaniment to the town of Grimley's industrial life. The miners' pessimism about the prospects of the mine is conditioned by their experience of defeat in the earlier strike of 1984–5. It is consequently the miners' wives who play the leading part in the campaign to keep the pit open, but their optimism is shown to be deluded; masculine realism triumphs.

The second, more commercially successful and less overtly political, film – for which industrial decline is a fact, not a process – focuses on former steelworkers who turn to stripping. Initially this is with a view to making a living, though ultimately it turns out to be for one symbolically transformative night only (as Cora Kaplan suggests, this 'is not a solution but rather a symptom of their plight'[107]). Through this they – and especially the central figure of Gaz – triumph over themselves by overcoming their aggressive resentment at their plight (becoming reconciled to more equal relations to women, *for* whom they ultimately perform), discovering sexual liberalism (two members of the troupe come out as gay) and incorporating racial diversity into their social lives. Gibson-Graham challenge Žižek's typically paranoid account of these films: he argues that, in spite of their divergent moods, they relate to the same neoliberal condition by together emphasising the processes of deskilling and reskilling that govern contemporary working life.[108] Gibson-Graham, by contrast, focus on the films' different dispositions towards the world: *Brassed Off* evinces that melancholic, pessimistic and masculine fixation on defeat by the all-powerful Economy, whereas *The Full Monty* discovers potential where once there appeared only to be limitation and destitution.

Gibson-Graham's reading of their preferred film, however, is facilitated by a problematic abstraction of *The Full Monty* from its context. They appear to believe that the men were employed by some private company,[109] whereas steel production in Britain took the form of a nationalised industry until its privatisation by the Thatcher government in 1988. Between 1981 and 1983, its workforce was notoriously decimated under the chairmanship of Ian McGregor, appointed because of his truly macho record of union-busting in the US mining industry. After his time at British Steel, he was appointed by Thatcher herself as Chair of the National Coal Board, where he was responsible for drawing up the pit closures programme that provoked the 1984–5 NUM strike whose outcome facilitated the all-but-total subsequent wipeout of that industry that is the context for *Brassed Off*. The miners' strike, moreover, was a confrontation the Tory Party had been planning since 1978, before they came to power, when Nicholas Ridley, MP – son of a coalmine-owning family in the days before nationalisation – drew up a plan for dealing with the kind of industrial action Thatcher's allies knew their policies would provoke.[110] Deindustrialisation and the defeat of the trade union movement in Britain was therefore actively pursued as state policy and involved global actors; it was crucial to the prototypically neoliberal project of Thatcherism. Moreover, *The Full Monty* allegorically draws our attention to the shift in the British economy – if I may be permitted such a singular, totalising reference – towards highly unequal, but predominantly low-wage service and entertainment employment that resulted from deindustrialisation. Both the film and its success, as well as the stripping it depicts, symbolise that. So does *Brassed Off*, for that matter – brass bands have survived or disappeared depending on their capacity to thrive as commercially independent entities – not to mention that other, similarly allegorical treatment of the miners' strike of 1984–5, *Billy Elliot*.[111] The men of *The Full Monty* become – at least temporarily – good entrepreneurial subjects of the sort Foucault has suggested are shaped by the neoliberal state:[112] they do not sell their bodies into alienated labour, but use them for narcissistically rewarding/reparative, if non-domineering, disinhibited display. In self-consciously performing their masculinity, they achieve a kind of liberation for all.[113]

Gibson-Graham's arguments are not without insight, of course. Habit is formative and the disposition it generates may be inhibiting in all sorts of ways, but it also more positively generates intuitions that can be crucial in figuring out what complex and bewildering changes portend. It is ultimately intuition that leads me to sense when I read Gibson-Graham's work that it resembles all too closely in tone and sentiment the kind of self-help guide that tells people to dust themselves off and start every day afresh, to be positive rather than negative all the time; Thatcher's arch-ally, Norman Tebbit, once notoriously advised the unemployed to get on their bikes in the midst of full-blown recession.

The people of Grimley have not disappeared, and they have had few reasons to cheer up; 'regeneration' has proved stubbornly elusive for towns that were constructed around industries such as coal. Their condition is that of people all over the world under what Raymond Williams once described in relation to the 1984–5 miners' strike as a 'nomad capitalism, which exploits actual places and people then (as it suits it) moves on'.[114] The language of deterritorialisation and reterritorialisation doesn't adequately capture the agency of such nomadism or the complex significance of it (exploitation or unemployment?) for those who are victim to its whims.

I write, indeed, in the immediate aftermath of the British vote to leave the European Union that has sent the kinds of shockwaves through the global economy that render it graspable as a totality. Generational, racial and ethnic, regional and class-based divisions are widely reported, and are disturbing and disorienting (though the statistics used to highlight these also both reflect and serve to consolidate entrenched perceptions and prejudices of the sort I dwell on here). Young people, who have been affectively engaged to tears by the result,[115] turned out in relatively smaller numbers than the rest of the population, while the elderly voted nostalgically *en masse* for everyone to return to the past they idealise. Blame and shame for the result is being heaped by the cosmopolitan areas and media on a white working class – respectable Home Counties Brexiteers largely escape scrutiny – that has increasingly become conscious of itself as such. Meanwhile 'Britons' are lauded by the Tory press for asserting their independence on the verge of a possible breakup of the UK. Yet that same press has in recent years revelled in other forms of stigmatisation – of scroungers and parasites – that inform the attitudes of many among a metropolitan middle class. As Owen Jones notes, overt disdain for the 'chav' is pervasive among those who are in other respects socially liberal.[116] And why should it not be? After all, the chav and his kind are no doubt responsible for the racist abuse and attacks that are widely reported to have increased exponentially since the vote – by 500 per cent according to one recent report of *recorded* incidents.[117] A march to reverse the vote, and in enthusiastic support therefore of a fundamentally undemocratic and neoliberal institution that has brought austerity, death and true despair to Greece and elsewhere, is attended by thousands of marchers in London (where else?), and is cheered on from a swanky hotel by migrant workers there.[118] If the white working class is abject – and it knows that it is and for whom – in what progressive sense might it be recognised?[119] There can be none for such a political identity, predicated on a residual sense of racialised entitlement – but that should not validate the abjection. Socialists, who were also divided over the vote, are united in despair; they know that this wholly unavailing situation results from the purposeful occlusion of their politics over decades. Sensing a general election, the response of the mostly right-wing Parliamentary Labour Party is to attempt to rid itself of its left-wing leader, Jeremy Corbyn, whose job it has consistently made impossible, but who has the overwhelming support of the membership at large.

In other words, the worsening situation in Britain, as elsewhere, demands a universalising politics that challenges the scapegoating encouraged by scarcity of resources. As a gay man from a working class background who has had some 'success' in the conventional, economic sense, and enjoyed a relatively cosmopolitan existence, I understand something of what it means to 'escape' confinements, but cheering on masculine disintegration in circumstances not of our own choosing is fraught with problems. Erich Fromm once spoke of the fear of freedom. He argued at length that the kind of liberty made possible by capitalism through its dissolution of traditional bonds may also be negatively experienced as uncertainty and isolation in ways that push people towards authoritarian solutions.[120] What Fromm did not emphasise sufficiently – perhaps because the point has become historically more significant – is that freedom and the fear of it are experienced in socially divergent ways. *Have no fear* seems to me the abiding counsel of contemporary antihumanism.

A very loosely analogous, but qualitatively different, project to Gibson-Graham's has been undertaken by Erik Olin Wright in a book called *Envisioning Real Utopias*. However, he presents the socialist case for transformation away from capitalism as the basis for examining a plurality of existing non-capitalist projects that, in combination, offer the potential through their extension, deepening and replication to achieve democratic, egalitarian control of state and economy. These various forms he lists under the titles of statist socialism, social democratic economic regulation, associational democracy, social capitalism, social economy, cooperative market economy and participatory socialism. Wright appreciates that the pursuit of such projects will ultimately meet powerful resistance from capitalist forces that will mean change cannot be merely incremental, but must also be ruptural. Organised political action and discipline, as well as solidarity, will therefore be necessary. Abstractly, I wonder what queers do or might think of such propositions through which we might seek self-consciously to reconstruct and organise our societies, propositions that must carry subjectively formative implications. Will they sound 'conservative'?

Answers to these questions are likely to be diverse, depending on which constituencies we have in mind when speaking of queers. Peter Drucker has recently argued for a distinction between gay normality and more radical queer identities that might be 'the starting point for developing an effective queer anti-capitalism and a global rainbow politics'.[121] That sounds optimistic to me for two reasons. First, because the stark subcultural dichotomy it proposes is based on an implausible avant-gardism that may well call into question what Drucker means by 'effective'. As Alan Sinfield has argued, we should expect subcultures to be heterogeneous in all sorts of ways, but they may be places in which ideas can be debated and persuasion can take place.[122] Any plausible counter-hegemonic socialist project will require a great deal of that all round; it cannot be a matter of berating people for failing to measure up to some radical agenda with which they have been previously unacquainted. (Perhaps this is not what Drucker has in mind, but it is familiar practice.) Second, participation by queers in a more general transformation will entail accommodation with others whose priorities are not immediately or even remotely focused on sexuality or gender dissidence. Perhaps we would have as much to learn from as we might hope to impart to them. I have drawn on Bourdieu to suggest that self-consciously queer identities, insofar as they perpetuate countercultural traditions, may thrive on their distinction from despised, supposedly 'assimilated' groups that are in fact comprised of real people who have often not been the beneficiaries of capitalism, especially as it has transmuted into neoliberal form: all of our social identities have been forged in conditions of class society, and we must anticipate that they will change. The Left used to believe it should shape precisely this process.

This brings me to the value for my purposes, at least, of Sedgwick's essay, which might be read as counselling a resistance to the sort of paranoia that serves to attach us to our persecuted identities, but also perhaps as encouraging a relaxation of other leftist avant-gardist rigidities, including the whole culture of rigid party lines and the denunciation of deviationism. It seems to me a matter of political urgency to cultivate in their place a generosity towards and presumption of goodwill on the part of others who are not avowedly reactionary in order to facilitate counter-hegemonic expansion. Not every infelicitous use of language or casual assumption should be regarded as evidence of one of the 'phobias' that are instructively multiplying in these times. Nick Srnicek and Alex Williams are among those who highlight the antagonism and puritanism that is prevalent in Left discourse on social media ('anti-social media' would surely be a better term): 'we are more concerned to appear right', they argue, 'than to think about the conditions of political change'.[123] Indeed, if the Left is to expand beyond its overlapping subcultures it must also find ways of engaging less judgementally with those who have become reactionary by habit and prejudice over decades of actual or perceived abandonment, and who may themselves articulate an identitarian language of suffering based on having been left behind. Socialist humanism might be a good name for such a project of overcoming, rather than accentuating, differences in order to appreciate what freedoms might be open to us all under egalitarian conditions.

## NOTES

1. Some degree of challenge to this is offered by the essays collected in the special issue of *differences: A Journal of Feminist Cultural Studies*, Vol. 26, No. 1 (2015), ed. Robyn Weigman and Elizabeth A. Wilson: *Queer Theory Without Antinormativity*.

2. Norman Geras, *Marx and Human Nature: Refutation of a Legend*, London: Verso, 1983.

3. Ibid., p. 115.

4. Jean-Paul Sartre, *Saint Genet: Actor and Martyr*, trans. Bernard Frechtman, Minneapolis: University of Minnesota Press, 2012 [1952], p. 49.

5. Marshall Berman explores the dynamism of capitalism as highlighted by Marx and Engels in *All That is Solid: The Experience of Modernity*, London: Verso, 1983.

6. Marcuse outlines these terms in *One-Dimensional Man: Studies in the Ideology of Advanced Industrial Society*, London: Routledge, 2002 [1964], pp. 6–8.

7. Judith Butler, *Bodies That Matter: On the Discursive Limits of 'Sex'*, New York: Routledge, 1993, p. 3.

8. Sara Ahmed, 'Interview with Judith Butler', *Sexualities*, Vol. 19, No. 4 (2016), p. 11.

9. David Harvey, *A Brief History of Neoliberalism*, Oxford: Oxford University Press, 2005, p. 11.

10. Judith Butler, *Excitable Speech: A Politics of the Performative*, New York: Routledge, 1997, p. 133.

11. Paul Passavant and Jodi Dean, 'Laws and Societies', *Constellations*, Vol. 8, No. 3 (2001), p. 381.

12. Ellen Meiksins Wood, *Democracy Against Capitalism: Renewing Historical Materialism*, Cambridge: Cambridge University Press, 1995, pp. 238–63.

13. For a critical consideration of this tradition's pervasive 'social weightlessness' (Bourdieu) and underestimation of the constraining effects of power, see Lois McNay, *The Misguided Search for the Political*, Cambridge: Polity Press, 2014.

14. Moya Lloyd, *Judith Butler: From Norms to Politics*, Cambridge: Polity, 2007, p. 148.

15. Judith Butler, 'Competing Universalities', in Judith Butler, Ernesto Laclau and Slavoj Žižek, *Contingency, Hegemony, Universality: Contemporary Dialogues on the Left*, London: Verso, 2000, pp. 178–9.

16. See Butler, 'Restaging the Universal', *Contingency, Hegemony, Universality*, p. 21.

17. Homi Bhabha, 'The Commitment to Theory', in *The Location of Culture*, London: Routledge, 1994, pp. 38–9.

18. Salman, 'In Good Faith', *Imaginary Homelands*, London: Granta/Penguin, 1991, p. 394.

19. Salman Rushdie, *The Satanic Verses*, London: Viking, 1988, p. 5.

20. Colin Leys emphasises the end of currency controls in *Market-Driven Politics: Neoliberal Democracy and the Public Interest*, London: Verso, 2001, pp. 8–79.

21. Stuart Hall, 'The Great Moving Right Show', *The Hard Road to Renewal*, London: Verso, 1988, p. 48.

22. Robert Spencer contrasts the novel with his comments in this respect in 'Salman Rushdie and the "War on Terror"', *Journal of Postcolonial Writing*, Vol. 46, Nos 3–4, (2010), pp. 251–65.

23. Judith Butler, 'Violence, Mourning, Politics', in *Precarious Life: The Powers of Mourning and Violence*, London: Verso, 2004, pp. 19–49.

24. Lauren Berlant, *Cruel Optimism*, Durham, NC: Duke University Press, 2011, p. 182.

25. Timothy Brennan provides a summary corrective to this in his Introduction to this volume.

26. Jasbir Puar, *Terrorist Assemblages: Homonationalism in Queer Times*, Durham, NC: Duke University Press, 2007.

27. Raymond Williams, 'Base and Superstructure in Marxist Cultural Theory', *New Left Review I*, No. 82 (1973), pp. 8–12.

28. Butler, 'Violence, Mourning, Politics', p. 35.

29. Slavoj Žižek, 'Da Capo senza Fine' in Butler et al., *Contingency, Hegemony, Universality*, p. 319.

30. Ernesto Laclau and Chantal Mouffe, *Hegemony and Socialist Strategy: Towards a Radical Democratic Politics*, London: Verso, 1985.

31. Harvey, *A Brief History of Neoliberalism*, pp. 19–38.

32. This is more explicit in Wendy Brown's essay, 'Wounded Attachments', on which Žižek bases his argument (though he doesn't do full justice to its complexity): see *States of Injury: Power and Freedom in Late Modernity*, Princeton, NJ: Princeton University Press, 1995, pp. 56–61. I return to Brown's important argument at various points in this chapter.

33. Kevin Floyd, *The Reification of Desire: Toward a Queer Marxism*, Minneapolis: University of Minnesota Press, 2009.

34. Judith Halberstam, *Female Masculinity*, Durham, DC: Duke University Press, 1998, p. 106.

35. Donna Haraway, 'The Cyborg Manifesto', in *Simians, Cyborgs and Women*, London: Free Association, 1991, p. 151. Sandy Stone was a student of Haraway's and author of 'The Empire Strikes Back: A Posttransexual Manifesto' (see Susan Stryker and Stephen Whittle (eds), *The Transgender Studies Reader*, vol. 1, New York: Routledge, 2006, pp. 221–36). Susan Stryker highlights and embraces the claim that 'the transsexual body is an unnatural body' and polemically identifies with Frankenstein's monster ('My Words to Victor Frankenstein above the Village of Chamounix', in Stryker and Whittle, *Transgender Studies Reader*, p. 245). One notable exception to this strand is Jay Prosser's *Second Skins: The Body Narratives of Transsexuality*, New York: Columbia University Press, 1998, which opens with a critique of Butler, and argues that 'Not simply costumes for our experience of our bodies, our theoretical conceptions of the body are foundationally formed

by and reformative of them' (p. 96). Significantly, Jacqueline Rose has suggested the book is regarded as conservative in trans studies ('Who Do You Think You Are?', *London Review of Books*, Vol. 38, No. 9 (5 May 2016): www.lrb.co.uk/v38/n09/jacqueline-rose/who-do-you-are.

36. Wendy Brown, 'Wounded Attachments', in *States of Injury: Power and Freedom in Late Modernity*, Princeton, NJ: Princeton University Press, 1995, p. 62.

37. See in general, for instance, David Harvey, *Seventeen Contradictions and the End of Capitalism*, London: Profile, 2014, and Wolfgang Streeck, 'How Will Capitalism End', *New Left Review II*, No. 88 (2014), pp. 35–64.

38. Timothy Brennan, *At Home in the World: Cosmopolitanism Now*, Cambridge, MA: Harvard University Press, 1997, p. 308.

39. In this section, I am summarizing, developing and, in some respects, modifying arguments explored in David Alderson, *Sex, Needs and Queer Culture: From Liberation to the Postgay*, London: Zed Books, 2016, chapter 3.

40. In this section, I partly summarize, but develop to different ends, points made more fully in Alderson, *Sex, Needs and Queer Culture*, especially pp. 152–83.

41. Alan Sinfield, *Literature, Politics and Culture in Postwar Britain* (London: Continuum), pp. 293–301.

42. Fredric Jameson, 'Periodising the Sixties', in Sohnya Sayres, Anders Stephanson, Stanley Aaronowitz and Fredric Jameson (eds), *The Sixties Without Apology*, Minneapolis: University of Minnesota Press, 1984, pp. 180–6.

43. See the documents collected in Karla Jay and Allen Young (eds), *Out of the Closets: Voices of Gay Liberation*, New York: Jove, 1977 [1972], pp. 205–50.

44. Dennis Altman, *Homosexual: Oppression and Liberation*, London: Allen Lane, 1974, p. 154.

45. Judith Roof, '1970s Lesbian Feminism Meets 1990s Butch-Femme', in *Butch/Femme: Inside Lesbian Gender*, London: Cassell, 1998, p. 30.

46. Stone, 'The Empire Fights Back', p. 232.

47. Maurice Isserman and Michael Kazin, 'The Failure and Success of the New Radicalism', in Steve Fraser and Gary Gerstle (eds), *The Rise and Fall of the New Deal Order 1930–1980*, Princeton, NJ: Princeton University Press, 1989, pp. 225–6.

48. See, for instance, James Miller, *Democracy is in the Streets: From Port Huron to the Siege of Chicago*, New York: Simon & Schuster, 1987, p. 54.

49. Timothy Brennan, 'The Organizational Imaginary', *Wars of Position: The Cultural Politics of Left and Right*, New York: Columbia University Press, 2006, pp. 147–69.

50. See, for instance, the account by Kirkpatrick Sale, *SDS*, New York: Vintage, 1973.

51. Brown, 'Wounded Attachments', p. 61.

52. Herbert Marcuse, *One-Dimensional Man: Studies in the Ideology of Advanced Industrial Society*, London: Routledge, 2002, p. 21.

53. Theodore Roszak, *The Making of a Counter Culture: Reflections on the Technocratic Society and Its Youthful Opposition*, Berkeley: University of California Press, 1968, pp. 1–5.

54. Dennis Altman, *Homosexual: Oppression and Liberation*, London: Allen Lane, 1974, p. 159.

55. Herbert Marcuse, *An Essay on Liberation*, Boston: Beacon Press, 1969, pp. 39.

56. Ibid., p. 48.

57. Ibid., p. 5.

58. Herbert Marcuse, *Counterrevolution and Revolt*, Boston: Beacon Press, 1972, p. 50.

59. Ibid., p. 31.

60. François Cusset, *French Theory: How Foucault, Derrida, Deleuze & Co. Transformed the Intellectual Life of the United States*, trans. Jeff Fort with Josephine Berganza and Marlon Jones, Minneapolis: University of Minnesota Press, 2008, p. 131.

61. See Alderson, *Sex, Needs and Queer Culture*, pp. 172–3.

62. Dennis Altman, *The Homosexualisation of America*, Boston: Beacon Press, 1982.

63. Elizabeth Wilson, *Bohemians: The Glamorous Outcasts*, London: I. B. Tauris, 2003, p. 22.

64. Pierre Bourdieu, *Distinction: A Social Critique of the Judgement of Taste*, trans. Richard Nice, London: Routledge, 1984, p. 251. Bourdieu is here speaking specifically of culture as art, but it seems to me legitimate to extrapolate from this sphere to culture in the broader sense.

65. Barbara Ehrenreich, *Fear of Falling: The Inner Life of the Middle Class*, New York: HarperCollins, 1989, pp. 97–143.

66. Susan Faludi, *Stiffed: The Betrayal of Modern Man*, London: Chatto & Windus, 1999.

67. For a refreshing critique of such unhelpfully misleading periodisations or trends, see Lynne Segal, *Why Feminism?*, Oxford: Polity, 1999, pp. 9–37.

68. Gayle Rubin, 'The Traffic in Women: Notes on the "Political Economy" of Sex', in Rayna R. Reiter (ed.), *Toward an Anthropology of Women*, New York: Monthly Review Press, 1975, p. 179. Rubin subsequently distinguished sexuality from gender as a category of analysis and focus for political intervention in 'Thinking Sex: Notes for a Radical Theory of a Politics of Sexuality', in Carole S. Vance (ed.), *Pleasure and Danger: Exploring Female Sexuality*, London: Routledge & Kegan Paul, 1984, pp. 267–319.

69. Rubin, 'The Traffic in Women', p. 199.

70. Joan W. Scott, 'Gender: A Useful Category of Historical Analysis', *Gender and the Politics of History*, Bloomington: Indiana University Press, 2011, p. 31.

71. For some of the considerations involved, see Joan Scott (ed.), *Women's Studies on the Edge*, the special issue of *differences*, Vol. 9, No. 3 (1997). I should acknowledge that I co-founded a master's programme in gender, sexuality and culture at the University of Manchester in 2003.

72. This is made clear, for instance, in Andrew Tolson, *The Limits of Masculinity*, London: Routledge, 1987.

73. Herbert Sussman, *Victorian Masculinities*, Cambridge: Cambridge University Press, 1995, p. 3.

74. Klaus Theweleit, *Male Fantasies*, 2 vols, Minneapolis: University of Minnesota Press, 1987–9.

75. See Alan Sinfield, 'Transgender and Les/bi/gay Identities' in David Alderson and Linda R. Anderson (eds), *Territories of Desire in Queer Culture: Refiguring Contemporary Boundaries*, Manchester: Manchester University Press, 2000, pp. 153–8; David Halperin, *How to be Gay*, Harvard: Belknap Press, 2012, pp. 69–81.

76. See Sally Munt and Cherry Smyth (eds), *Butch/Femme: Inside Lesbian Gender*, London: Cassell, 1998.

77. Rubin, for instance, advocates androgyny in 'The Traffic in Women', p. 204.

78. Judith Butler, *Gender Trouble: Feminism and the Subversion of Identity*, New York: Routledge, 1991, p. 9.

79. Ibid., p. 146.

80. Annamarie Jagose, 'The Trouble with Antinormativity', in Weigman and Wilson (eds), *Queer Theory Without Antinormativity*, p. 44.

81. Ibid., p. 147.

82. Ibid., p. 149.

83. Žižek, 'Da Capo senza Fine', p. 216.

84. Toril Moi, 'What Is a Woman?' in *What Is a Woman?: And Other Essays*, Oxford: Oxford University Press, 1999, p. 42.

85. Ibid., p. 72.

86. The essays in *Undoing Gender*, New York: Routledge, 2004, consider ways in which such formations can or should be challenged.

87. Eve Kosofsky Sedgwick, 'Gosh, Boy George, You Must Be Awfully Secure in Your Masculinity', in Maurice Berger, Brian Wallis and Simon Watson (eds), *Constructing Masculinity*, New York: Routledge, 1995, p. 16.

88. Ibid., p. 13.

89. Judith Halberstam, *Female Masculinity*, Durham: Duke University Press, 1998, p. 272.

90. Deborah Cameron, 'Body Shopping', *Trouble and Strife: The Radical Feminist Magazine*, No. 41 (2000), pp. 21–2.

91. On the distinction between transgression and transformation, see Elizabeth Wilson, 'Is Transgression Transgressive?', in Joseph Bristow and Angelia R. Wilson (eds), *Activating Theory: Lesbian, Gay, Bisexual Politics*, London: Lawrence & Wishart, 1993, pp. 107–17.

92. Leslie Feinberg, *Transgender Warriors: Making History from Joan of Arc to Dennis Rodman*, Boston: Beacon Press, 1996, p. x. On the significance of the book, see Susan Stryker, '(De)Subjugated Knowledges: An Introduction to Transgender Studies', *The Transgender Reader*, vol. 1, New York: Routledge, 2006, p. 4.

93. See www.lesliefeinberg.net/self/ (accessed June 2016).

94. Feinberg's account does, however, clearly challenge Rubin's anthropological claims about the origins and rigidity of the sex/gender systems.

95. Introduction to Leslie Feinberg, 'Transgender Liberation: A Movement Whose Time Has Come', in Susan Stryker and Stephen Whittle (eds), *The Transgender Studies Reader*, New York: Routledge, 2006, p. 205.

96. Halberstam focuses on the novel, and in a footnote regrets the 'sweeping generalizations' of *Transgender Warriors* (*Female Masculinity*, p. 291). See also Jean Bobby Noble, *Masculinities Without Men? Female Masculinity in Twentieth-Century Fictions*, Vancouver: University of British Columbia Press, 2004, pp. 90–141.

97. Rubin, 'The Traffic in Women', p. 180.

98. http://genderqueerchicago.blogspot.co.uk/p/gqc-policies.html (accessed June 2015).

99. Jack Halberstam, 'You Are Triggering Me! The Neo-Liberal Rhetoric of Harm, Danger and Trauma, https://bullybloggers.wordpress.com/2014/07/05/you-are-triggering-me-the-neo-liberal-rhetoric-of-harm-danger-and-trauma/ (accessed June 2016).

100. Even Kosofsky Sedgwick, 'Paranoid Reading and Reparative Reading; or, You're so Paranoid You Probably Think This Introduction Is About You', in *Novel Gazing: Queer Readings in Fiction*, Durham, NC: Duke University Press, 1997, p. 4.

101. Donald Morton, 'Pataphysics of the Closet: Queer Theory as the Art of Imaginary Solutions for Unimaginary Problems', in Mas'ud Zavarzadeh, Teresa L. Ebert and Donald Morton (eds), *Marxism, Queer Theory, Gender*, special issue of *Transformation: Marxist Boundary Work in Theory, Economics, Politics and Culture*, No. 2 (2001), p. 25.

102. Sedgwick, 'Paranoid Reading and Reparative Reading', p. 18.

103. Gibson-Graham, *A Postcapitalist Politics*, Minneapolis: University of Minnesota Press, 2006, p. xxxiv.

104. Lisa Henderson offers a more positive spin on Gibson-Graham's work and argues for modes of solidarity in ways that have influenced my arguments here, but which I have sadly not had the space to engage with directly. See *Love and Money: Queer, Class and Cultural Production*, New York: New York University Press, 2013; also 'Queer and Class: Toward a Cultural Politics of Friendship', in David Alderson (ed.), *Queerwords: Sexuality and the Politics of Culture*, special issue of *Key Words: A Journal of Cultural Materialism*, No. 13 (2015), pp. 17–38.

105. Wendy Brown, 'Resisting Left Melancholy', *Boundary 2*, Vol. 26. No. 3 (1999), p. 20.

106. Ibid., pp. 23–7.

107. Cora Kaplan, 'The Death of the Working-Class Hero', *new formations*, No. 52 (2004), p. 107.

108. I have not been able to locate the source Gibson-Graham cite for this argument, but Žižek describes both the apparently opposing gestures at the end of each of these films as 'the acts of losers' in *The Ticklish Subject: The Absent Centre of Political Ontology*, London: Verso, 1999, p. 352.

109. Gibson-Graham, *A Postcapitalist Politics*, p. 16.
110. For details of this, see Huw Beynon and Peter McMylor, 'Decisive Power: The New Tory State Against the Miners', in Huw Beynon (ed.), *Digging Deeper: Issues in the Miners' Strike*, London: Verso, 1985, p. 35.
111. On this, see John Hill, 'A Working Class Hero is Something to Be? Representations of Class and Masculinity in British Cinema', in Phil Powrie, Anne Davies and Bruce Babbington (eds), *The Trouble with Men: Masculinities in European and Hollywood Cinema*, London: Wallflower Press, 2004, p. 108.
112. Michel Foucault. *The Birth of Biopolitics: Lectures at the Collége de France 1978–1979*, trans. Graham Burchell, New York: Picador, 2008, p. 236.
113. Judith Halberstam, for instance, claims that 'minority [especially female] masculinities can expose mainstream masculinity as a dangerous myth of potency, invulnerability and violence' (*In a Queer Time and Place: Transgender Bodies, Subcultural Lives*, New York: New York University Press, 2005, p. 141).
114. Raymond Williams, 'Mining the Meaning: Key Words in the Miners' Strike', *Resources of Hope: Culture, Democracy, Socialism*, London: Verso, 1989, p. 124.
115. Toby Helm, 'Poll Reveals Young Remain Voters Reduced to Tears by Brexit Results', *The Guardian*, 2 July 2016: www.theguardian.com/politics/2016/jul/02/brexit-referendum-voters-survey.
116. Owen Jones, *Chavs: The Demonization of the Working Class*, London: Verso, 2011.
117. Nazia Parveen and Harriet Sherwood, 'Police Log Fivefold Rise in Race-Hate Complaints Since Brexit Result', *The Guardian*, 30 June 2016: www.theguardian.com/world/2016/jun/30/police-report-fivefold-increase-race-hate-crimes-since-brexit-result.
118. Ed Vulliamy, 'We Are the 48%: Tens of Thousands March in London for Europe', *The Guardian*, 2 July 2016: www.theguardian.com/politics/2016/jul/02/march-for-europe-eu-referendum-london-protest.
119. William Davis, adopting Nancy Fraser's terms, similarly remarks that even New Labour had offered its own heartlands '"redistribution" but no "recognition"' ('Thoughts on the Sociology of Brexit', *The Brexit Crisis: A Verso Report*, London: Verso, 2016, p. 16).
120. Erich Fromm, *The Fear of Freedom*, London: Routledge, 2002 [1942]. I endorse the general argument, if not all aspects of the analysis and methodology.
121. Peter Drucker, *Warped: Gay Normality and Queer Anticapitalism*, Chicago: Haymarket, 2015, p. 307.
122. Alan Sinfield, *Gay and After*, London: Cassell, 1998, p. 199.
123. Nick Srnicek and Alex Williams, *Inventing the Future: Postcapitalism and a World Without Work*, London: Verso, 2015, p. 8.

# Conclusion

## David Alderson and Robert Spencer

It is now often said that democracy will not tolerate 'capitalism'. If 'capitalism' means here a competitive system based on free disposal over private property, it is far more important to realise that only within this system is democracy possible. When it becomes dominated by a collectivist creed, democracy will inevitably destroy itself.

Friedrich von Hayek[1]

I said to him that if people were communists it was for the sake of happiness. In substance, his reply was: you mustn't say that. It is in order to bring about a change in the mode of production.

Pierre Victor on Althusser[2]

Where it concerns basic human needs, whether for adequate nourishment and other physical provision, for love, respect and friendship, or for a freedom and breadth of intellectual and physical self-expression; where it concerns the identification of suffering and oppression associated with their non-fulfilment, and the attempt to change or remove such institutions as may be responsible for frustrating them – this is surely a central part of any socialist politics worth the name: the fight against what is inimical to human happiness.

Norman Geras[3]

The contributors to this volume for the most part speak of and defend the traditions of socialist or Marxist, rather than liberal, humanism. In concluding, we as editors feel it would be helpful to reflect on this distinction at greater length, both through a return to defining moments in the history of theory and politics engaged with in the foregoing chapters, and in order to bring those engagements up to date. We ultimately wish to speculate, not too fancifully we hope, on what manner of transcendence of liberalism is both possible and desirable.

As should be clear by now, we do not underestimate the liberal tradition's achievements through its promotion of human rights. The limits of liberalism reside in its failure to grasp the systemic nature of the power its principles otherwise consolidate, rendering its finer commitments inadequate: it presumes a necessary tension between individual and society, and privileges the privacy of the former over the needs of the latter, not least through the defence of property rights that facilitate accumulation for some through the exploitation of nominally free others. But precisely because we do not underestimate liberalism, we wish to distance ourselves from the ultra-leftist rejection of the discourse of rights as such as *merely* a bourgeois smokescreen for exploitation and defence of the status quo. The socialist humanist commitment is to a general expansion of the liberty of individuals, though in a qualitatively different form from the individual*ism* to which people are currently taught to aspire. This will, of course, entail the curtailment of the extravagant freedoms that the few currently enjoy at the expense of the many, but redistribution is a matter of justice, not (as is alleged) jealousy. To whatever extent Nietzsche was right to suggest that *ressentiment* – the moralistic desire to call one's superiors to account – is grounded in inequality, then the socialist project, which he rejected along with all other forms of modern egalitarianism, is to abolish the conditions for *ressentiment*. The rationality of such a project consists in the belief that human beings are capable of achieving determinate transformations of their societies.

Attitudes towards liberalism have been crucial in determining antihumanist agendas, in part because of the tendency at one time sneeringly to run together liberal with humanist as if the two were inseparable, and to the discredit of both. Althusser is again a key figure in this respect, but in dealing with his legacy we should first say something appreciative about his intentions. The rigorous analyses of Marx's works in *For Marx* and the two volumes of *Reading Capital* contributed hugely to the thawing out of Marxist theory after the prolonged ice age of Stalinism. He championed 'the right of such theory not to be treated as a slave to tactical political decisions'.[4] Specifically, Althusser called into question an overly simplistic 'economism' – the doctrine that a gradually sharpening conflict between the forces and relations of production and the resultant transformation of modes of production straightforwardly determined the course of history – and historicism – the notion that historical development is inevitable, more or less uniform and directed at the behest of some sort of agent or prime mover like reason (for Hegel) or the party and its leaders (for Stalinism). Althusser challenged the misleading and conservative humanism peddled in the USSR under Khrushchev, which claimed 'Man' was now in the saddle and riding into the truly communist future, while actually the Soviet economy was still warped by inequality, isolation, shortages and bureaucratic superintendence. As Gregory Elliott's 'anti-anti-Althusserian'[5] account demonstrates these were genuine motivations, though compromised by his fidelity to the Parti Communiste Français (PCF).

But there was another reason for Althusser's antihumanism. Khrushchevite humanism was not only hypocritical in relation to the Soviet Union, but licenced the liberalisation of European Communist Parties.[6] Althusser was committed both to a scientific Marxist, rather than moralistic, analysis of Stalinism, as well as a revolutionary stance in the face of substantially transformed social conditions in France and the popularity of de Gaulle. Of course, he elaborated a general philosophical opposition to humanism, but the specific conditions we have described generated his sense of the importance of doing so. This explains why Althusser invoked the category of socialist humanism exclusively to refer to the Communist Party of the Soviet Union's post-Stalin project and the PCF's adherence to it, while for others the label signalled dissidence from the regime and its influence.[7] It is confusion on this point that led E. P. Thompson to misrecognise himself in Althusser's critique, though his consequent exaggerated attribution of Stalinist intent to Althusser did find warrant in the writings themselves: in the abandonment of the very terms – alienation, exploitation – that explained why anyone should be motivated to become a Marxist in the first place, and the introduction of an indefensibly rigid distinction between science/theory and ideology that led Althusser to argue that, under communism, the people were to be directed in their tasks by a (scientific) elite truly in the know.[8]

Key to understanding Althusser's project is his relationship to the Maoism that proved such a lure to PCF dissidents. Not only did Althusser sympathise with the Chinese Communist Party's criticisms of Khrushchev's 'revisionism' at the time of the Sino-Soviet split in the early 1960s (philippics in which Koba was held up by the Chinese leadership as the acme of revolutionary authenticity), his work began to make barely theorised references to 'class struggle' as the 'motor of history'.[9] In his later career, Althusser appealed to the anti-bureaucratic potential of the 'Great Proletarian Cultural Revolution', which insofar as it was ever anything more than a tactical move on Mao's part to reassert his hold over the party after the calamity of the Great Leap Forward was in practice an anarchic cure even worse than the bureaucratised revolution it professed to be restoring to health.[10] In the eyes of the Red Guards, class struggle meant vendettas and purges, the burning of books, the wanton smashing up of artefacts, a grotesque personality cult that made the worship of Stalin look like a mild round of applause, the torture and humiliation of intellectuals and others, as well as the summary murder of whoever might conveniently be dubbed a 'capitalist roader' and then kicked to death. A point in Kevin Anderson's chapter also bears repetition: the anti-imperialism of the Chinese regime was a paper tiger, given that the regime cosied up to Nixon and Kissinger while they razed Vietnam and then assailed that country again after the United States had finally left it alone. While little was known in France at the time of what the Cultural Revolution actually entailed, and Althusser cautioned against violent tactics,[11] he has ended up appearing *plus Staliniste que les Stalinistes* through the supposed alternative he endorsed.

The Cultural Revolution, Althusser writes, is 'a *revolution of the masses* that transforms the ideology of the masses and is made by the masses themselves'.[12] The task consists 'in identifying and criticising leaders who cut themselves off from the masses, who behave in a bureaucratic or technocratic manner, who ... abandon the "revolutionary road" and take the "capitalist road"'.[13] What is both instructive and extraordinary about such statements is the way in which the pessimism of Althusser's emphasis on ideological interpellation of the individual gives way to a spontaneist belief in the masses' autonomy, insight and efficacy. The oscillation is wholly typical of antihumanism, though it emerges in different ways in different kinds of theorist: if ideology/power is so thoroughly constitutive of the modern subject then it is either difficult to see how it may be escaped, or can only be comprehensively challenged by some implausibly undetermined force – a kind of *deus ex machina.*

Radical humanism, by contrast, argues that human beings' possession of a shared if dynamic nature offers the possibility of and justification *for* a transformed social order; socialism is not wholly unprecedented. Nor can the existing social order be criticised, as Noam Chomsky observed in a famous conversation with Foucault on Dutch television in 1971, without the aid of a 'humane' grasp of that nature as frustrated and repressed.[14] Foucault responded to this truism by claiming that, to the contrary, any characterisation of a future society in terms borrowed from our current perspectives debars the possibility of fundamental and qualitative social change.[15] 'Popular justice', he says in another interview from the same year with Maoist interlocutors, will have nothing to do with 'bourgeois' or (what he says amounts to the same thing) 'fascist' principles and rituals of justice. The 'masses' apparently, 'when they perceive somebody to be an enemy, when they decide to punish this enemy – or to re-educate him – do not rely on an abstract universal ideal of justice'.[16] In such a situation, they will have no resort to any state or judicial apparatus, says Foucault, proving himself even more 'radical' than his questioners. They will be guided not by ideals of justice but solely by their own grievances. Foucault could see nothing wrong with this; socialist humanists who acknowledge their indebtedness to liberalism emphatically can.

Foucault's attraction to Maoism, his belief as an activist in the Groupe d'information sur les prisons (GPI) in the early 1970s that prisoners' voices should be heard without mediation, and the appeal for him of the 'non-Western' Islamist revolution in Iran discussed in Kevin Anderson's chapter, all betray his occasional faith in spontaneism. It contrasts with the lesson that has proved more congenial to the more timid Left in recent years that only micro-political resistance – no real departure from liberalism – is either possible or desirable. Many of the particular causes Foucault took up – against the death by garrotting of ETA activists under Franco, in support of the Vietnamese boat people and, later, of the Polish Union, Solidarity – were human rights ones. Inconsistent with his *Maoisant* pronouncements, they were quite straightforwardly liberal.

As all of this serves to illustrate, the question of Foucault's politics is a thorny one. What were they? Describing them vaguely as 'Left' is surely insufficient, and antihumanism is not itself a mode of politics, as many appear to believe these days, but rather of subscribing to various political options. What is clear is that Foucault's alignments shifted during the 1970s along with those of other French intellectuals; revolutionary commitments abated. Few of his works are more interesting in this respect than the lectures he gave on neoliberalism in 1978–9. The timing of these was remarkable, but we should be wary perhaps of attributing too much prescience to him. He believed, after all, that neoliberalism was already dominant by that time,[17] and so he did not anticipate the enormity of what was about to unfold and that through this process neoliberalism would more obviously disclose itself as what David Harvey and others have suggested it has been all along: a class project designed to restore power to an elite, even if the nature of elite has been reconfigured in the process.[18] Of course, such an explanation would have been thoroughly uncongenial to Foucault, as his occasional polemics against Marxism and socialism in the lectures – defining him negatively at least – make clear.

The tone of them is significant in other respects, because the discussion of economic liberalism is remarkably dispassionate by contrast and betrays little sense of *critique*. Indeed, some quite plausibly claim that this is because Foucault was sympathetic to a phenomenon that obviously fascinated him. According to Michael C. Behrent, Foucault was attracted to economic liberalism as something quite distinct from political liberalism: it did not rely on normative humanist assumptions about subjects and the kinds of rights they demanded, but rather consisted in the art of understanding how not to govern – how not to intervene, too much. In this way, Behrent argues, 'it offered a compelling terrain upon which [Foucault's] practical aspiration for freedom might merge with his theoretical conviction that power is constitutive of all human relationships'.[19] Wendy Brown abruptly dismisses this case by reminding us of Foucault's argument in *Discipline and Punish* that the idea of freedom of the subject is *the* ruse of modern power,[20] but this fails to take note of Behrent's detailed argument that Foucault had moved on from his analysis of disciplinary power to an understanding of biopower, as this focused more on populations and touched more lightly on the subject. Moreover, Behrent's case acquires its power from the larger context he establishes for the lectures: the economic crises of the 1970s, the fear of totalitarianism sparked among the French intelligentsia by the threat of an alliance in government between Communists and Socialists in 1978,[21] and the spreading influence of neoliberal thought through its active promotion – including through anti-statist Left circles in which Foucault circulated – now that Keynesian orthodoxies had ceased to serve the interests of capital.[22]

Nonetheless, Behrent's case relies on an overarching concept of 'economic liberalism' that fails to register sufficiently the distinction that Foucault draws extensively between its laissez-faire and neoliberal manifestations. The latter is said to be characterised by its indebtedness to the ordoliberal conviction that markets are not natural, but rather need to be cultivated and sustained by states, which thereby play an active role in the entrepreneurialisation of everyday life. Wendy Brown's work represents the most impressive, neo-Marxist critical elaboration and development of Foucault's arguments, though she does not convince us to abandon the view of neoliberalism already outlined above and discussed below as hegemonic in a properly speaking Gramscian sense relating to class –

and therefore as actively formative rather than passively reflective of what is taking place in a determining economic base. We should be deeply impressed by the resourcefulness and imagination of neoliberals in the transformations they have brought about in order to achieve the tricky task of using the state to roll itself back. The Left, by contrast, has largely abandoned attempts to elaborate any positive, systemic alternative, focused as it has substantially been in its intellectual endeavours on anatomising human passivity (interpellation) in the social construction of identities.

Behrent claims that the neoliberalism Foucault was attracted to represented 'liberalism without humanism'. True or not, the phrase is a wonderfully succinct way of characterising the brutal project that has unfolded since the 1970s, and it is to this that we now turn in order to suggest that if there is to be a future fit for humans, it can only take a socialist form. Pace Althusser, this is certainly because of contradictions between the forces and relations of production, and we would hope that reason may prevail through the political organisation and agency of peoples.

The prolonged crisis into which the world economy entered in that decade provoked what David Harvey refers to as a worldwide 'neoliberal counter-revolution'[23] against the democratic and egalitarian aspirations of the global Left. 'However much camouflaged by economists' diagrams and equations and the homilies of conservative, social individualism, neoliberalism was also', as Neil Smith has argued, 'a quite direct strategy of class struggle. A weapon of reaction and revenge – revanchism – it was designed to take back for the ruling classes and their professional and managerial consorts the "losses" that twentieth-century "liberalism" has visited on them.'[24] Since the 1970s, we have witnessed an attempt to free capitalism from the demands of democracy, whether those demands have been pressed by social democratic movements in the Global North or in different ways and to varying extents by the myriad of reformist and revolutionary regimes that came to power in the 'postcolonial' world. The world's peoples have been asked to forfeit the civil and social rights they have dreamed of and fought for over the last hundred years and more.

Still, just as neoliberalism emerged out of crisis, its own increasing exhaustion offers opportunities for the Left to develop ambitious alternatives. Wolfgang Streeck is convinced that we have now entered the period of capitalism's protracted but inexorable 'decay'.[25] He places the collapse of the American financial system in 2008 and the continued 'disequilibrium' of the advanced capitalist world in the context of what he calls 'the crisis of democratic capitalism' since the 1970s. There is an underlying tension between democracy and capitalism, Streeck argues.[26] Indeed the idea that capitalism is compatible with democracy was widely countenanced only for a relatively brief period in the three decades after World War II, just as the compromise formations of welfare capitalism that mixed together these two contradictory imperatives in unstable compounds took place only in a small corner of the globe at that time. Neither before nor since was it considered possible to combine democratic aspirations such as full employment, universal public services and social justice with the distorting effect of capitalist markets. The 'democratic capitalism' that prevailed in every First World economy during the *trentes glorieuses* welded together two clashing regimes of resource allocation, one operating according to the criterion of social need and the other according to 'market forces' serving privacy. The crisis of profitability that befell the world economy in the 1970s has seen an end to this truce and the onset of a concerted offensive of capital against the democratic aspirations of labour, in which profitability and class power have been restored but at the expense of the system's legitimacy. Where once there may have been a reasonable expectation that capitalism might preside over '[s]teady growth, sound money and a modicum of social equity',[27] there is now only a persistent decline in the rate of economic growth, an unprecedented and unsustainable rise in public and private indebtedness even in leading capitalist states in addition to massive and growing economic inequalities within and between states. Either neoliberal 'reforms' will protect profits and rents at the expense of democratic aspirations for redistribution and publicly funded services, *or* explicitly socialist measures will defend and advance democratic aspirations for redistribution and publicly funded services at the expense of profits and rents. We can have a capitalist economy or a properly democratic polity but we can't have both. Walden Bello calls this situation 'capitalism's last stand'.[28]

States now find themselves in a muddle because they continue to serve two very different and incompatible masters: the one demanding a 'stable investment environment' of low taxes for the wealthy and corporations, as well as low wages for the mob, and the other demanding equality, decent public services and a secure income. In 2008, as Streeck reminds us, 'no democratic state dared to impose on its society another economic crisis of the dimensions of the Great Depression of the 1930s'.[29] So the financial sector was bailed out with vast quantities of public money. This public indebtedness as well as the private indebtedness that has resulted from financial deregulation and the easing of access to private credit is the tell-tale sign of Western governments' fear that they must continue to ensure relatively substantial levels of security and prosperity for the sake of 'social peace'.

Indebtedness is a 'temporary stopgap' that indicates 'that a lasting reconciliation between social and economic stability in capitalist democracies is a utopian project'.[30] This fragile balancing act cannot continue forever. National states have the function of mediating, to use Streeck's terms, 'between the rights of citizens and the requirements of capital accumulation'.[31] But the global interdependence of states has reduced their capacity to shelter citizens from those requirements. Will massively indebted states not capitulate to them, as Ireland, Greece and any number of economies in the periphery and semi-periphery have done? The incompatibility of democracy and capitalism is now at least visible. 'In my view,' writes Streeck, 'it is high time, in the light of decades of declining growth, rising inequality and increasing indebtedness – as well as of the successive agonies of inflation, public debt and financial implosion since the 1970s – to think again about capitalism as a historical phenomenon, one that has not just a beginning, but also an end.'[32] In response to the existential crisis of late capitalism, ruling classes since the 1970s have sought to postpone the final reckoning, in Streeck's phrase to 'buy time', whether through increased government borrowing, the expansion of private loan markets and most recently through central bank purchases of bank liabilities.[33] But 'the means to tame legitimation crises by generating illusions of growth seem to have been exhausted'.[34]

Hence, as David Harvey points out, capitalism's various contradictions are becoming ever more acute, but there is no reason to believe that the capitalist mode of production will somehow simply expire or fade away. Dystopia is an option. The Left therefore requires a compelling vision of the future as *more* just, democratic, ecologically sustainable and subjectively satisfying around which it will be possible to construct a viable counter-hegemony. To this end, we would lend our support to utopian ideas that are adumbrated in Marx and find further elaboration in writers such as Herbert Marcuse, André Gorz and, most recently, Nick Srnicek and Alex Williams. The latter pair's cry of 'Full Unemployment!'[35] wonderfully turns the logic both of the system and of ameliorative responses to it on their heads. The aim of the Left should not be freedom in work, or freedom to work, but freedom *from* work, or at least from the reified and alienating forms of it through which we are made to serve the obsolete regime of capital.

Technological advances have massively increased the efficiency of labour and reduced the amount of necessary toil. The price for this is automated production processes that have made paid work less interesting, more alienating and scarcer. The Left's goal, in Gorz's words, must be to do away with the myth that paid employment is the source of identity and fulfilment and to reduce working hours for everybody, thus broadening 'the field of non-work activities in which we can all ... develop that dimension of our humanity which finds no outlet in technicised work'.[36] Other pursuits, far less amenable to the instrumental rationality of the market than the alienating consumerism, with its bogus rhetoric of 'choice', might then be given priority. This is the human*ist* alternative to a harried life. Free time, once work has been reduced to a minimum, will be a 'realm of freedom', to use Marx's splendid phrase,[37] not the sorry domain of unfreedom in which time is 'consumed' by the search for gratuitous commodities or else sucked into a void by the inane distractions of the culture industry and the choleric babble of social media.

What we have now in what we should refer to as the overdeveloped world is a phony 'elite' of managers, rentiers and affluent but overworked salaried employees, alongside a much larger group of unskilled or semi-skilled workers toiling in what David Graeber calls low-paid and precarious 'bullshit jobs' in the service sector.[38] There is an even vaster reserve army of unemployed or informally employed workers living in gigantic slums in the rapidly industrialising though still underdeveloped world. Indeed, Fredric Jameson reminds us how difficult it can be to maintain a commitment to utopian thinking and politics in such circumstances. In large parts of the globe 'the disintegration of the social is so absolute – misery, poverty, unemployment, starvation, squalor, violence and death – that the intricately elaborated social schemes of utopian thinkers become as frivolous as they are irrelevant'.[39] The depth of the crisis and its intolerableness is precisely why a politics of transformation rather than a politics of mere resistance is so urgently necessary.

It is estimated that somewhere between 47 and 80 per cent of current jobs will be automatable within the next two decades.[40] One explanation for the dire productivity that is a persistent feature of the UK economy is that jobs that could easily be automated are still being done, pointlessly but profitably, by people on low wages and with insecure terms of employment.[41] The staged reduction of working hours, with no reduction of income, will liberate us from such drudgery and set us free for meaningful activities of free and creative self-realisation. Who knows what form they will take? 'We have to ensure the means of life, and the means of community', as Raymond Williams once declared. 'But what will then, by these means, be lived, we cannot know or say.'[42] But we can say with confidence that lives no longer shackled to the regime of capital will be free to make and remake themselves at will, to find the time and resources necessary for aesthetic and intellectual undertakings as well as new relations with nature and with each other.

That is the utopian aspiration with which we wish to end this book, and it transcends anything on offer from liberalism. How can we reduce work and expand free time while equalising incomes in a vastly unequal world? Such a proposal obviously requires human beings to find ways of providing the basic necessities of life for all people on earth. We have neither the space nor the competence to set out in detail the strategies required to bring such a society into being, but we welcome the increased commitment to thinking about such things from a range of thinkers and economists whose work deserves more urgent consideration than that of the undialectical social constructionists who continue to insist on power's primacy as a formative principle.[43] A universal basic income will undoubtedly be part of the solution, not least because it will greatly increase the bargaining power of labour against capital and thus make it immeasurably harder for capital to use the threat of impoverishment and destitution to coerce us into a state of inhuman subservience. Moreover, we rather like the idea of imposing a use-by date on money so that its virtue in facilitating choice is preserved while its potential for antisocial accumulation is suppressed. Rational control of a socialist society will be necessary: Gorz, for instance, proposes that a democratic state should be responsible for ensuring the production of indisputable necessities – which may be very complex, like health – while 'civil society' might produce other diverse 'goods and services'[44] (the inverted commas here are designed to signal the inadequacy of these contemporary terms to the future we envisage).

It is clear, though, that the development of such a society would meet with concerted resistance from the regime of capital. We depart from Gorz in believing that class politics remain indispensable,[45] both because it is perfectly reasonable to assert that those who are most exploited and least rewarded in order to achieve the efficiencies of the system have most to gain through its transformation, and because we believe that ordinary workers whose emotional and intellectual capacities have been disdained should be at the centre of any project to achieve their own emancipation. However, we neither wish to reify the proletariat nor to underestimate the potential for all sorts of alliances with those who have reason – whether based on interest or ethics – to challenge capitalist instrumentality. If utopians have been right to reprimand Marx for his resistance to providing a blueprint for the future, he at least understood that visions count for nothing without any identifiable forces to bring them into effect. Many people's attachment to the work ethic has been truly virtuous. It has given them dignity, solidarity and a sense of service, but self-sacrifice is unnecessary – it is now the very ruse of capital – and a world without traditional work need not be absent of endeavour, community and fulfilment. People need to be convinced of this.

In such a future free time will be massively augmented. Freedom, according to Adorno's brilliant essay on that subject from the late 1960s, is not the obverse and counterpart of alienated work. Freedom is not another word for distraction or 'fun', but it may consist in climbing mountains for the sheer sensuous joy of doing so, in playing and writing music, dancing, erotic discovery, or in having the time to care for others or to mourn; it names a world in which liberation has come about through the drastic reduction and redistribution of necessary toil.

'If the world were so planned that everything one did served the whole of society in a transparent manner, and senseless activities were abandoned, I would be happy to spend two hours a day working as a lift attendant', wrote Adorno.[46] But no more than two hours! Functional work, Gorz makes clear in his *Métamorphoses du travail* (oddly translated into English as *Critique of Economic Reason*), in such a highly automated system of production and such a vastly complicated division of labour, cannot be anything other than alienating.[47] How could it be otherwise, unless we somehow rescinded the industrial revolution and again directly controlled our labour and its products? Adorno will doubtless be given a great deal of autonomy by the cooperative that oversees Frankfurt's lifts and be allowed to work flexible hours. He will even, we trust, be permitted not to wear a uniform and also to share his job (though we wouldn't like to say with whom). Indeed, since lifts too have become fully automated, one of the last century's greatest philosophers might be excused his duties as a bellboy and invited to assume some other task entirely, albeit one that makes a similarly negligible demand on his talents. 'Free time' should not be 'shackled to its opposite', and used mainly 'for the recreation of expended labour-power'.[48] In a pleasingly Sartrean turn of phrase Srnicek and Williams call this future condition in which it will be possible for individuals and groups to explore their diverse and versatile species-being 'a humanism that is not defined in advance'.[49]

There is, then, an urgent need to move beyond political nostalgia for social democracy and say good riddance to it. The compromise formations of capitalism's 'golden age' in the three decades after World War II were, as Srnicek and Williams remind us,[50] predicated on the principles of endless production and accumulation, on a sexist division of labour, on the bourgeois and heteronormative model of the family, on racist ideologies of social order, on the availability of exploitable colonies and neocolonies, and on the painful repression and sheer boredom of wage labour and consumerism. Goodbye to all that. Every single one of those features of the social democratic compromise with capital had already shown itself to be intolerable and unsustainable at the time of the emergence of the New Left in the 1960s. Sadly, much of that Left's agenda has been co-opted, as market libertarians at the time and since believed it could be; there are endless complaints now about 'assimilation'. Today, then, the Left's distinctive aim should not be to 'resist' the faltering regime of capital, in the sense of absorbing capital's blows or organising in its margins, but to do those things more purposefully in preparation for *overturning* it in the name of a different kind of future.

## NOTES

1. Friedrich von Hayek, *The Road to Serfdom*, Abingdon: Routledge, 2001 [1944], p. 73.
2. Pierre Victor, *On a Raison de se Révolter*, cited in Gregory Elliott, *Althusser: The Detour of Theory*, London: Verso, 1987, p. 181n.
3. Norman Geras, *Marx and Human Nature: Refutation of a Legend*, London: New Left Books, 1983, pp. 95–6. On these themes, see also David Leopold, *The Young Karl Marx: German Philosophy, Modern Politics, and Human Flourishing*, Cambridge: Cambridge University Press, 2007.
4. Louis Althusser, *Essays in Self-Criticism*, trans. Grahame Lock, London: New Left Books, 1976, p. 169.
5. Gregory Elliott, *Althusser: The Detour of Theory*, London: Verso, 1987, p. 10.
6. Ibid., pp. 32–3.

7. See Kate Soper, *Humanism and Antihumanism*, London: Hutchinson, 1986, p. 113.

8. See E. P. Thompson, *The Poverty of Theory: Or an Orrery of Errors*, London: Merlin Press, 1995 [1978], p. 173, on this misrecognition. In 'Marxism and Humanism', Althusser claims that in a socialist society 'men must be ceaselessly transformed so as to adapt them' to conditions of existence (*For Marx*, trans. Ben Brewster, London: Verso, 2005 [1969], p. 232).

9. Althusser, *Essays in Self-Criticism*, p. 47.

10. Elliott, *Althusser*, pp. 187–97 and 260–74.

11. Louis Althusser, 'On the Cultural Revolution', trans. Jason E. Smith, *Décalages*, Vol. 1, No. 1 (2010), p. 8.

12. Althusser, 'On the Cultural Revolution', p. 7; emphasis in the original.

13. Ibid., p. 17.

14. Fons Elders et al., *Reflexive Water: The Basic Concerns of Mankind*, London: Souvenir Press, 1974, p. 172. See also Noam Chomsky, *Language and Politics*, ed. C. P. Otero, New York: Black Row, 1988, p. 246.

15. Elders, *Reflexive Water*, p. 174.

16. Michel Foucault, *Power/Knowledge: Selected Interviews and Other Writings*, ed. Colin Gordon, Brighton: Harvester Press, 1980, p. 8.

17. Michel Foucault, *The Birth of Biopolitics: Lectures at the Collége de France*, ed. Michael Senellart and trans. Graham Burchell, London: Picador, 2008, p. 149.

18. David Harvey, *A Brief History of Neoliberalism*, Oxford: Oxford University Press, 2005, pp. 9–36.

19. Michael C. Behrent, 'Liberalism Without Humanism', in Daniel Zamora and Michael C. Behrent (eds), *Foucault and Neoliberalism*, Oxford: Polity, 2016, p. 31.

20. Wendy Brown, *Undoing the Demos: Neoliberalism's Stealth Revolution*, New York: Zone Books, 2015, p. 234n.

21. Michael Scott Christofferson charts the complex emergence of this antitotalitarian moment in *French Intellectuals Against the Left: The Antitotalitarian Moment in the 1970s*, New York: Berghahn Books, 2004.

22. Behrent, 'Liberalism Without Humanism', pp. 31–9.

23. David Harvey, *Seventeen Contradictions and the End of Capitalism*, London: Profile, 2014, p. 129.

24. Neil Smith, *The Endgame of Globalization*, London: Routledge, pp. 143–4.

25. Wolfgang Streeck, 'How Will Capitalism End?', *New Left Review II*, No. 87 (2014), p. 38.

26. See also Ellen Meiksins Wood's superb *Democracy Against Capitalism: Renewing Historical Materialism*, Cambridge: Cambridge University Press, 1995.

27. Streeck, 'How Will Capitalism End?', p. 37.

28. Walden Bello, *Capitalism's Last Stand? Degloblization in the Age of Austerity*, London: Zed Books, 2013.

29. Wolfgang Streeck, 'The Crises of Democratic Capitalism', *New Left Review*, No. 71 (2011), p. 20.

30. Ibid., p. 24.
31. Ibid., p. 25.
32. Streeck, 'How Will Capitalism End?', p. 45.
33. Wolfgang Streeck, *Buying Time: The Delayed Crisis of Democratic Capitalism*, London: Verso, 2014, p. xiv.
34. Ibid., p. 46.
35. Nick Srnicek and Alex Williams, *Inventing the Future: Postcapitalism and a World Without Work*, London: Verso, 2015, pp. 107–27.
36. André Gorz, *Critique of Economic Reason*, trans. Gillian Handyside and Chris Turner, London: Verso, 1989, p. 88.
37. Karl Marx, *Capital: A Critique of Political Economy*, vol. 3, trans. David Fernbach, Harmondsworth: Penguin, 1981, pp. 958–9.
38. David Graeber, 'On the Phenomenon of Bullshit Jobs', *Strike!* 17 August 2013: http://strikemag.org/bullshit-jobs/.
39. Fredric Jameson, 'The Politics of Utopia', *New Left Review II*, No. 25 (2004), p. 35.
40. Srnicek and Williams, *Inventing the Future*, p. 88.
41. Sarah O'Connor, 'UK Productivity Falls by Most since Financial Crisis', *Financial Times*, 7 April 2016: https://next.ft.com/content/e8b0639c-fcaa-11e5-b5f5-070dca6d0a0d.
42. Raymond Williams, *Culture and Society, 1780–1950*, Harmondsworth: Penguin, 1961 [1958], p. 321. Göran Therborn has recently reiterated a crucial point about equality. Equality is not about sameness, as the Right believes, but about the possibility of pursuing meaningful difference (*The Killing Fields of Inequality*, Oxford: Polity, 2013, p. 1).
43. There is clearly more of this material than we are aware of, but in addition to the works discussed elsewhere in this conclusion we would mention in particular: Michael Albert, *Realising Hope: Life Beyond Capitalism*, London: Zed books, 2006; Pat Devine, *Democracy and Economic Planning: The Political Economy of a Self-Governing Society*, Oxford: Polity Press, 1988; Erik Olin Wright, *Envisioning Real Utopias*, London: Verso, 2010.
44. See André Gorz, *Farewell to the Working Class: An Essay on Postindustrial Society*, London: Pluto, 1982, especially pp. 90–104.
45. Gorz (ibid.) argues both that the proletariat was a philosophical category that never matched empirical reality, and that post-industrial conditions now demanded an emphasis on individuality rather than class.
46. Theodor Adorno and Max Horkheimer, *Towards a New Manifesto*, trans. Rodney Livingstone, London: Verso, 2011, p. 22.
47. Gorz, *Critique of Economic Reason*, pp. 39–61.
48. Theodor Adorno, 'Free Time', *The Culture Industry: Selected Essays on Mass Culture*, ed. J. M. Bernstein, London: Routledge, 1991, pp. 162 and 164.
49. Srnicek and Williams, *Inventing the Future*, p. 82.
50. Ibid., p. 46.

# Index